ICELAND
SEROW SAGA

Big Adventures on a Small Motorbike

Helen Lloyd

Take On Creative

Copyright © 2020 Helen Lloyd

All rights reserved.

No part of this book may be reproduced or transmitted in any form whatsoever without the express written permission of the publisher except for use permitted under UK copyright law.

For the purposes of anonymity and to protect privacy, some names have been changed.

First published in 2020
by Take On Creative

Cover design, maps and photographs
by Helen Lloyd

ISBN 978-0-9576606-4-9

www.takeoncreative.com

Icelandic Language

The Icelandic alphabet has 32 letters, of which several are accented vowels. There are also three letters not used in the Roman alphabet:

> Ð or ð sounds like a soft 'th' as in *thing*
> Þ or þ sounds like 'th' in *this*
> Æ or æ sounds like *eye* or the 'ai' in *aisle*

For the names of places, the Icelandic spelling is used for authenticity and to aid locating them on a map, if desired.

However, for people's names, 'Þ' is replaced with 'Th', as this is more commonly seen in English text. I.e. Thor, not Þor (god of thunder).

Icelandic names for roads are used and, where they exist, the road numbers are included in brackets.

See the Glossary at the end of the book for a list of some Icelandic words and their definitions. It may help with understanding the names of some of the places described.

THE AUTHOR

Helen Lloyd grew up in Norfolk, England. She studied engineering and has worked in industry. Travelling has been a part of her life since she was sixteen. She has cycled 45,000 kilometres through 45 countries on four continents and has written two books about her experiences in Africa and Siberia. She has also made remote journeys by river, on foot and horseback. Her most recent adventures have been by motorcycle. Between journeys, she lives in her camper van in the UK.

PHOTOGRAPHY AND VIDEOS

Helen Lloyd is an avid photographer and strives to capture the journeys she makes through photography. She has also made a series of fifteen videos of riding in Iceland. All her published photographs and videos are available to view on her website:

www.helenstakeon.com/iceland-photos
www.helenstakeon.com/iceland-videos

CONTENTS

EUROPE AND THE FAROE ISLANDS Page
1 The Beginning 5
2 Across Europe 14
3 Small Islands in the North Atlantic 25

ICELAND - PART ONE
4 Arrival 43
5 Driftwood and an Abandoned Village 55
6 Waterfalls, Whales and a Hoofprint Canyon 65
7 Breakdown and Recovery 73
8 Trails and Turf Houses 82
9 Coffee and Executions 92

ICELAND - PART TWO
10 Rough Tracks and a Herring Factory 107
11 The Sagas 118
12 Geysers and Greenhouses 128
13 Into the Highlands 137
14 Pirates and an Eruption 153

ICELAND - PART THREE
15 Highland Traverse 165
16 A Barbecue and Bike Problems 173
17 Lunar Landscapes 183
18 A Hot Pool and Rum 191
19 Bike Repairs 198

ICELAND - PART FOUR
20 In Deep Water 209
21 Company on the Trails 220

		Page
22	Mountains of Colour	229
23	A Reindeer and More Rain	239
	Tribute	249
	Glossary	250
	Acknowledgements	252

ROUTE MAPS

Europe and the Faroe Islands	2
Iceland - Part One	40
Iceland - Part Two	104
Iceland - Part Three	162
Iceland - Part Four	206

Thule, the period of cosmography,
Doth vaunt of Hecla, whose sulphureous fire
Doth melt the frozen clime and thaw the sky;
Trinacrian Aetna's flames ascend not higher.
These things seem wondrous, yet more wondrous I,
Whose heart with fear doth freeze, with love doth fry.

Thule, the Period of Cosmography
Thomas Weelkes (*c*.1575–1623)

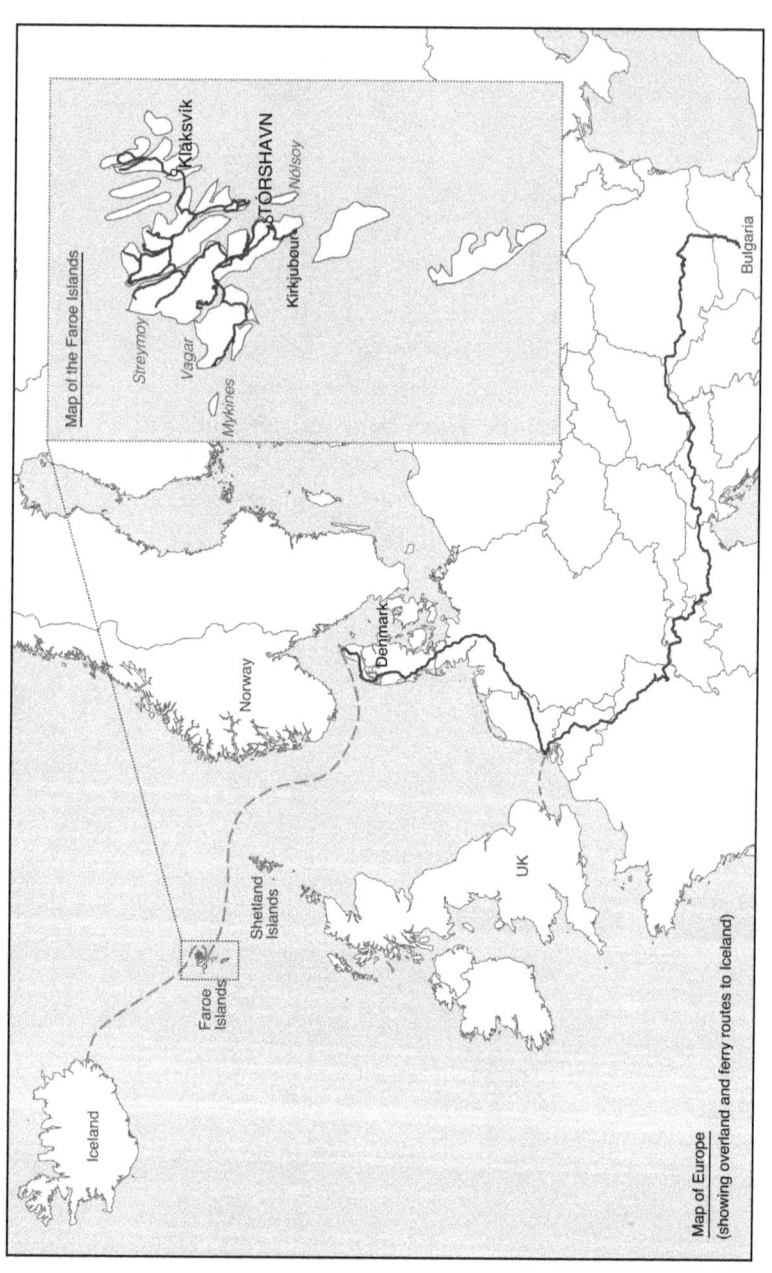

EUROPE and the FAROE ISLANDS

St Magnus' cathedral in Kirkjubøur.

Camping above Mykines village.

1

The Beginning

UK

The idea of riding a motorcycle in Iceland was a long time in the making. It began with a dream and was shaped by a decade of adventures and experiences.

I haven't always ridden a motorcycle. I secretly wanted one as a teenager but my parents would never have allowed it. Instead, at seventeen, I got a car and the bike dream faded, forgotten as my life steamrollered ahead: school, exams, university, more exams and lots of drinking. Then I entered the world of work and lots more drinking until, one day, I woke up and wondered why I was wasting my life doing what other people did when I didn't want what everyone else I knew wanted. I wanted to go on a long journey.

I had already been travelling: trekking in India and Morocco, backpacking in South America and along the old Silk Route through China, hitch-hiking the Karakoram Highway, cycling in Ireland (fuelled by Guinness) and Cuba (fuelled by rum and mojitos). These trips had been of varying lengths, crammed between term-time studies or into my annual leave, usually three or four weeks, never more than a few months. There was always a deadline and a return flight booked, the end point looming as certain as a full stop finishing a sentence. I envied those people I met who journeyed without end, unconstrained by plans, free to travel wherever the fancy took them, their paths like a toddler's scribbles on a blank canvas. When I met cyclists on a long tour of Asia, it struck me that this was a great way to see the world.

It took until I was twenty-six to realise that I could do it too. I was single and independent; no one could stop me from taking control of my life and setting it on the course I desired. For two more years,

ICELAND Serow Saga

I worked, saved up money, pored over maps – maps of Africa – and dreamt bigger than I'd ever dared before. Then I quit my job, picked up my bicycle, packed my panniers and began pedalling.

Twenty-six countries and 25,000 kilometres later, I arrived in Cape Town, certain that I could not return to a life of comfort and a career that I had abandoned two years before. At heart I was a nomad and travelling was in my blood.

Subsequent years followed a routine of going home to work as an engineer to save money to fund my habit, then disconnecting from society in favour of a rootless existence unfettered by unnecessary possessions, carrying everything I needed – shelter, clothing and food – on my bicycle. It was a simple life; the less I owned, the happier I was. Sleeping beneath the stars and waking to watch the sun rise, savouring the refreshing taste of water sipped straight from a stream, and feeling the gentle touch of the breeze on my bare skin and a bead of sweat trickle down the back of my neck were the things that filled me with joy.

I loved travelling through changing landscapes of oppressive forest and arid desert, windswept coasts and snow-covered passes. I loved meeting people, no matter that there was no common language. The gnawing hunger to discover new places, understand foreign cultures and learn about the history of everywhere I visited was as unceasing as my ravenous appetite induced by long-distance cycling.

As much as I loved cycling, there were times on long, monotonous roads when I wondered what other opportunities and experiences might exist if I were travelling some other way. Instead, sometimes I walked, paddled a river or journeyed by horseback. When I met people travelling overland in a 4x4 or on a motorbike, I thought that I would like to do that too, one day.

Paradoxically, it was because I wanted to travel more slowly that I decided to 'upgrade' to a bike with an engine. A motorbike would take me on a fast, direct route to the places that interested me the most, so I could spend more time exploring them in-depth.

UK

It took until I was thirty-one to realise that no one could stop me from fulfilling the dream I'd had as a teenager. I did the Compulsory Basic Training ('CBT') followed by a four-day fast-track Direct Access course to get my full, unlimited motorcycle licence, ready for when the time came.

I wanted a motorcycle that could handle any trail. I knew it needed to be cheap, easy to fix, small enough that my feet could touch the ground, so that I felt comfortable and confident, and light enough to pick up when I dropped it. The Yamaha XT225, also known as a Serow after the Japanese mountain goat, was the perfect fit.

I found one on eBay, which had been recently imported. I was still in Russia having spent the winter cycling through Siberia. Knowing little about motorcycles, there seemed no point in going to see it. A cursory glance and kick of the tyres wouldn't tell me anything more than the photos. I bought it over the phone. It looked in excellent condition and had done, according to the odometer, barely 8,000 kilometres despite being a 23-year-old bike.

The night before I went to collect the Serow from Devon, I typed 'How to ride a motorcycle' into YouTube and watched a video. It was two years since I'd taken my test, the last time I'd ridden a bike. I wasn't sure I could remember how to start one, let alone change gears or brake.

In my new shiny helmet and protective bike gear, I made a couple of wobbly practise laps around the industrial estate before venturing nervously onto the main roads. My confidence grew during the long ride back. By the time I reached Oxfordshire, I was hooked. The following weekend I rode to Norfolk; the one after that to Wales. The third weekend was the start of a ten-day break; I rode to Scotland to visit friends. They had big adventure bikes, and I buzzed along behind like a mosquito on my small Serow. I loved it.

I joined the Trail Riders' Fellowship and accompanied the local group for a weekend riding the byways of the Wiltshire Downs. After a morning of dropping the bike several times, I crash-landed on my shoulder and hip. Besides a bruised ego, the only real damage was to my thumb. It had got caught on the handlebar as I was propelled inelegantly over the top. The pain, swelling and purplish hue of my hand suggested a trip to A & E was in order. The doctor diagnosed a torn ligament. He let me choose what colour bandage I wanted – blue – and put my forearm in a cast. It matched the colour of the bike that I'd be unable to ride for six weeks. I was gutted.

As the weeks of inactivity passed, my hips and back started to hurt. Sitting for eight hours a day working at a desk takes a greater toll on me than putting my body through long periods of physical endurance. I began to feel imprisoned by the office and the tiny room I was renting. I'd stare out of the window, longing to be outdoors in the fresh air with nature my companion. I hated being cooped up when there was a world to explore. The recent death of my grandfather and also two friends made one thing clear: life was short, not to be wasted.

As I'd saved enough money over the summer, I bought a van that had been converted into a camper. It enabled me to explore new places at weekends. When my work contract neared an end, I requested a month off unpaid before renewing it. Then I escaped to Scotland in my van. I loved parking in a different place each night, going for walks wherever and whenever I fancied, watching the stars and feeling the fresh air of freedom fill my lungs. I spent hours writing, with a mug of tea and a scenic view for company.

I loved this van life. Why couldn't I live in my van all the time? There were showers at work and places to park nearby, even a peaceful campsite with direct access to footpaths and bridleways through the Chiltern Hills. I hadn't many clothes and could easily fit everything I needed into the reduced living space. The only things stopping me were convention and what other people might think. Neither are good reasons not to do something. So I gave up the rented room and moved into my home on wheels.

UK

It was hard to keep clean when it was wet and muddy outside. In winter, I needed an extra duvet and sometimes slept in my woolly hat. If I woke in the morning with frost on the inside of the windscreen and could see my breath, I'd quickly brew up a mug of tea on the gas stove to take the chill off the air. The freedom gained more than compensated for these hardships. It had the added benefit of saving me money, which I could put towards my next adventure. There was no doubt; this time, it would be by motorcycle.

With sufficient savings after the following work contract ended, I spent five months riding through Europe with the guy I'd started seeing. Our paths had first crossed in Mongolia the year before; he was going east on his motorcycle and I was cycling west. We'd stayed in touch and had been meeting up now that we were both back in the UK.

We got as far as Bulgaria when my Serow broke down. We spent the next week disembowelling the engine one bolt and screw at a time using the Haynes manual and YouTube as our guides until we found the problem: three bolts in the starter clutch gear had sheared. From there it was easy: get the bolts drilled out, replace them, reassemble the engine and refit it to the bike. The starter motor had also burned out, so I kick-started the Serow back to the UK and got it replaced there.

Ever since I'd cycled through Africa, I'd known I would return to explore more of that continent. We shipped the bikes to Cape Town and spent fifteen months riding back to Europe. There were no major mechanical problems with the bikes during the journey, mostly worn out parts that needed replacing: chain and sprockets, tyres, clutch plates and spokes.

Unfortunately, the underlying problems in our relationship could not be repaired. We had spent every day of the journey through Europe and Africa together. But I need moments of solitude, especially in nature. I explained repeatedly my desire for occasional time alone, independence and freedom. It never happened. Communication between us began to break down until, at the end of the trip, we broke up. With it came an overwhelming sense of relief at being released.

With my funds running low, I returned to work and van life. The summer came and went in a flash. As the leaves on the trees turned golden and fell to the ground, I was left with the stark, bare-branched reality of a long, cold winter. There were several freezing nights when the snow flurried outside as Storm Caroline hit, bringing Arctic weather that disrupted travel and forced schools to close. I still loved van life, but the novelty had worn off. I arranged to house-sit for a friend who was going travelling in January. Having a real bed, central heating, a proper toilet and shower felt like a real luxury. As the Beast from the East blasted the UK with a Siberian chill, I began to wonder where to go next.

The seed was sown as I listened to friends' stories of their travels to Iceland. If I craved sun and warmth, Iceland's very name suggests the polar opposite. But after a few weeks of living indoors, isolated from the weather's whimsical ways, I forgot that I hate the rain. Dulled by comfort and security, I began to long for a life closely connected to nature. Iceland, by far the most sparsely populated country in Europe, had that in abundance.

I imagined finding a scenic riverside to camp beside, with only the sound of water flowing over rocks and the birds' cries piercing the air; I could relax, isolated and content in my solitude with the luxury of time to fill. There, I could continue working on the manuscript for another book on Africa that I was writing, which I'd struggled to focus on in a constantly connected world. Above all, Iceland seemed a place I could be free.

It would have been easy to book a budget flight from London to Reykjavík and be at my destination in less than three hours, but I'll never tire of travelling by motorcycle. I wanted to ride my Serow.

I pulled back the curtains onto another wet day, jumped back into bed, lost in its king-size oceanic expanse, then pulled my laptop onto

UK

my knees. 'Ferry to Iceland' I typed into Google. From there, it was a few simple steps to completing my summer escape plan.

First, I had to collect the Serow. It had been stored in Bulgaria since the end of the African trip. Not only had it been a long winter; it had been a long year with no motorcycle to ride.

The Serow needed an oil change, and a new battery and spark plug to get it running. It wouldn't start reliably on the button, so I kick-started it across Europe again. I could have raced back taking the highways, stopping only to refuel, eat and sleep, but why rush when there's a continent full of rich history, a mingling of cultures intertwined and merged, a network of winding back lanes and trails to get lost in? I spent a month riding across Romania, Croatia, Slovenia, through the snow-capped Alps and up through France towards the Netherlands. I would have been happy to spend longer.

Travelling alone for the first time since being single again felt wonderful. I could choose when and where to go, ride at my own speed, stop whenever I fancied. I could nip off the route at any moment and see what was to discover in another direction. There were no chains holding me back. I'd been let loose. *Watch out world, here I come.*

I visited friends I'd met on previous journeys and made new ones, mostly other bikers. I love meeting people, and even for an introvert like me, it's easy to meet other bikers. The bike is my confidence-boosting sidekick. Being kitted out in bike gear seems to encourage other bikers to introduce themselves, which I find easier than starting the conversation myself. Bikes have a way of connecting people, even those who to all appearances have nothing in common beyond the motorbike. It's like being part of an extended family. No matter where in the world I end up, there's a fellow biker who will drop everything to lend a hand if needed, as will I.

My parents collected me and the bike from the port at Harwich. The last MOT had been three years and 60,000 kilometres earlier, so

ICELAND Serow Saga

I couldn't legally ride it in the UK. At home, I worked on the bike to get it roadworthy enough to pass the MOT, so I could tax and insure it. In the past, there'd been someone else to do most of the bike maintenance. I was capable, but I couldn't care less who did it as long as the bike worked. Now I had to do the maintenance myself, which was fine by me.

I got oily jeans, dirt under my fingernails and a splash of petrol in my eye requiring a trip to A & E. The bike got new tyres, chain and sprockets, and a new rear shock absorber since the old one had given up somewhere in East Africa and squeaked beneath my weight ever since. I put new spokes on the rear wheel since several had broken and been replaced by mismatched make-do ones that were bent to fit.

Then, out of laziness, I took the bike to the local mechanic for further work. He walked around it and, with a superficial inspection, commented, 'It'll need a new number plate.'

I laughed. The first split had been duct-tape repaired three years ago, but the second break could not be hidden; now it dangled by a thread like a kid's loose tooth.

The mechanic dutifully carried out all the repairs I requested. He changed the headlight assembly since the old electrics had burnt out. He fitted a new intake manifold since the original one had perished and the on-the-road repair of sealing it with gasket sealant had started to fail. The rear drum brake got replaced; it had been ineffectual since somewhere in Ethiopia. I'd made do with the front brake and dragging my heels, only marginally less effective than a good drum brake anyway. And the bike got treated to a new air filter because I knew how full of dust and African dirt the old one was. To determine the problem with the starter, the mechanic took the left casing off and inspected the parts. He said the starter clutch was fine but fitted a new starter gear. It didn't help and was most likely a problem with the starter motor. Unfortunately, I was out of time; I had a ferry to

UK

catch. I'd have to continue kick-starting it. It failed the first MOT, but with new wheel bearings, it passed.

'The air filter I removed was a little oily,' the mechanic informed me when I went to collect it.

'I'd noticed that too. I meant to ask, is it a problem?'

'It's probably a sign that the piston rings are beginning to wear.'

'Will it be alright to ride like this?'

'If you haven't felt any loss of power, it should be OK for a while,' he said optimistically.

'I only need the bike to last this little trip. Then I'll have time to fix it up properly.'

'What are you doing?' he asked.

'Going to Iceland for three months.'

'Oh,' he said, his confidence in the bike vanishing.

'Well, I haven't time to do anything now. Do you think the bike'll make it?'

'Do you keep a blog? I'll be interested to see if it does.'

2

Across Europe

Bulgaria to Denmark

It's a foggy five o'clock start as I haul the fifty-litre roll bag onto the back of the bike and strap it down tightly together with my rucksack. My kit weighs a lot more than I travelled with through Africa. For Iceland's inclement weather I need extra clothes, a warmer sleeping bag and a decent tent. It all adds up. I also need good boots for walking and my laptop for writing. Over the last year living in my van, I expanded my collection of belongings for comfort and luxury. It was a challenge to downsize back to little more than essentials that will fit on the bike. I fretted endlessly over what to pack, but I know that once I hit the road it won't matter. I will make do with what I have. Life will be simple again. I just have to leave.

I tug at the straps one last time, check the bags are secure and pat my pockets to feel for my passport-wallet-phone. I swing my leg over the saddle, stomp down on the kick-start, tap into first gear and wave to my parents as I roll down the driveway. I pass the village sign, take a left at the end of the road, accelerate to cruising speed and smile at the freedom of the road.

One small part of me cannot fully relax. This is the first real test of all the repairs to the bike. But the Serow is as reliable as ever and gets me to Harwich port on time.

I ride up the ramp and onto the ferry. Bikes directed to the back, I tie the Serow down securely with straps and take the stairs up onto the deck. The day disappears in the Channel, an uneventful blur of coffee, reading in the comfy lounge chairs and dozing in the sun. Eight hours later, I ride out of the Hook of Holland in the evening light, which is rapidly vanishing, sucked into an ominously black, brooding sky. When the first thick drops of rain hit my visor, I pull onto the hard shoulder and struggle into my waterproofs.

Lightning lights up the sky ahead. The rain pelts down and the congested commuter roads turn into waterways. My gloves are soon sodden. The lightweight off-road ones that did me well in Africa are no match for Europe's weather. I feel the first trickle of water run down my forearm to my elbow and shiver as another slithers down my right shoulder blade. The waterproof hiking jacket I brought is clearly not waterproof enough for riding in. It doesn't bode well.

I have no plan of where to stop for the night. I only know that I have four days to get to Hirtshals in the north of Denmark for the ferry to Iceland via the Faroe Islands. It's over 1,000 kilometres taking a direct route, so I want to cover as much ground as possible before the first nightfall. As usual, I'd prefer to avoid the motorways, taking quieter minor roads instead. I'm still nervous that the bike will develop a problem and want time to fix it if it does.

Teasingly, the rain eases off at one point, only for the skies to open and release a deluge that turns the road into an unrideable lake. I take shelter at a petrol station. Rain streams off the roof and oil swirls on the surface water. When a gentle patter resumes, I ride in search of a place to camp. Taking a track into the forest, I pitch my tent atop a soft, damp mattress of fallen leaves. I take off my new boots, which have thankfully kept my feet dry, and remove my sodden jeans and fleece top. Then I crawl into the sleeping bag in my base layers, thankful to be dry and warm.

With the past long winter a faint memory and my summer destination of Iceland intangible in the far-off distance, the near-perfect, clear blue skies back in England had erased from my mind the possibility that it could ever be anything other than hot and sunny. This evening's downpour has reminded me of the reality of life on the road, when not every day is an easy holiday.

My friend Louise, who recently set off on a cycle tour around Europe, is also in the Netherlands now. I message her about meeting

ICELAND Serow Saga

up. She replies that she will soon be cycling into Germany. I catch up with her at the border sign, and we ride to the first town for coffee and a lively chat.

She tells me that a couple of days before at one of the free campsites in the Netherlands, she met Constantinos from Cyprus. He's riding his motorcycle across Europe and heading to Iceland too. Iceland being half the size of Great Britain, it seems feasible our paths might cross; although, with almost 13,000 kilometres of national and other public roads, it's not guaranteed. I message him and check his Facebook profile, so I'll recognise him if we do meet.

I wave goodbye to Louise, wish her good luck on her journey and continue on my own. I make good progress until the evening when the sky blackens, and I'm greeted by another deluge. Soaked to the skin, I take refuge in a bus shelter. My attempts to find a wild camping spot in densely populated Germany have been thwarted by endless villages. When the rain subsides, I go in search of a campsite. It's late by the time I pitch my tent at the edge of the large duck pond. I go to bed certain of one thing: I need to buy some decent waterproofs.

At daybreak, I'm rudely awakened by a resounding guffaw and splashing as the ducks take to the sky. With long summer days in more northerly latitudes, I will have to get used to sleeping through daylight or make do with a lack of sleep.

It's no surprise that after lunch at a roadside picnic table, I have to lie down and rest my heavy eyelids. An hour later I wake, the intense sun burning my face. There's not a cloud in the sky. No doubt this change in weather was caused by my visit earlier in the day to a large motorcycle store in Hamburg to procure good quality waterproof jacket, trousers and gloves.

By evening I'm in yet another country, Denmark. In all my years of travelling, I've rarely covered ground so fast. The bike is running smoothly; with two days remaining and around 300 kilometres to the ferry, I can afford to slow down.

Bulgaria to Denmark

Multitasking the cooking of dinner with pitching the tent, I change out of my bike gear and shovel down some pasta. Then I set out on foot to explore the area around the campsite near Esbjerg before dark.

By the long beach of rust-red, iron-rich sand, people sit outside a bar watching the sun set. Couples walk their dogs, weaving in and out of the shallow water lapping at the shore. Two brave women bathe in the cold water, only their heads and shoulders exposed to the gentle evening breeze. I wander with flip-flops in hand, toes digging into the cool, moist sand, leaving footprints between the churned-up tracks from two horses.

Where the land turns northwards, gulls chatter noisily, silhouetted on the sandy spit where the water has carved wavy patterns. I head inland over the pebbles, brush the sand off my feet and try not to step on the pink and white flowers carpeting the upper shore. Then I climb up the eroded bank and into the dark plantation behind. When I emerge again into the evening light, I'm on open heathland. The trail passes over a small rise that gives views of the sea in one direction and the forest extending to the horizon in the other. Skylarks sing their hearts out from amongst the heather, cattle graze by a small pool and a few horses stand below a lone tree. Besides a couple of joggers, who soon disappear into the woods, I have the place to myself. It's peaceful and serene. After the pace at which I've been travelling these past days, it feels good to slow down. I watch the sun inch lower, its reflection glittering in the pool, until it vanishes below the horizon.

I wind my way back through the plantation. It's the twilight hour belonging to nature. I listen to the birds' final chatter of the day. A roe deer stands frozen on the footpath ahead until, released from its stunned surprise, it bounds out of sight. A fox roaming a recently mown field, the loose grass almost dry enough to be baled, speeds off at the sound of my footsteps, wary of my intrusion into its kingdom.

ICELAND Serow Saga

Because I wake the next morning to the dawn chorus, there's time for another walk. Morning dew drips down the tent and soaks my shoes as I step through the moisture-laden grass. The low-lying landscape and big sky remind me of the Breckland heath and fens of Norfolk. The skylarks are singing again. A kestrel hovers overhead, hunting on the heath, while a jay darts through the pine trees. Shelducks bob on the small lakes by the Varde stream where egrets stand tall, and black-headed gulls cruise past along the coastline. Two hours later I return to the campsite, the sun warm and sweat trickling down my neck. I wash, brew up some coffee and devour a well-earned big breakfast of muesli, fruit and yoghurt.

As I pull on the heavy-duty straps to secure my bags onto the rear rack of the bike, one snaps. I'd noticed they were worn prior to setting off but couldn't find the new ones I'd bought online months before. I figured that since they lasted three years, they'd surely survive this three-month trip. I was wrong. There's a motorcycle store with identical replacements a few kilometres away. If this is the only thing to break on the trip, I'll have done all right.

Riding north the next day, the road passes through wetlands, the freshwater lakes a haven for wildlife and birdwatchers alike. I arrive at the harbour town of Hirtshals with an hour to spare before needing to head to the ferry port. I stock up on food supplies at Spar. The prices are eye-watering. I shudder at the thought of further inflated prices in Iceland. Then I park beside a bench overlooking golden sands and crystal-clear turquoise water, the kind I associate with a tropical island paradise.

I look out across the water to the horizon. It's hard to imagine that somewhere beyond there is more land, not wave after wave of endless ocean. How did those first people who set sail from Europe and settled on the remote islands of the North Atlantic feel? To leave what is familiar and enter a void beyond the edge of the known world sounds a daunting prospect. But for people whose livelihoods revolved around the sea, setting sail would be like me getting in my

Bulgaria to Denmark

van and driving down the motorway. Where I see emptiness, they saw a source of food and transport. Wind offered power, and they could navigate by the sun, the stars and the subtleties of nature, skills long lost by land-focused people of the twenty-first century.

On the ferry's lower deck, the ratchet straps for tying down the bike are different from the ones I've used before, with confusing loops and too short to go over the bike seat and attach to the floor. I walk over to a group of guys with BMWs to ask for help. Despite appearances, they haven't a clue how to use them either.

Being in a relationship and having someone to turn to has made me lazy. I smile as I return to my bike, reminding myself that I'm capable of figuring it out. Besides, if I'm going to head off into remote wilderness alone, I'd better get used to solving my own problems again. Ratchet straps are a minor inconvenience compared to all the possible things that could go wrong on the rough, rocky trails and big river crossings of the Icelandic Highlands.

When I think about the reason why there are loops in the straps, it becomes obvious. Soon I have the bike secured.

A Polish biker parks next to me.

'Do you know how these work?' he asks, holding up a strap towards me like an offering.

The guys with the BMWs are still bent over their bikes tying knots in theirs. I explain, then sling my rucksack containing sleeping bag and food over my shoulder and wander towards the stairwell to find my couchette.

On the *MS Norröna* ferry, deep in the boat's bowels and well below the waterline are a series of small rooms with simple bunks on each wall, a hostel dorm downsized into a shoebox. No frills, you must provide your own bedding and sleep head to toe with some stranger. 'Couchette' describes a thin mattress and not enough height to sit up without banging your head. But this budget option makes transport to Iceland more affordable.

ICELAND Serow Saga

I ditch my rucksack on my cattle-class bed as the engines rumble into action and head up to the top deck. I watch from the stern until Denmark is an inkblot on the tissue paper horizon. I've made it through the first part of the journey, no need to look back now. I turn around and stare out across the water wondering about what's beyond the horizon and under the surface. The sea is a mirror reflecting my hopes, desires and fears back at me as I think of the adventures to come.

Sun worshippers have dragged deck chairs into the daylight; others are hugging the strip of shade along one side of the boat. A few people are taking photos. Others are relaxing in the armchairs of the upstairs bar, quenching their thirst on extortionately priced beer.

Mmm … beer. In the rush to reach the ferry on time and the worries about whether the bike would work and if I've brought the right kit, I haven't had time to sit and relax in carefree contemplation. I run my tongue over my dry lips. I can think of nothing else except a cold draught beer.

I order one, glad to be unsure of the conversion of Danish kroner to pounds. I tap my credit card on the machine, which makes it much easier to ignore the price than when paying with cash. I fear this will become a familiar necessity in Iceland.

As evening draws on, I return below deck and crawl into my couchette. Not tired enough to sleep, I indulge in my addiction of binge-watching back-to-back episodes of whole TV series, downloaded onto my phone.

The owner of the other bags in the room, a German lady, enters soon after me, pulls out her sleeping bag and goes to sleep. A couple of hours later, another woman stumbles into the box, the swing doors banging behind her. I glance up.

Mumbling and slurring a jumble of words, she presses her nose to each bedpost. With a short-sighted squint, she fails to find her bed number. Then she leans over me, her face so close to mine I can smell her stale breath over her cheap, pungent perfume and see her smudged mascara, the roots of her dyed blonde hair and the creases in her face.

After she tumbles out into the corridor, all is quiet for a while. Thirty minutes later she returns. The German lady in the bed at my feet sighs audibly, rolls over to face the wall and pulls her sleeping bag up round her head. I wish the drunk English woman would be quiet for my room-mate's sake.

'Where are my fucking bed sheets? I paid for sheets …'.

When she utters venomous words at me as though it's my fault her bedding hasn't been delivered, I want to give her a sobering slap.

'You'd better go and ask at reception,' I comment politely and lay back down.

With a slew of profanities, she crashes back through the swing doors.

Unable to keep my eyelids open any longer, I turn off my phone and roll over to sleep, only to be ripped from my dreams when a young man in uniform places a pile of white linen on the mattress above. An hour later, the woman returns, giving an unintelligible running commentary. The German lady and I both pretend not to hear. Eventually, there's silence.

In the middle of the night, the drunk lady sits up, bangs her head on the bunk above, swears loudly and leaves the room. Five minutes later she reappears. I peer through one bleary eye as she turns on her bedside light and rummages through her belongings until she's found her towel and wash bag.

'What are you doing?' the German lady comments gruffly. She coughs to clear her throat, then adds, 'It's three o'clock.'

'Oh hell!' The drunk woman throws down her towel and clambers back into bed, failing to duck low enough. She bangs her head and swears again. I stifle a snigger.

In the dark room, isolated from the world with no sunlight or cheerful chirping birds to wake me, I sleep later than normal after the disturbed night. The snoring drunk woman stirs and asks the time. 'Seven-thirty,' I reply.

'Ugh! It's going to be a long day. I need coffee to get through it,' she moans.

I then realise it's only six-thirty on ship's time, which runs in sync with our first destination, the Faroe Islands. The cafe on-board doesn't open until eight. I don't say anything.

I'm looking forward to a whole day at sea with time to read and write, perhaps peruse my maps and plan a route. First, I go up on deck for fresh air. The blue sky of the previous day has gone. A grey mist blotting out the view gradually clears until the horizon appears, a narrow strip of light below a blanket of clouds. When the cafe opens, shivering against the chill of the damp dawn and the stiff breeze as the ferry ploughs through the water, I go back inside, sit by the window and sip my coffee.

It's so calm I can't feel any ocean swell. The horizon remains perfectly horizontal, framed by the window. Whenever I glance out, it's as though the sea is rushing past and the ferry is stationary. Only the waves breaking at the bow and the white trails behind belie this vision. It's a long time since I felt this detached from the rush and chaos of the daily rat race. Without internet and with only a calming sea to connect to, the forces of nature are having a pacifying effect on my soul.

A fulmar soars past, effortlessly contouring the sea's surface. A gannet, sleek and white with ink-dipped wing tips flies alongside at eye level like a faithful dog at heel. A woman shuffles past muttering something inaudible except for a loud f-word that punctuates the calm like a pin bursting a balloon. It's the drunk woman from the couchette clutching a glass of white wine. I turn back to the seabirds.

Late in the afternoon, writing snippets between long, vacant stares out of the window, I spot the long, black, glistening dorsal fin of a whale nearby … and then a second one … and another. Five orcas in all, gracefully dipping in and out of the ocean. I watch in awe and want to point and shout out, 'Look! Look!' like an excited child. I glance around the cafe but everyone's ensconced in conversation or dinner. I prod the nearest person to me, eager to share my sighting.

The rotund, soft-at-the-edges, white-haired German looks bemused until his stare follows the line of my arm. When he sees the whales, he leans over enthusiastically to get a better look, almost crushing me into the corner. His bulk on the move catches the attention of his friends, who stand up to see what the fuss is about. With a murmured ripple through the cafe, soon the window is covered in faces, food forgotten. Oohs and aahs rise up as with fireworks on Bonfire Night.

As the evening draws in, more gannets appear following the ferry. Occasionally, one veers off and circles up, brings its wings in tight to its body and makes a sharp dive into the sea. Its activity often attracts the attention of a couple more who approach, hoping for a piece of the fishy prize. Then along comes an Arctic skua, alone and mischievous. With powerful wingbeats, it chases after a gannet that's flying apart from the main group. With dogged determination, it attacks the lone gannet at least three times its size and seizes onto its wing tip. Together, tussling, they tumble towards the sea. Oblivious to its diminutive size, the black bird continues scrapping even when their wings hit the waves, ceasing only once the gannet regurgitates its latest catch, which the skua will eat. Then it takes off again and, like a yapping Jack Russell biting at one's heels and not afraid of a good kicking, goes in pursuit of another hapless Goliath for more regurgitated goodies. Again and again, it chases and attacks. You've got to admire the underdog. It makes me think of the Serow on the trails when trying to keep up with bigger enduro bikes.

There is only one passenger ferry that goes to Iceland. Run by Smyril Line, a Faroese shipping company, it takes three days and two nights from Denmark. It stops at the Faroe Islands long enough for passengers to disembark and explore the capital. It's a good ploy to

ICELAND Serow Saga

boost the economy. The ferry line also makes an attractive offer to motorcyclists: stop for three days in the Faroe Islands when returning from Iceland and the motorcycle is transported for free, though only during the short summer season when prices are highest. Travelling either side of this peak period, which is what I'm doing, the ticket cost is similar even though paying for the bike. My three-month trip includes ten days to explore the Faroe Islands. It's unlikely I'll be so close again.

Knowing little about the Faroe Islands, I looked at photos online before leaving home: vivid green pockets of beauty under bright blue skies, dramatic cliffs, gushing waterfalls and quaint, colourful turf-roofed houses. It was not only a windswept and harsh environment, as I had imagined. After two decades of travel, I am no longer surprised by my own ignorance. I travel to learn about and understand the world in which we live. Yet the more I learn, the more aware I become of how little I know.

Debatable credit for the Faroe Islands' discovery goes to the Irish abbot St Brendan. He spoke of an 'Island of Sheep and Paradise of Birds' several days' sailing from Scotland during his voyages around AD 560.

Føroyar, the Faroese name for the country, means 'The Sheep Islands' in old Norse. It was the name given by the Viking Norsemen who are considered the first settlers around the ninth century, a time when infighting and population increases encouraged people to look beyond their own country for land suitable for farming.

I look on Google Maps to visualise where we are. With the Faroe Islands centre-screen, Scotland is at the bottom of the page with the Shetland Islands on a straight line between the two. The Norwegian coast bounds the right and Iceland dominates the top left corner. Zooming out, Greenland and then North America come into view beyond Iceland. The Faroe Islands no longer seem like an isolated outpost with Iceland at the edge of the world.

3

Small Islands in the North Atlantic
Faroe Islands

From the top deck at five o'clock, the Faroese capital Tórshavn is lit up in a gentle golden glow of morning sunlight, the lighthouse silhouetted. The small boats in the marina reflect in the water, shimmering and dancing on the rippled waves.

The rocky promontory of Tinganes jutting into the harbour is where the Viking *ting*, or people's assembly, first met. This parliament, where disputes were resolved and punishments for law-breaking issued, continued to be held annually until 1816. Now, Tinganes is a web of narrow streets and well-kept red-painted buildings that house government offices.

The medley of impressions and emotions at seeing a destination approach is wonderful, lasting until the descent to the noisy, dirty car deck below. Usually, it's followed by a drive through some characterless concrete port with queues and security checks, but entry to the Faroe Islands is different.

I ride off the ferry and onto Streymoy, the largest island. Directed immediately out of the parking area by the harbour's pretty waterfront, I turn right up the hill past the lighthouse and continue out of town. It takes less than five minutes before all vestiges of urban life – if this laid-back, sleepy capital can be called urban – vanish behind me. Ahead, there is only the winding coastal road and low hillsides across the water. Without looking at a map, I can't tell if they are separate islands or the other side of a fjord.

Even in the sun, the air is bitterly cold. Riding along, my hands are soon freezing. I've always had poor circulation, but recently suffer from an increased sensitivity to cold, perhaps an after-effect of my Siberian winter cycle trip. The longer I ignore the pain, the longer it takes to bring feeling back to my extremities. I stop to put on another layer and thaw out my whitened, waxy fingers, shaking my arms and rubbing my hands to kick-start the blood flow. If this is a typical day, I fear I'll be unable to do much riding this summer.

Around the first fjord, I find Kaldbak, a pretty village with neat houses scattered over a hillside of vibrant green grass. It appears deserted; I suspect people are still tucked up in bed. A few sheep graze between rocks on the hill. Down by a jetty, small boats bob in the water, gulls fly over and a couple of mallards float by. The picturesque black-walled, turf-roofed church dates back to 1835. The door is locked. Peering through the small windows, cloudy with windblown salt and dirt, I can make out new wooden pews, somehow out of character with the old building.

Returning the way I came, at the small bridge at the head of the fjord I stop to photograph an oystercatcher pecking in the stream. The black and white bird with a distinctive long red beak flies away a short distance, then turns its back as I remove the lens cap.

Each year the oystercatcher's arrival in the Faroe Islands is warmly regarded. It signals the beginning of spring and the end of a long battle against the elements as the winter storms of sleet, snow and wild Atlantic gales abate and the battering of the shores by the ocean waves subsides. It brings hope after months of near darkness

The oystercatcher, the national bird of the Faroe Islands, is highly defensive of its young. It will deter you if you walk too close by making repeated circular aerial attacks, swooping at your head whilst piping loudly. Other birds often nest close by to benefit from their protection. It is this characteristic that led the Faroese poet Nólsoyar Páll to compose *Fuglakvæði*, 'The Bird Ballad', wherein birds of prey are symbolic of the Danish authorities and the oystercatcher is the defender of the more vulnerable birds, the Faroese themselves.

I return to Tórshavn and pitch my tent at the coastal campsite beside a small embankment, offering scant protection from the notorious winds known to blast these islands. Too cold to ride any more, I walk through town, then up and over the hills. It's impossible to ignore the collie dog lying beside the path, its tail tapping the ground expectantly. I crouch down as it rolls over to have its belly rubbed. A fat cat plods over from the farm for its share of affection. It's a friendly ambush.

The path crosses a small stream running through a lush grassy field covered with marsh marigolds. Called sólja in Faroese, they are the national flower. Higher up, it's rockier, rougher like the Scottish Hebrides with cairns marking the trail. Beyond the rise, a couple of small lakes fill the dips in the land. Kittiwakes, shining brilliant white in the sun, float on the water until a hooded crow disturbs them. As the path contours around the hillside, the islands of Hestur and the conical Koltur come into view to the west.

I descend to the picturesque coastal village of Kirkjubøur. The houses overlook a verdant meadow and calm blue water. They're painted black to resemble the historical tarred look, have matching make-up of red window frames and doors, and each is topped with a close cut of turf, the traditional roofing material. I suspect that every village in the Faroe Islands is romantically charming and pretty.

It's likely that the first inhabitants of the country, Irish monks around AD 800, eked out an existence at this place. Due to the tidal currents around the islands, the quantity of driftwood and seaweed washing ashore here was incomparable to elsewhere. On a land devoid of trees, the driftwood provided a vital source of building materials, whilst the plentiful seaweed could be used to fertilise the land for farming. Presumably, the monks had hoped for a hermit-like, peaceful life. When Vikings arrived more frequently in their longboats from Norway, the monks fled.

At the end of the village, the whitewashed St Olav's church stands a hair's breadth from the sea. Originally constructed around the twelfth century, it's the oldest church still in use in the Faroe Islands. It was built under the orders of Gæsa, a wealthy woman whose father owned half of the island. With the arrival of Gudmundur, the first bishop, Kirkjubøur's importance was assured.

Set back from St Olav's, nearer the hillside rock face at the foot of an old scree slope that's now grass-covered, is the stone-walled, roofless St Magnus' cathedral. The ruined grandeur of the largest medieval building in the Faroe Islands, which is undergoing a leisurely renovation, is diminished by the internal scaffolding. Building of the cathedral was stopped before its original completion around 1300, most likely in revolt against the Church's hefty taxes. Despite an avalanche in 1772 causing significant damage, the 1.5-metre thick walls still stand defiantly against the forces of nature.

When I emerge from the neighbouring building, a farmhouse that has been in the same family for seventeen generations and now houses a small museum, a Danish couple are looking around the cathedral. We talk as people do when outdoors and enjoying life, not encumbered by deadlines or distracting thoughts.

Torben and Eva became enamoured with the country on their first visit the year before and have returned to learn more about the history of the islands. I listen enviously as they tell me about families they stayed with and their insights into Faroese island life. We part ways when they get on the bus for Tórshavn. I prefer to walk back.

The concept of almost continuous light at these northerly latitudes is wonderful. There's no rush to fit everything into the daytime when it stretches out into the night. The reality is different. My body clock is confused. I'm wide awake and bright-eyed at four o'clock, despite having stayed up past midnight. Daily routine, however, continues according to normal working hours, shops shut and public transport not running until later. It's too cold to ride. Instead, I make coffee in the communal kitchen, settle indoors and write. By the time everyone else is getting up, an overwhelming tiredness washes over me. I return to my tent and sleep until the afternoon, waking in time to get a boat to Nólsoy, the nearest island.

Faroe Islands

I wander down to the harbour and wait at a picnic bench. A notice states that boarding for Nólsoy begins twenty minutes before departure. There are two boats moored beside it. One is a sizeable trawler more suited to fishing in the Atlantic; the other is so old and rusted, I'm surprised it still floats.

'Are you waiting for the boat to Nólsoy?' It's Torben and Eva, the Danish couple I met the day before.

'Oh, hello again! Yes; although, I'm not sure which boat that is.'

They join me at the bench and ask about what brought me here. I explain my plan to spend the summer in Iceland. As usually happens when people hear that I have so much time available to travel, they ask what I do for a living.

'I'm an engineer, work short-term contracts, live cheaply and save up so that I can spend more time doing the things I love. It's amazing how little money you need to get by and still enjoy life. It helps that I don't have a mortgage or kids.'

'Where do you live when you're not travelling?' Torben asks.

'In my camper van. I love it! Although it can be hard in winter,' I explain.

'It sounds like you have the right approach to life. Our son's a bit like you. He's living in Australia now,' Eva says.

'Yes, life is too short,' Torben interjects. 'Who knows what will happen tomorrow? I wish we had done the same thing when we were your age.'

I hear the same sentiments repeatedly, always from older people, usually because they have experienced health problems or the loss of someone close.

'There weren't the same opportunities then as now,' I say. 'Saving for a pension was a priority as well as having a family.'

'Perhaps, but you don't have the same securities as we did. I don't envy young people today ...' Torben says.

'Excuse me,' a lady interrupts. 'Are you going to Nólsoy? The boat's leaving soon.' She points to a small, smart-looking passenger ferry docked by the marina. 'You wouldn't be the first to miss it. It's a replacement while the usual ferry is being repaired.'

Inside, we join the short queue for tickets. Torben chats with the captain in Danish while they wait for his card payment to process.

'How much is it?' I ask Eva.

'Oh, for English women today, there's no charge,' she replies with a smile.

It takes a second to realise what she means. 'You didn't have to do that.'

'We know,' she says.

We walk along the aisle and take window seats on the starboard side.

'Please, let me give you money for the ticket,' I urge Torben, wallet in hand.

'Certainly not. It's just a little,' he replies.

Having done similar things myself, I know that it is as much about the giving as receiving; refusing can appear rude or ungrateful.

'We admire the way you're choosing to live your life,' Eva adds.

Compliments, like gifts, can be hard to accept graciously. I thank them, knowing it will never convey how much I appreciate their words. I promise to pay forward their kindness and generosity in the future.

The ferry docks at the quayside of Nólsoy village, situated at the narrow isthmus joining what looks almost like two islands. The smaller northern part is low-lying, but the larger chunk of land rises steeply to a summit before descending gradually to the south.

Torben and Eva go to explore the village, heading towards the whalebone arch around the quay. I walk in the opposite direction.

The path climbs upwards, then skirts along the western plateau between the range rising steeply to my left and a vertiginous drop to the sea on my right. I follow the cairn way-markers where the trail isn't obvious. All the countryside in the Faroe Islands is grazing land, which would soon be extensively damaged if every visitor walked wherever they pleased.

Besides a handful of sheep, there's only me and the birds enjoying this pleasant summer's day with the sun shining and a soft breeze blowing. The oystercatchers are ever-present. A golden plover seems oblivious until a gate I pass through slams shut behind me. Then it runs from its high rock and vanishes into the dips and troughs of the contoured ground. Whimbrels make their rippled peep-peep-peep-peep-peeps of alarm. I can hear them nearby in the grass, their calls coming one moment from in front, the next behind, but I rarely see them.

I pass a couple of tarns, then descend to two longhouses. Two hours after setting off, I reach the brightly painted red-and-white lighthouse, a shining beacon under the sun at the southern tip of the island. Sitting on the grass and eating my sandwich, I watch the fulmars glide along the cliff face and the gulls perched on the black, rocky promontory below.

As I amble back along the same path, I see a flash of movement on the hillside. I stop, motionless, and wait. *What was it?* There it goes again: a mountain hare. This time it pauses in plain view, its long ears pricked and alert to every sound.

Hares were originally introduced from Norway in 1855 for hunting. They thrived; within nine years, thousands were reportedly roaming wild. Together with brown rats and house mice, they are the only wild mammals that still live on the islands.

Introduced hedgehogs never established a breeding population, whilst any Arctic foxes and American minks that escaped from farms had no opportunity to mate and survived only until found and shot.

It's unknown when black rats first appeared, but they are blamed for spreading the bubonic plague in 1349. Eventually, they were overridden by the brown rat, which first landed from on board the Norwegian ship *Kongen af Preussen*, which wrecked on the Scottish Isle of Lewis and drifted here in 1768.

ICELAND Serow Saga

I feel fortunate to have seen a hare; I can live without encountering the other wild mammals. Besides, there are more birds to spot. Torben and Eva told me that the best place to see puffins is on Mykines, the westernmost island. Transport to and from Mykines is by boat or helicopter and soon gets fully booked. Despite my aversion to planning and scheduled timetables, I quickly make arrangements. The services are often cancelled in bad weather, leaving visitors stranded for days at a time. Keeping a couple of days in hand before my ferry to Iceland, there's only availability to spend one night on the island.

Over the next few days, I explore the main islands on my motorbike. I ride from one picturesque village at the end of a road to the next in another fjord. Wild camping is forbidden, but there are enough village campsites. In the evenings, I pitch my tent, then explore each surrounding area on foot. The slower pace of travel has a calming effect. I enjoy simply sitting and watching the wildlife.

In Gjogv, I eat lunch by some rocks where the stream enters the bay. A family of eider ducks play in the current. One fluffy brown duckling holds its head underwater with its webbed feet waving in the air, only coming up for breath. Two fishermen set off in a small boat, a tern hovering above hopefully.

Hours disappear meandering down small winding roads. Tired at the end of the day, I take a more direct route on the main roads used by commuters and for transporting goods around the country. Journey times have been greatly improved through investment in infrastructure, by digging tunnels through the mountains and building bridges between the closest islands. As I cross them, it's easy to forget that I'm travelling between islands and not taking a shortcut across a fjord.

Seventeen land tunnels range from 220 to 3,240 metres on seven of the islands. The first was built on Suðuroy in 1963. More recently, two subsea tunnels have been constructed.

Faroe Islands

The newest one is over six kilometres long and has a psychedelic display of pink, purple, blue and green lights halfway through. As far as I can tell, they serve no purpose except to make you feel as though you're travelling back in time, straight to a nineties school disco.

In the unlit single-lane tunnels, I always give way to larger vehicles, which being on a Serow means everything. I have serious doubts about how visible I am with the bike's candle-like headlight, so I pull into the passing places whenever I spot approaching lights.

The green countryside and idyllic quiet life make it seem as though the Faroe Islands is a safe place to visit. Don't be fooled. With the unlit tunnels, the questionable driving skills of foreign tourists unused to the narrow, winding lanes and the wandering sheep that frequently race across the road as a vehicle approaches, getting around on a motorcycle has inherent dangers.

Leaving most of my gear at a hostel, I carry the bare essentials in my rucksack for camping overnight on Mykines and board a small motorised boat from Sørvágur harbour with twenty other tourists and locals.

The harbour disappears from view, the fishy stink replaced by fresh salty air as the boat bounces over the fjord waters. A small road contours the northern hillside, passes through a hamlet of quaint black houses with turf roofs, then disappears into the mountain. Further along the coastline, a waterfall plunges off the cliff face into the sea below. Hiding in the next valley is the isolated hamlet of Gásadalur, the last settlement to be made accessible by road when a tunnel was built in 2003. Before then, the only land route was over the mountains along a precarious path, which the postman walked three times a week.

We pass the two sea stacks of Drangarnir, then the jagged shark-tooth ridge of Tindhólmur, hinting at a more savage and wild side of the country than I've experienced. The boat passes close to the dark cliffs of Mykines where fulmars nest on narrow ledges, keeping their eggs warm and protected. We pull into a small cove and moor at the jetty.

Enquiring about the campsite at a guesthouse, which also serves as cafe, bar and tourist information, I'm directed to an area above the village. I walk up a narrow alleyway between a house and outbuildings with chickens pecking in the dirt, then climb up the grassy bank beside a stream that runs through a cluster of brightly painted traditional houses. I pitch my tent with a view towards the lighthouse in the distance. Continuing along that line of sight is Newfoundland on the Canadian east coast, thousands of kilometres away.

Having waited until most of the day-tripping visitors are returning, I walk over to the islet where the puffin colony resides. The short, stocky, black-and-white birds with their clown faces, bright orange-tipped beaks and matching webbed feet stand on the grassy hillsides looking this way and that. Some disappear into their burrows that pit the ground; others throw themselves off the steep slopes and, with little wings beating rapidly, torpedo towards the sea until I lose sight of the distant specks. Some loop back to the cliffs, their bulky bodies and stumpy wings defying gravity. How each one tells which burrow is its own, I've no idea.

Mykines' ten permanent residents are greatly outnumbered by the bird population. It's hard to believe that seabird numbers have fallen drastically in recent years. It's estimated that the Faroe Islands had a puffin population of 1.5 million in 1997. Twenty years later, it has declined by about eighty per cent. The primary cause is thought to be a shift in the distribution of marine food sources due to the changing climate and warmer waters in the North Atlantic.

The following day, hoping to go for a hike up the hill behind the village, I set off up a farm track but am thwarted by relentless attacks by Arctic terns. They circle above with cries of alarm and take turns to dive at me ferociously. I wave my jacket frantically in the air to protect my head but am defeated and turn back.

Faroe Islands

I leave Mykines by helicopter. Heavily subsidised by the government, it's inexpensive. Before take-off, I sit with the handful of other passengers in the small office to watch a safety video. There's no confirmation of tickets, no security check or baggage search. Once the helicopter has landed and the arriving passengers disembarked, the gate to the helipad is opened and we step aboard. We fly close to the cliff and so low that the downdraught of the rotating blades creates eddies on the surface of the sea.

The regular boat and helicopter services make the smaller islands accessible, essential for the few people who still live on them. Without these connections, the population would decline further.

Reunited with the Serow, I ride as far east across the islands as it's possible to go without taking a ferry, then turn back. I stop for lunch in Klaksvík and sit by the harbour eating fish and chips from a van. The British were posted to the Faroe Islands during the Second World War and some of their traditions have been adopted. With Cadbury's Dairy Milk and tea, I feel quite at home during mealtimes.

By my last full day in the Faroe Islands, the weather has turned, the last remnants of sunshine obliterated by low grey clouds and damp mist. My visit coincided with a period of unusual weather. According to a middle-aged Faroese lady I chatted with, it has not rained for fourteen days. It's the longest dry spell she can remember.

I spend the day writing indoors. I enjoy having something to focus on as the rain is discouraging me from going outside. Although, I suspect I'm going to do less writing during this trip than I'd imagined. When the weather allows, the urge to explore new places is proving too great to ignore.

Tórshavn campsite is busy with backpackers and a few bikers spending their last night on the island. I talk to two Germans who are heading to Iceland for a week on their motorbikes. Holgar's Honda Shadow cruiser is older than mine. Tomas's Ducati, parked alongside, makes an unlikely partner. I saw them a couple of times earlier today, each time refuelling at a petrol station, surprising given the limited roads. I haven't needed more fuel yet, thanks to the oversize tank on my Serow.

We sit outside on a picnic bench, drink beer and laugh lots. Tomas's dry humour and Holgar's exuberance are infectious. When we erupt again in raucous laughter, one lady shouts from her tent for us to keep quiet. So we whisper for a while, but Holgar's volume control is faulty and the decibels rise. With the third remonstration, I have to sympathise and go to bed too. I recognise the khaki rucksack outside the tent as belonging to the German lady who was in my couchette on the ferry. She isn't having much success in getting quiet nights' sleep.

Familiar with the ferry, I ditch my gear in the couchette, change out of my two-weeks-since-last-wash bike gear and into my shorts and flip-flops, then head straight to the top deck. Several bikers are already ensconced at the bar. Some wear jeans and black t-shirts with white logos and writing on the front, tattoos on their arms; one couple wear pristine, expensive adventure bike gear; two guys have outfits that look as though they haven't been removed since they bought their first bikes in the seventies. Everyone dresses according to their tribe.

One guy stands out. He looks twenty years younger than everyone else. A larger than life character, he attracts people like filings to a magnet. He's the kind of person who will talk to anyone, loves to know everyone, would never understand how difficult some find it to strike up conversation with a stranger. He's regaling his audience with a story that looks like it could go on a long time.

I'm almost certain I recognise his face: someone I expected to see on the ferry. It's Constantinos. I overcome my innate shyness and wander over, hoping he'll recognise me as Louise's biker friend. In animated story-telling mode, he doesn't notice when I give him a timid tap on the shoulder. Most of the other guys are looking at me. *OK, this is awkward.*

I give a solid prod. 'Hi!' I shout, which is still much quieter than his normal talking level. He looks up.

'Hi,' I begin again. 'Are you Constantinos?'

'Yes,' he replies warily.

'I'm Helen, Louise's friend …'.

Before I can get another word in, he booms, 'Great to meet you! Come and sit down. Everyone, this is Helen. She's a friend of this girl I met in the Netherlands. Helen's cycled all around the world …'.

'Not exactly,' I peep, but it's lost in the ongoing introduction.

'And she cycled in Siberia in the winter, would you believe. Now she rides a motorcycle and is coming to Iceland …'.

I shrink into the uncomfortable, plastic sofa-style chair (yes, that's a thing), and try to drown out the relentless high praise.

'Helen, this is Boris from Germany next to you.'

'Hi,' I shake his hand.

'And this is Ari and Dirk from the Netherlands; Friedrich, Karl, Jurgen from Germany and Fillipos from Spain …'.

Of course, these aren't their real names. I struggle to remember anyone's name on first meeting let alone ten at the same time.

Once everyone's beer is drained, Constantinos announces that he is going to make use of the free on-board hot tub. Knowing that Iceland has a lot of natural hot pools, he has planned his route using an online map that shows all the locations of free ones. He hopes to stop at a different one each evening.

Since striking up conversation in a bar makes me uncomfortable, being forced to talk (because not talking would be even more awkward) to strangers sitting well within my personal space in a pool of questionably clean water while wearing limited clothing is an experience I'm keen to avoid. Being a curious traveller at heart and generally living with the mantra of trying everything at least once, I shoved my bikini into the bottom of my clothes bag. I suspect it will be my least-used item but don't want to be ill-equipped should I end up in a situation that warrants it.

While Constantinos goes for a soak, I go back to my couchette. Descending deep below the water-line, I try to deflect images of the Titanic and getting locked down here in a sinking boat.

I was warned of the violent storms that can hit these seas turning the ferry into a cork bobbing helplessly as giant waves wash over it. I've been on rough seas before and take a mild sadistic pleasure as those around me turn pale and green and stumble towards the toilets, knocking from wall to wall as the ferry lurches with the swell. One by one the hurling wretches go to their cabins to curl into a foetal position on their bunks, hoping sleep or death will save them. It leaves the bar open to the unaffected few, whose laughter is their weapon against the storm. Ultimately, though, everyone is taken down. Those of us that weathered the gale usually find ourselves in pain and discomfort much later, suffering the ill-effects of a hangover; whilst the rest, now recovered and famished, dig into a hearty breakfast to refill their empty stomachs.

I eat the bread and cheese I brought with me and watch the rest of the TV series on my phone. There's no tilt or sway of the ferry to be felt as it glides smoothly across the flat sea. I soon fall fast asleep.

My couchette companion, who hasn't peeped a word until now, wakes me to say that we should be disembarking soon.

'What?' I raise my head and fumble for my phone, the fear that I've overslept dragging me out of my sleepy fog. I stare at the screen until the clock comes into focus, then crash back onto the pillow. There's still an hour and a half until I need to pack. I can't begrudge anyone when they have good intentions; except, perhaps, at five-thirty in the morning.

If I thought there might be a sunrise to see, I would have raced up to the top deck. But the forecast is for rain. I hate the rain. *What on earth induced me to come to Iceland for the whole summer?* The prospect of a

Faroe Islands

three-month downpour drowns out my usual enthusiasm. I roll over and fall back to sleep, my curiosity a damp squib.

I wake this time to the crackling voice over the tannoy informing us of our imminent arrival. Suddenly I'm anxious that I'm missing the part of ferry travel I enjoy the most: watching the approach to land, seeing a new country form in front of my eyes. Energy bubbles within me. I leap into action.

Ouch! My head bashes the upper bunk. I lay back down and wait for the throbbing to subside before making a second attempt. I dress quickly and stride up the stairs two at a time, then heave open the door onto the deck. Squinting and blinking, I emerge into the bright light of day.

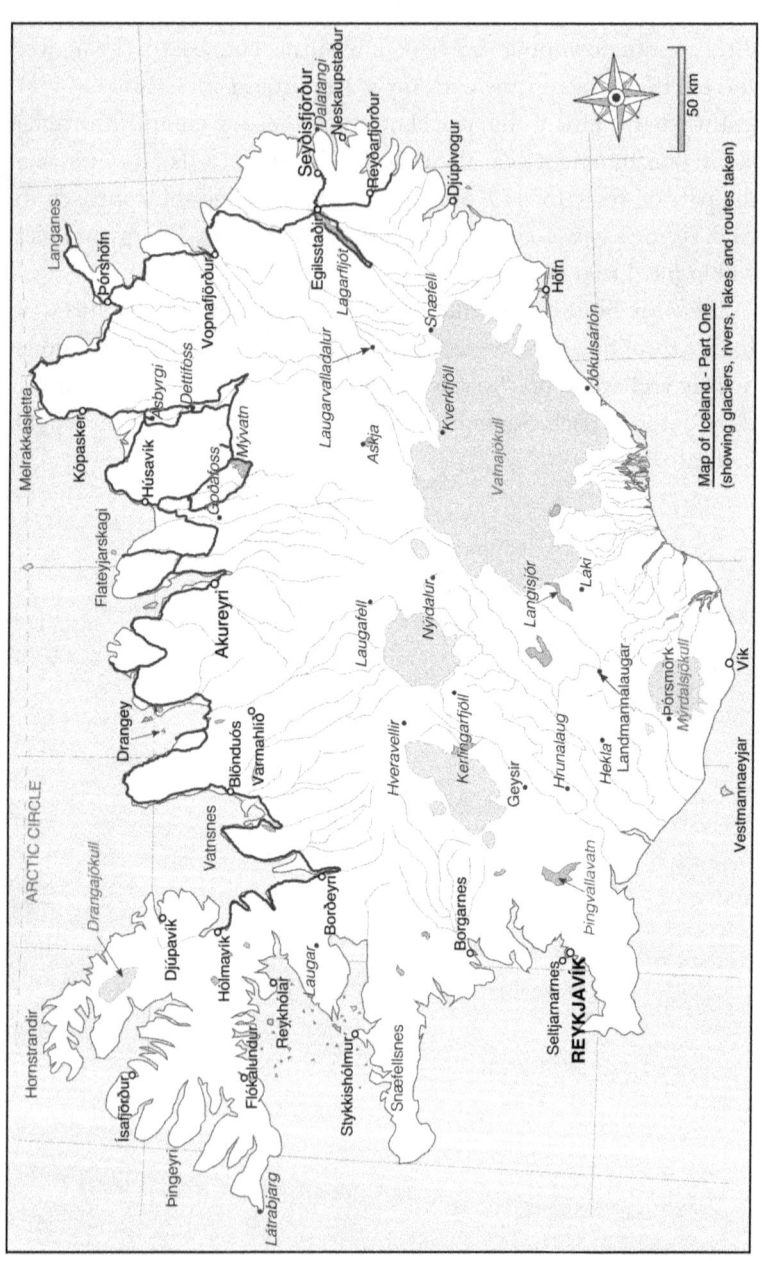

ICELAND
-
Part One

Breakdown recovery vehicle heading for Akureyri.

Camping in Flateyjardalur.

4
Arrival
East Fjords

The land appears as an impregnable barrier, rising formidably into low-lying cloud that obscures the mountaintops. Black rocks glisten on the steep ridged walls of the fjord that disappear into the deep-sea oblivion of dark water. A powerful waterfall cascading into the sea has me transfixed.

If this vision is the opening line of a thriller, I'm hooked. It's wild and raw and beautiful. There's a vast landscape awaiting my discovery. *I think I'm going to like Iceland after all.*

The ferry cruises parallel to the land. We are funnelled deeper and deeper into the fjord as though being pulled in with no hope of retreat. The air is heavy with moisture; a damp chill penetrates my clothes. I zip my jacket tight under my chin and pull my hat down over my ears. I hope the weather improves and the clouds clear. I want to see more.

After struggling into multiple layers of bike clothing and waterproofs, I disembark with the other passengers at the pretty town of Seyðisfjörður. The vivid red and yellow, pale blue, turquoise green and brilliant white houses are a cheerful contrast to the grey day. Buoyed on, I ride past the small lake and keep going on the only road out of town, over the mountains, on never-ending switchbacks rising into ever-thickening fog. In clearer patches, around pools of inky water, I can see snow and ice even though it's mid-June.

My plan for the trip extends as far as having a place to stay tonight. Beyond that, I have no idea which route to take or what to see. With over a decade of travelling and wild camping experiences, the uncertainty of not knowing where I will sleep doesn't concern me.

ICELAND Serow Saga

I enjoy the freedom, excited to wonder what each day has in store because nothing is planned and anything can happen.

A friend had put me in touch with an Icelandic couple she knew. I emailed them, not expecting a bed for the night (although I would never pass up an offer of a shower or use of a washing machine) but because a country is always more interesting when you know people who live there. They replied instantly, saying I was welcome to stay on arrival as they lived in a village just south of where the ferry docks.

Knowing that in less than two hours I can be safely ensconced in a warm, dry home drives me on. I hope the Icelanders are similar to the Russians and keep their houses well heated so that, no matter how chilly it is outside, you can lounge about in skimpy clothing inside. It might be my last opportunity to wear the shorts I packed.

I clench the heated grips, trying to force what little heat they emit through my gloves to my fingers. Then I feel the road changing. No longer climbing, the engine is not straining. The bike accelerates even though my grip on the throttle hasn't changed. We've made it out of the fjord and begin to descend. The country is spread out below me, I presume. Trapped in the white fog, my vision is limited. I see the hairpin bend almost too late. Breaking as hard as I dare on the wet tarmac, I lean in slightly and ease on down, down, down …

It's fitting to start my Icelandic travels in the East Fjords. It's where Naddoddur, credited with the discovery of the island, first landed. According to *Landnámabók*, a medieval text detailing the settlement of the country by the Norse in the ninth and tenth centuries, the Norse-Faroese Viking got lost on his way from Norway to the Faroe Islands. He came ashore near present-day Reyðarfjörður and climbed one of the mountains to look for rising smoke or another sign of human habitation. He found none and decided to continue to the Faroe Islands. As he was turning to leave, it started to snow. He named this country Snæland (Land of Snow). Unlike the snow on the mountaintops, the name didn't stick for long.

East Fjords

The next man to come was a Swede, Garðar Svavarsson, whose ship was forced to the eastern coast by a storm. (Getting lost and blown off-course proved a successful method of discovering new land for the Vikings.) He sailed west along the south coast, then headed north, wintering near today's Húsavík. He eventually completed the first circumnavigation, thereby proving the landmass was an island. On his departure in the summer, he renamed the land Garðarshólmur (Garðar's Island).

It was the next man to visit, Flóki Vilgerðarson, who gave this island its present-day name. From near the Faroe Islands, the Norseman released three ravens. The first returned to the Faroe Islands, the second flew up and came back to the ship, but the third flew in front of the bow, so he followed it. Because of this, he was known by the nickname Hrafna-Flóki (Raven-Flóki). He sailed up past Reykjavík and came ashore at Vatnsfjörður in the Westfjords where he spent a harsh winter that killed all his cattle. He cursed the country, and when he saw drift ice in the fjord, he decided to call it Ísland (Iceland). I'm not sure what I would have called this country; Cold-wet-n-misty doesn't roll off the tongue as smoothly.

My initial enthusiasm at the approach to Iceland on the ferry has been tempered now I'm on the bike, can see little through the fog, and the pain in my cold fingers is clawing for my attention. I clear my visor again with the rubber wiper blade on the forefinger of my glove, hoping to improve my visibility through the low cloud.

At least I made it over the mountain road, the only way out of Seyðisfjörður from where I disembarked. It's not uncommon for this road to be blocked in winter due to snow, making escape impossible. Some people arriving by ferry for a short holiday may never see more of the country. There is an Icelandic crime series, *Trapped*, based on this scenario. Fortunately, I didn't watch it before coming. The murderer was suspected of arriving on the *MS Nörrona*, the ferry I took. *Trapped* meets *Titanic* and the idea of having a murderer on board a sinking ship would not have been conducive to sweet dreams in my couchette.

I am surprised when Egilsstaðir emerges below like a ghostly apparition. With a population of roughly 2,500, it's the largest town in the east. The two budget supermarket car parks are full of camper vans and motorhomes. The ferry's arrival must be a major boost to both the population and economy each week. I'll make do with my leftover bread and cheese for lunch rather than face the inevitable queues in Bónus or Nettó.

At the main junction, I stop to check my map and rub my hands together vigorously to get the circulation flowing. The German lady with the khaki rucksack is waiting, hoping to hitch a ride north. She's only got two weeks, so can't linger long if she wants to see everything she hopes to. I'd like to be able to offer a lift, but we're going in different directions. Besides, there's no space for a passenger on my loaded bike. I wave goodbye, expecting this will be the last time our paths cross.

It's stopped raining, although the grey clouds remain. The improvement entices me to explore the area before rushing to Högni and Unnur's home, where I'm staying tonight. Knowing little about Icelandic weather, I fear that this could be a good day. Resigning myself to the possibility of a grey summer, and with as much enthusiasm as I can muster in going to the dentist, I set off to tour around Lagarfljót, the long lake on which the town is situated. Like Loch Ness, it's said to have a giant worm-like monster living in it. Sightings have been dismissed as floating ice.

Icelandic folklore is rich in mythical creatures. Elves are said to inhabit the rocks and hills, whilst there's a world of *Huldufólk*, hidden people, that can only be seen if they want to be. Stories of the first settlers as told in the sagas are full of trolls and giants and ghosts. If you believe these tales, a Lagarfljót worm is not so unlikely.

I only know about the elusive Lagarfljót worm from my guidebook. I see no signs informing me about it. There are no books in the

East Fjords

garage, cuddly toys or memorabilia in shop windows, certainly no exhibition centre about the lake and its monster of the deep.

It's a prime example of the untapped Icelandic tourist market. With creative marketing, this could be a significant attraction. I'm glad it's not. The East Fjords are the least developed region in terms of tourism. Far from Reykjavík, they are often driven through in one day of a driving tour or viewed only from the motorhome window on the way to and from the ferry.

People have been visiting Iceland for centuries and as tourists in the modern sense for decades. Until the eighties, it was a slow and steady trickle. Gradually more foreigners came until, in 2000 for the first time, annual tourist numbers exceeded the Icelandic population. After the financial crisis of 2008 plunged the country into hardship, Iceland came onto the international radar, and when Eyjafjallajökull erupted in 2010 disrupting flights around Europe, it made headline news. Once the smoke had settled, with an aggressive marketing campaign and cheap flights to Reykjavík, people began to visit in droves. In 2017, there were around 2.2 million foreign visitors to this country with a population of only 335,000. The proportion of tourists to locals is higher in summer when most Icelanders prefer to escape abroad to more tropical destinations. If today's weather is anything to go by, I can't blame them.

I ride past Reyðarfjörður where Naddoddur first came ashore and take the tunnel through to the next fjord, though the old road around the headland would be a welcome detour on a dry, sunny day for a visitor with lots of time. Historically, because getting from one fjord to the next took a long while, people's work and careers would have been determined by where they lived, according to the industry of the fjord rather than what they would like to do. A tunnel makes journeys quicker for locals in the summer and possible in winter when rockfalls and avalanches can block the coastal road.

It's easy to find Högni and Unnur's home. There are not many streets in a village of little more than 750 inhabitants. There is no obvious centre to the village; it spreads along the coast, hemmed in between sea and mountain. There's one home with a 'Motorcycle Parking Only' sign on the garage. I park, walk up the wooden steps to the front door and knock. Unnur welcomes me in. I leave my waterproofs and bike gear dripping in the entrance hall.

'Would you like coffee?' she asks first. Coffee is an Icelandic obsession.

As this is my first day in Iceland, I probably shouldn't be considering a day off. Yet, my last day at work was nine weeks ago, after which I flew straight to Bulgaria to be reunited with my bike. Since then, I've ridden through fifteen countries, overhauled the bike and only slept in the same place more than one night on a handful of occasions. So, later that evening when Högni says I'm welcome to stay longer and Unnur nods in agreement, I don't need persuading.

I don't need an excuse for a day off, but the bike needs an oil change and the forecast is for more rain. Besides, the football World Cup is on. Although I usually have as much interest in football as I do in watching paint dry, I remember how entertaining it was to watch Ghana play in the 2010 World Cup from their home country. It might be similarly fun here. It's a historic event, the first time Iceland has qualified. The country is disadvantaged on the world stage by having a small population from which to draw their professional footballing stock. They are drawn to play Argentina in their first game. The odds are against them. The whole of Iceland is rooting for their success. Tonight, there are almost as many Icelanders in Moscow, where the match is being held, as in Iceland. I have a soft spot for the underdog. They win.

The next day Unnur takes me to the neighbouring village, a half-hour drive away in the next fjord, where an archaeological dig is underway, now in its third season.

The rectangular plot contains several large stones that, to my inexperienced eye, could be old foundations or simply rocks scattered haphazardly by nature. Six guys in workmen's clothing, woollen hats,

East Fjords

fleece jumpers and checked flannel shirts, with rough hands and reddened, wind-worn faces, work at a leisurely pace armed with a bucket, spade or trowel. Another person kneels apart from the rest. She's a student with model looks, make-up and straightened blonde hair, who manages without trying to make work clothes look stylish and digging in the dirt glamorous. She's working with meticulous care.

At the end of each summer, the turf is re-laid to protect the remains from environmental damage over the winter, during which time the summer finds are processed. The whole plot has to be dug out again for the excavation to resume the next summer. Icelandic summers are short. No wonder progress is slow.

I once held ambitions to be an archaeologist, inspired by the adventures of Indiana Jones, the untold riches and discoveries of the ancient Egyptians, and the more down-to-earth stripy-jumper quirkiness of *Time Team*. The reality is right in front of me. Kneeling on the cold ground, painstakingly brushing away earth from stone remains in a fine drizzle is not appealing.

They've uncovered an unusually large Viking longhouse. What's of particular archaeological interest is the location beneath what is, in geological terms, called the 'settlement layer', a sedimentary layer of volcanic tephra that fell around AD 869–873. This can be used as a date marker. According to *Landnámabók*, the first permanent settler arrived in AD 874. As this longhouse pre-dates that by several decades, it throws into question textbook Icelandic settlement history.

The popular version is that the first permanent settler was Ingólfur Arnarson. Undeterred by Raven-Flóki's earlier visit, he made an exploratory journey to Iceland with his foster-brother. They spent the winter here, then returned in AD 874 to settle. When they were approaching land, Ingólfur threw overboard his high seat pillars, the pair of wooden poles placed on either side of the seat belonging to the head of the household. They were a revered symbol. It was determined that where they washed ashore would be the place they should settle. This was a common method, according to the written sagas.

Ingólfur spent three winters exploring the south coast while his slaves went in search of the pillars. When they were found, Ingólfur built his permanent homestead at the place he named Reykjavík, meaning 'Smoky Bay', after the steam that rose from nearby hot springs. The location of the country's capital was not therefore selected for reasons of defence or good food supplies but a completely random event, which resulted in subsequent families moving to this original farm.

History of the early settlers is mainly drawn from two written sources, *Íslendingabók* (Book of Icelanders) and *Landnámabók* (Book of Settlement). *Íslendingabók* is the first history of Iceland written in the vernacular. The author was Ari Thorgilsson, an Icelandic priest born in AD 1068. Historians widely agree that *Landnámabók* was also written, at least in part, by Thorgilsson. *Landnámabók* tells the stories of some 430 principal settlers, focusing on the families, their farmsteads, and what brought them to Iceland. It tells of the friendships and feuds that developed and contains a wealth of information that was later used by the saga writers to describe the many colourful characters, their adventures and misdeeds.

Unnur tells me about her grandmother, Petra, who lived in the village. Always with an interest in nature, Petra collected stones as a child. When she married and had a house and garden with space, her obsession with mineral rocks and stones grew. She used to go walking regularly in the northern slopes of the fjord, staying out all day. Already knowing where to find many interesting rocks, her collection soon expanded. As roads were primitive and with no bridge across the river, her collecting was mostly confined to the East Fjords.

On the day of her husband's funeral in 1974, Petra decided her home and garden should be opened to the public so that her collection could be seen by everyone. Petra's home is now a museum containing many of her finds, the majority on display in the garden.

East Fjords

Surrounding a wooden sculpture of Petra in gumboots and a holdall slung over her left shoulder are rows of rocks of all shapes, sizes and colours. It's possibly the biggest private collection of geological finds in the world. I try to focus on the uniqueness of each stone despite the sheer quantity. There is a story behind each one; how they were found and where. Was it summer with the plover calling or winter with a harsh wind blowing? And what was happening in the rest of the world beyond the fjord that day?

It seems amazing that so much history and interesting geology is associated with this one small village. While Petra's stone collection is unique and the Viking longhouse a rare find, I suspect that every village, fjord, waterfall and mountain in Iceland has its own extraordinary story.

What I like most about the stone museum is about Petra herself. A modest woman, she went through life doing what she loved, yet creating something beautiful that the rest of the world can enjoy. It reminds me that everyone has a fascinating story to tell. We are privileged that Petra told us hers.

I was writing, but am easily distracted and have ended up perusing an adventure motorcycle touring book belonging to Högni and Unnur. The route descriptions are in Icelandic, but I understand the maps, distances, difficulty level and best times of year to travel them. Högni's given me an old road atlas to use and pointed out their favourite trails. I've been made to feel so at home here, it would be easy to stay longer, but I'm eager to explore the country and don't want to overstay my welcome.

Over Sunday morning coffee, Unnur says, 'We were chatting last night about the possibility of adopting you.'

We laugh. 'You just enjoy my dishwashing services,' I say.

'You may as well stay for lunch. We'll have my favourite,' Högni says. 'English fry-up.'

They're not making it easy for me.

ICELAND Serow Saga

In the afternoon, full up on sausages, I wheel my bike out of the garage, load up and say goodbye. It's not a final farewell but the see-you-again-soon kind.

'You must stay on your way back before you get the ferry or anytime you pass,' Högni adds.

I set off along the coastal road back towards Egilsstaðir. It's supposed to be better weather in the north. I shall let the forecast be my guide. Unnur recommended making a detour along one of her favourite roads: to the lighthouse at Dalatangi.

The wide track runs alongside the meandering river and leads invitingly towards the mountains. Snow clings doggedly to the upper slopes, only on the steepest rock faces and cliff edges has it melted, the dark lines like the chocolate layers of Viennetta ice-cream. The river makes a sharp bend around the hillside where two valleys meet. I stop to photograph water gushing through a small ravine. When I look up, there are only small patches of snow visible on the lower slopes. The rest is obscured by a white blanket of fog creeping towards me. Reluctantly, I put on my new waterproofs. Already I'm thankful for those evening storms in the Netherlands that prompted me to buy them. At this rate, I'll be wearing them permanently and needn't worry about them taking up space in my bag. And I can ditch the bottle of suncream.

Five minutes later I can barely see the trail ahead. From the strain on the engine easing, I know when I've reached the pass. Pools of frozen water edged with snow show faintly through the fog. I ride with the visor up to see better, my cheeks windblown red. My gloves are wet and my fingers painfully cold. *It'll be clear once I descend.*

It's worse on the other side. The fog reaches down to the sea. It's pointless continuing. I'm cold and wet and can't see a thing. If this turns out to be my favourite road, I'm in for a disappointing holiday. I turn around, the lure of town and my tent more appealing.

When I get to town, there is a hint of sunshine to the north. It is teasing me; I fall for it. I set off towards Borgarfjörður in an

East Fjords

upbeat mood. The farmland is bathed in a warm evening glow when the sun breaks through the cloud. Then I cut across the estuary to find a wall of mountains ahead, the tops hidden by black clouds that threaten to swallow up a Serow and its hapless biker. I'd be thrown out on the other side wet and miserable, I'm sure. I turn back, not to be distracted from my tent this time. I'm soon safely ensconced and warm in my sleeping bag, in a dry tent, drinking hot coffee. Tomorrow will be better.

Tomorrow is not better. It's raining when I wake and the forecast is for worse. I take a day off and watch the whole season of *Trapped*. It's how I feel. Trapped because of rain rather than snow, but still trapped. At least there's not a murderer on the loose. And I'm happy because I'm warm and dry.

I harbour concerns about the durability and water-fastness of my twenty-year-old tent, though. Occasionally I look up from the screen when the drumming of rain intensifies and notice a drop of water running down from the flysheet seam into a growing pool on the roof of the tent inner, somewhere above my left kidney when I'm lying down. I resist the urge to poke at it, knowing that to do so will release the bulge onto me.

I didn't bring my new hiking tent because the ultralight material is as thin as crepe paper and I doubted its durability in high winds, which I have been promised Iceland provides in abundance. This old tent has been tested in strong Patagonian winds. It's a good quality one but has had little use as it's too heavy for carrying on a bicycle. With the motorbike, weight is not such a limiting factor. My assumption that it is waterproof because it has never let in water before is flawed. I don't think it's ever rained when I've used it.

The pool of water is growing into a big, flashing red button that's shouting 'Press me!'

My forefinger hovers below it. *Don't do it.*

I can't resist.

ICELAND Serow Saga

I raise my finger slightly and give the faintest of pokes. Water trickles down my hand. I grab my towel, which like all my belongings for the next three months is within arm's reach, and quickly rub the inner roof fabric, attempting to erase my misdeeds. I look about me slyly as though checking no one caught me in this heinous act, which is ridiculous because there's only me, only enough space for me, in this supposedly two-man tent.

I go back to watching *Trapped*. A full five minutes pass before I notice the first drop of water drip onto my sleeping bag. *Sigh.*

The next morning, hyperactive from too many cups of coffee and suffering cabin fever, I decide I must leave. I'm not raring to ride; it's cold and dreary grey. Importantly though, it's not raining; this might be as good as it gets. Besides, I do want to see more of this country.

Oh Iceland, I want to love you. You're not making it easy, but you're going to have to try harder if you want to deter me.

5
Driftwood and an Abandoned Village
Langanes

Buzzing from the caffeine overdose, I pack up and hit the road. The forecast still looks better further north, the bright yellow sun teasing me on the weather map, while Egilsstaðir and the East Fjords are wallowing under clouds. My initial plan is to follow the coast in an anticlockwise direction. Being low-lying, the coast is most likely to be cloud- and rain-free. There is just one little mountain range to get over first.

I think I'm being mocked. 'You think the rain is bad? Well try this!' I hear the heavens bellow above the wind. It blasts down the mountains and pummels me from the left.

I hurl abuse back at it. *Is that all you've got!*

But then I reach a section of road that is being re-laid, the top layer of gravel not yet bedded in. I move over to avoid the lone workman driving heavy machinery straight towards me. The rear tyre fishtails in the loose gravel. I veer off, the wind pushing the bike into the side channel full of water. I slow to a crawl, fighting for every metre of forward progress. Then the trail becomes hard-packed and gives a moment of relief as I turn towards the mountains, the wind hitting me face on. I relax my grip on the steering. As the switchbacks start, I resume my rigid, tight rein on the bike as though it's a wild horse trying to break free. It'll take more than this to unseat me. Then the rain turns to hail, trying to batter me into submission. *Should I turn around?* There's no alternative way to the other side; it's either give up or go on. I step down a gear and open the throttle in defiance. *Come on little bike, help me out.*

The switchbacks end; the road continues upwards more gradually. The pellets of hail soften to sleet. There is snow on what I can make out of the hillside. The road is frozen. I slow to a crawl, both feet scraping along the ice as stabilisers on the slippery surface. *Surely I'm near the top.* I consider turning around again, but the thought of having to repeat this another day convinces me to push through. My gloves are saturated. In the icy wind, my hands begin to freeze. Cold toes too.

Eventually, the road peaks and begins a gradual descent. Snow falls thickly and settles on the road and gives some semblance of grip on top of the ice. I had been following a set of car tracks but those have faded into obscurity. My bike tyres leave two dark trails behind me, snaking one over the other like a ragged double helix.

But this isn't the top; it's merely the start of a winding route through the mountains. With every rise and fall, I think I am stupid for continuing and ought to turn back, but now the ride back is equally unappealing. *What if I get stuck?* I know how to survive. Besides, this is just some unpleasant weather in the hills and will be over soon.

Not soon enough.

My toes have gone numb. The throbbing pain of frozen fingers brings tears to my eyes. Do I stop and run to warm up or persevere and get out of here as fast as I dare? At least the wind has lost its power, unable to twist its tendrils and search me out in the heart of these mountains. I shake my left arm violently, hoping to force some warmth to my fingers. On the downhill, I take my right hand off the throttle and rattle some feeling into it too. The burning pain intensifies until I'd happily chop off my fingers right then if someone handed me a knife. Fortunately, there's only me up here – no one else seems foolish enough to be out today.

Then I realise that I'm going down. There's no longer snow on the road, and I'm getting drenched by rain again. Emerging from the cloud veil, I see a bridge at the bottom of the valley. I speed up, cross it and head towards the coast. The clouds look less threatening there. They end just offshore, the blue sky beyond tormenting me.

Langanes

With the bike parked in a lay-by, I run up and down the road waving my arms and jump up and down while shrugging my shoulders. Eventually, my hands and feet thaw out. I sometimes have wistful memories of the winter I spent cycling in Siberia and dream of going back there; it's moments like this that remind me of the reality.

In Vopnafjörður I wring out my sopping gloves and blow warm breaths to revive my fingers again. There's a sculpture of a sailing ship by the water, signifying the importance of the town as a major trading port in the eighteenth and nineteenth centuries. The tourist information place is shut; I can think of no other building to enter that won't involve spending money. All I want is somewhere warm. I pour tea from my Thermos and grip the mug of tepid fluid tightly, hoping to transfer warmth to my fingers.

At the next village, Þórshöfn, meaning 'Thor's Harbour', the tourist information is at the swimming pool. The reception area is blissfully heated. I remove my dripping waterproof clothing and boots and take a seat near the radiator. I've heard that swimming pools are something of an Icelandic institution, not to be missed. As I've been wet for most of the day and am now dry, I've no desire to jump into a pool of water, however hot it may be.

At the reception desk there is a folder with information on things to see and do locally. When the friendly receptionist has finished talking on the phone, I ask about heading along the Langanes peninsula. She tries to deter me from going until she realises that I'm on a trail bike. Then she says it'll be a lovely ride tomorrow as better weather is forecast.

Checking the weather forecast is already becoming an obsession bordering unhealthily on addiction. I check the weather app more times than I drink cups of coffee. When it comes to coffee and weather forecasts, I successfully assimilate Icelandic habits. It helps being British, as we probably come second after the Icelandic for obsessing about the weather. They say here, if you're not happy with the weather, wait ten minutes. It's like Scotland having four seasons in one day. I'm still waiting, though, for a glimpse of Icelandic summer.

Two hours later, the sun emerges. *It exists!* The campsite, behind the village, looks to the church over a field with horses grazing. A fresh meadow of long grass with buttercups glows golden in the evening light. A couple of redshanks repeatedly fly over my tent like guardian angels keeping watch over me. It's as if, after freezing in hell, I've risen straight to heaven.

I anxiously endured many rainy-season African storms in a badly leaking tent. (No wonder I don't like the rain!) I would make sure anything that needed to stay dry was in one of the panniers and not drowning when my Thermarest became an island in the lake of my tent. To save weight I'd not brought tent pegs so would lie with arms and legs outstretched to the four corners, giving support to my panniers that acted as anchors in the strong gusts of wind, and I'd worry that I'd left something outside but was unable to check because if I moved, the tent would probably blow away. Years later, with a familiarity for tent life, I enjoy the sound of gentle rain pattering on the roof. Now, I'm in a country where dry days can never be taken for granted. When the sun appears, a swell of pent-up energy bursting to be released makes me as restless as those African storms.

The next morning when I awake to sunny blue skies, I can't relax and enjoy the morning over a leisurely breakfast, maybe read a little. I scoff my muesli while the coffee is brewing, drink the coffee while loading my bag onto the bike and check the forecast on my phone while fastening my jacket and putting on my helmet. Then I zip up the tent, which can stay where it is because it's a dead-end trail on Langanes. I'll collect it on my way back to save some weight. The lighter the luggage, the more fun the ride. And all the while I'm smiling because it's sunny and it's going to be sunny all day, and days in northern Iceland the day before the summer solstice go on without end, night indistinguishable from day.

Langanes

Soon out of Þórshöfn, the tarmac turns to dirt. The Serow is in its element. Without dropping speed, I continue on the trail beside the coastline, slowing only for the sheep. In kamikaze fashion, they love to run across the road in front of the bike as though they're playing chicken. Either the ewes are trying to get to their lambs or the lambs race to their mothers and don't stop bleating in frenzied fear until they're contentedly sucking milk. I don't understand how they can never be on the same side of the road and stay there.

Gradually, the trail rises until it's skirting clifftops. I stop and wander a well-worn trail to the edge of the land, stand on a platform protruding from the vertigo-inducing cliff and look to the horizon where the deep-blue sea meets the sun-bleached sky. Below, water crashes against the foot of the cliffs. The rock-faces are flecked with white where fulmars nest on precarious perches. Gannets soar, their white arrow bodies sharply outlined against the dark water. On a single stack, thousands cluster as though they've been corralled and have no choice but to live shoulder-to-shoulder.

I ride on, the trail descending again to sea level. On white sand beaches, driftwood is piled high like giant matchsticks. Siberian pine trees from Russian sawmills have washed ashore, making an effective flood barrier. Earlier I passed Sauðanes church perched on a low rise, the tallest structure for miles. With this ready supply of building materials, it was a prized parsonage. Together with good grazing for sheep, plentiful eider ducks for down and a helping of seaweed for nutrition, it lacked nothing for someone to comfortably live off the land.

At the end of the peninsula where the ground flattens out into grassy steppe, there's an imposing lighthouse: white column, red helmet.

On my return, I detour down a track that ends on the east side at Skálar. The grass is lush green and blanketed with yellow buttercups. It's picturesque, albeit windswept. The flat land offers little protection. No one has lived here for decades. Now, there are only ruins; overgrown foundations of stone, remnants of concrete walls and a crumbling pier. An old finned radiator, possibly an old oven, and other unidentifiable rusting metal objects litter this abandoned village.

At the time of settlement, Skálar comprised a number of farms belonging to the church. A village formed when a man called Thorsteinn arrived in 1910 with an oared boat and three men. With the help of one of the farmers, they set up a fishing enterprise. They gradually acquired more boats, began extracting cod liver oil and opened a store. More boat owners came to fish. In 1923 a freezing plant was built. By 1924 there were 117 people living here. At its height, this would have been a lively place, especially when the fishermen returned from sea and dances were held.

Attempts to improve the landing stage resulted in the ruin of the original one. Then when fish prices plummeted during the worldwide depression of the thirties combined with the migration of fish stocks away from Skálar, the village's decline was assured.

A coastal observation station here was manned by British soldiers and then the US marines during World War II. It was also at this time that two naval mines broke loose from the East Fjords minefield, drifted around the coast and exploded on the beach, destroying a couple of buildings. After the village was deserted, one family moved here in 1948 but stayed only seven years in this isolated location.

This is a typical story of an Icelandic village or farmstead: originating from the time of settlement and growing into a thriving fishing village, only to later decline when fish stocks migrated or when the Ring Road, which circumnavigates the country, was constructed, thereby replacing traditional sea routes and cutting off any villages it bypassed.

In a hollow beyond the ruins, there is a small wooden chalet fenced within a small plot near the stream. It looks like a perfect writer's retreat. I wonder who owns it; perhaps I could come back and rent it over the winter. For years I have contemplated creating my own Walden somewhere; solitude guaranteed, nature my only distraction. On closer inspection, I see there is no chimney, no stove. It would be cold. Cut off by snow and with the nearest neighbours nine kilometres away, it might be too lonely a place to weather the winter storms and long, dark nights, even for me.

On the way back, I collect my tent and gear from the campsite and at the small supermarket buy a banana and biscuits, which I devour outside by my bike. It's sunny still and I don't know how long it will last and I want to do everything today – see the whole of Iceland – while it's bright and warm.

Melrakkaslétta, meaning 'Arctic Fox Plain', is the next peninsula around the coast. It's much broader and deeper than Langanes. In search of dirt trails, I turn off the tarmac road onto what looks like a shortcut on the map but will surely take longer. The road descends to a broad valley with rich grazing land and a couple of farmhouses, but soon out the other side, the ground is drier, rockier, unsuitable even for sheep.

The bare tundra inland is bleak and flat, unlike any other peninsula. There are a handful of farmhouses along the coast road; otherwise, this land is the reserve of birdlife taking advantage of the hundreds of inland lakes and almost uninhabited shoreline. In places, the road passes over a causeway, the only thing separating large lakes from the sea.

I turn right onto a faint jeep track towards the lighthouse of Hraunhafnartangi. (This is the correct name; I haven't accidentally leant on the keyboard.) Situated around three kilometres south of the Arctic Circle, I had thought the lighthouse was at Iceland's northernmost point on the mainland. It was considered so until 2016, when *Landmælingar Íslands*, the National Survey of Iceland, identified the point at Rifstangi further along the coast as being sixty-eight metres closer, which is where the lighthouse used to be situated until it was moved in 1945.

ICELAND Serow Saga

I progress slowly over rough terrain. Large rocks hidden in the long grass send the front end of the bike leaping wildly. Then the trail rises onto an embankment along the shoreline where the rocks are smooth and round. Pieces of driftwood lie where they washed ashore. Green netting trapped under rocks spans the high tidemark. At the tip of the headland, there is a ruined shelter dug into the ground; only the wooden timber of the apex roof remains. The brilliant white, nineteen-metre tall lighthouse appears more imposing by the relative flatness of the terrain, its straight lines juxtaposed with the natural environment.

I stop to get water in Kópasker. I had been hoping to wild camp in the peace and quiet of my own company. Apart from that one wet night in the Netherlands, I've not wild camped since leaving the UK three weeks ago. Suddenly overwhelmed with tiredness, I decide spontaneously to stay at the village campsite instead. Choosing wild camping spots when tired is like shopping for dinner when hungry; I am indecisive, unable to decide exactly what I want and, in the end, grab anything.

I pitch my tent in a grassy dip beside the thicket of stunted trees that offer shelter from the wind and nesting for small birds. A neighbouring camper approaches carrying an army-issue mess tin.

'We cooked too much, would you like this bolognese?'

I never turn down free food, especially in a country where my supermarket purchases are dictated by price, not nutritional value or what I actually fancy. Staying on campsites has its moments.

It takes ten minutes to cook some pasta and reheat the sauce; it takes two minutes to devour it and another one to be certain I've scraped every last morsel from the tin, even though it was two portions. My gluttony could be excused if I had been cycling all day, but riding a motorbike does not warrant such a huge calorific intake. I certainly don't need dessert.

Langanes

On my way to the washing-up facilities, I notice a hiker has just pitched his tent. He's sporting a full beard under a multi-coloured woollen hat with ear flaps like travellers wear in South America.

'Walked far?' I ask.

'Thirty-seven miles,' he replies. 'I set off from the lighthouse at Hraunhafnartangi yesterday. Today was long because there wasn't any water en route. I walked the last eighteen miles without any.'

I choke back my surprise. He appears none the worse for wear. I would be lying in a crumpled heap, crippled, blistered and nursing bruised soles while cooking up a massive meal or greedily eating a large bar of chocolate. I decide not to mention that if he'd arrived fifteen minutes earlier he could have had a filling meal of pasta bolognese.

Leo, from Italy, is walking from the north to south of Iceland over the next month. A long-distance walk is something I've been seriously considering for some time. I'm curious as to what gear he's brought, and how much water he has to carry, especially across the interior.

I find it interesting what different people consider important to take on a trip. Some buy ultralight gear, each gram saved costing a disproportionate amount. When space and weight are limiting factors, some prioritise extra clothes over a fully equipped kitchen, others like gadgets with bags full of cables. There are websites, magazines, blogs and online TV channels dedicated to marketing and reviewing the overwhelming variety of bike and camping gear.

I notice Leo's quality tent, an expensive brand. All his kit looks new and shiny. Over the years, I have accumulated a substantial amount of gear. Now I take and make do with what I've got, preferring to save my money for the trip. If I realise there's something I don't have and absolutely need, I can buy it along the way or get it shipped by international courier.

I'm not easily impressed by feats of endurance; the human body is capable of much more than we usually give it credit for. It is mental fortitude that overcomes difficulties, and it is what drives someone to undertake such a challenge that interests me.

Leo is walking to better understand Iceland. It is not to say he has done it but to see the country in a way that is impossible from the comfort of a car or even a motorbike. I am envious. I had intentions of doing lots of hiking here myself, yet I suspect the allure of the lazier and more thrilling two-wheeled ride will prove hard to overcome.

Kópasker sits on a sheltered bay, black sand arcing from the lighthouse at one end to a pretty white-washed farmhouse at the other. I sit on a wooden bench and watch ducks splashing in the shallows. To the west across the water, there are snow-capped mountains. I imagine it will be a lovely sunset, the sun gradually dipping to the horizon, a gentle kiss at the end of one day before lifting its head and welcoming the next. Since this happens around half past one in the morning, I won't see it. I'm too tired; my sleeping bag beckons.

After tomorrow the days will begin to shorten until there's little light shining on the land except from the moon and stars. Right now it's impossible to imagine that darkness will ever come to these shores.

6
Waterfalls, Whales and a Hoofprint Canyon
Around Mývatn

Many movies have been filmed in Iceland. The otherworldly landscapes make it ideal for sci-fi films; the lunar-like terrain of the interior works for extra-terrestrial settings. Because Iceland benefits from eternal summer daylight, scenes can be filmed in towns in the middle of the night so they appear deserted, which is perfect for the zombie-apocalypse genre. The Lara Croft and James Bond films, *Batman*, *Star Wars*, *Captain America*, *Star Trek*, *Oblivion*, *Stardust*, *Beowulf* and perhaps not surprisingly considering the Norse myth link, *Thor: The Dark World* all have scenes shot in Iceland.

I recently watched *The Incredible Life of Walter Mitty* starring Ben Stiller, partly set in Iceland and filmed from multiple locations here. The most iconic scene is of Walter long-boarding down a winding road of seemingly endless hairpin bends. This is the road to Seyðisfjörður that I ascended in the fog when I first arrived. Based on the number of sunny days I've had so far during my time in Iceland, I suspect they were on location a long time to capture the scene.

According to the tourist map, I am close to Dettifoss. They are *the* waterfalls that are the backdrop in the classic shot from the film *Prometheus*. The German friends I made in the Faroe Islands told me it was one of their three must-visit places on their week-long whistle-stop tour of Iceland. Holgar said he wanted to recreate the scene from the film by standing naked and drinking beer in front of the waterfall. I'm hoping that if I see Dettifoss without any naked Germans, the mental image can be reset.

Arriving at a massive car park, my expectations are tempered. I follow the line of couples, families and tour groups weaving through the rocky land on foot. The immense power and beauty of Iceland's largest waterfall are detracted by the hundreds of footsteps and camera clicks reducing it to a novelty postcard image. I also realise that the film shots (I watched the classic opening scene online to know what the fuss was about) were taken from the other side of the river.

I continue south and join the Ring Road, the longest and most significant road in Iceland. It circles the island and connects most of the major towns. It's this road that many tourists use to circumnavigate the country. With vehicles passing at regular intervals, it's a veritable highway compared to the coastal roads I've been riding whilst exploring the peninsulas. The wind blasts across the open plain. I grapple to keep the bike upright, my arms burning from the effort. I'm riding at a constant lean, seemingly defying gravity. With all the bends and having to lean against the wind, there's no chance of the bike tyres ending up with a squared profile.

I head towards Mývatn, another tourist hotspot. Its name, meaning 'Midge Lake', I consider deterrent enough but dismiss my discouraging thoughts on the assumption that the masses must know best. It must be utterly spectacular. Before I reach the lake, I see a cluster of vehicles parked off the roadside. My curiosity is piqued.

Steam rises from vents in the red and orange iron-rich earth. Rocky mounds taller than me and smeared with yellow-white sulphur stains emit a steady stream of stinking, choking, suffocating gases. These fumaroles occur when magma close to the earth's surface interacts with and superheats groundwater with the sulphurous gases escaping through cracks and fissures in the earth's crust. I hold my breath and pull my headscarf around my nose as I pass, walking quickly upwind.

This inhospitable landscape is free to roam with the exception of a few low rope cordons. Only the careless or stupid would step beyond if they value the skin on their body. Metallic grey pools of mud bubble and boil where the highly acidic compounds and gases have dissolved the clay earth into a gloopy toxic slurry.

Around Mývatn

The same processes that result in the formation of fumaroles, create geysers and hot springs. Geysers spout water rather than steam and require a sufficiently large body of groundwater as well as rock hard enough to withstand the pressures that build up. Where the heated groundwater can reach the surface without building pressure, there are hot springs.

With the threat of rain on the horizon, I head north towards a campsite I intend to use as a base for a few days. It can get tedious having to pack up and take down a tent at the start of every day. In a country spoilt for choice for beautiful or unusual scenery, this place is spectacularly unimpressive, made less appealing because this is where the black flies are.

I take a short ride into Húsavík, the nearest town, a hub for whale-watching tours. The tours are too expensive for my budget, but it's a pleasant town with a picturesque harbour. Tall wooden sailing ships and smaller white motorboats, equally beautiful princes and paupers of marine travel, sparkle in the sunlight against a backdrop of snow-capped mountains across the bay.

The whale museum here has, unsurprisingly, a lot of whale skeletons on display. There is also a reading area with free coffee. I split my time between the exhibits and the caffeine. On one dimly lit wall is a replica of the first good map of Iceland. Drawn by Bishop Guðbrandur Thorláksson in 1585, it was added to the *Theatrum Orbis Terrarum*, the first modern atlas. It shows an island of long, spindly, mountainous peninsulas spreading out like fingers, the interior dissected by long rivers, lakes and volcanic fires. Artistic licence takes precedence over accuracy. It's unlikely there were ever giant sea monsters prowling the ocean or fifteen polar bears on ice cubes invading from the northeast.

Another museum has a collection of stuffed animals and local artefacts from the early twentieth century. Go to enough cultural museums and the objects on display showing how people lived a hundred years ago start to look the same. It's uncanny how people

ICELAND Serow Saga

around the world, seemingly disconnected, have lived in similar fashions. Some items and ideas will have been traded throughout the centuries, but others were undoubtedly arrived at independently. Humans, regardless of creed, colour or race are the same the world over, always have been. I prefer to be reminded of this by meeting people on my travels.

One display attracts my attention: the stuffed polar bear. Polar bears are not native to Iceland but occasionally one makes a trip here from its home above the Arctic Circle, transported on an iceberg significantly larger than those depicted on the 1585 map. Sadly, because they can carry parasites and have no way of returning home once their floating berg has melted, but also because they are a threat to people, they do not survive long, shot before they get too hungry and start hunting sheep or humans.

The museum is in the same building as the library. There is little point me trying to read any of the books since they're mostly in Icelandic, but I am drawn in by the free coffee and sofa, which is comfier than my tent. It's a good place to write.

It's raining when I leave. I don't have my waterproofs. I'd had the foolish notion that because it was sunny when I left the campsite it would remain that way all day. The twenty-kilometre drenching ride back is awful. I won't make the same mistake again.

The clothes I washed are wetter than when I hung them out to dry. I wring them out and dump them in a pile in the porch, then lie down in the tent and watch the water pooling above my head. Rather than waiting for it to drip on me, I push the inner tent fabric to smooth out the natural dip and the water dissipates down the sides.

I wake in the middle of the night with the sun shining on the tent. I force myself from my sleeping bag and hang out my laundry again. By morning, it's all dry.

With my waterproofs stowed in my rucksack, I set out on a day-ride loop of the Tjörnes peninsula. The coastal cliffs and rocky beaches piled high with driftwood are like those I saw on Langanes.

Around Mývatn

The road descends into a wetland delta where the glacial river, Jökulsá á Fjöllum, empties into Öxarfjörður. Arctic terns swoop over the shallow marsh waters. The rocky hillside behind is reflected in an emerald green lake, the only ripples on the surface from two whooper swans elegantly gliding past.

Before the bridge, I turn off to Ásbyrgi. The visitor centre contains a wealth of information on the region and a seating area where you can drink coffee. A bearded young man looks up from one of the tables and smiles at me.

'Leo!' Without his hat on, I barely recognised him, let alone expected him to walk here so quickly.

'At this rate, you'll make it to the south coast before I do,' I joke.

'Maybe,' he replies, 'but you'll have travelled further and seen other things that I will not.'

I ask if he'd like to come for a walk. He declines; he's tired and would rather rest. I know from my cycle-touring days how unappealing it is to cycle on a day off because an eager host wants to take me on a short sight-seeing ride. Even if you're used to cycling one hundred kilometres every day, thirty kilometres on a rest day can still take its toll. I leave Leo to his journal.

At the end of the canyon, I walk through the woodland of willow and birch and several imported species such as spruce, larch and pine. In the shadow of the cliffs is a small pond. A group of walkers sit on the low wooden fence around the viewing platform eating their sandwiches.

A flat-topped island with sheer cliffs dominates the central part of the canyon. I follow a trail up one sloping side, sweating in the rare warmth of the sun and squinting in the bright light. From the top are distant hazy views to the north.

The formation of this horseshoe-shaped canyon began with catastrophic glacial flooding soon after the end of the last Ice Age. Legend, however, drawing on Norse mythology, says that Ásbyrgi is the hoofprint of Sleipnir, Odin's eight-legged flying horse. Odin was the supreme god and creator. As god of death, he decided the fate of warriors and travelled between the living world and that of the dead on his horse. Considering Odin's importance in Norse mythology, I'm surprised I don't come across his name more often in Iceland. By contrast, Odin's eldest son Thor has his name given to many places and is the basis for many common Icelandic names such as Thorsteinn, Thorgeir and Thóra. This hammer-wielding god of thunder, the weather, agriculture and the home had control over everything important to a Viking farmer of the ninth century. Farmers called upon him for good crops, and seamen for safe passage upon the water. His strong, powerful persona fit well with the Scandinavians, as though they had been created in his image, or he in theirs. He had a more human aspect to him than Odin.

Much of what we know today about Norse mythology comes from the *Prose Edda*. One of Scandinavia's best-known works of literature, it is generally agreed that the *Prose Edda* was written by Snorri Sturluson, the thirteenth-century Icelandic historian, poet and politician, although the stories existed long before and the original manuscript has been lost.

The epic stories of heroes fighting supernatural forces were brought across the seas by the Viking settlers. From these, new myths and legends about giants and elves emerged. Tolkien was immensely interested in Norse mythology and used the stories as inspiration for creating his own fantasy kingdom, Middle Earth.

Until now, I've been following the shoreline-hugging roads around the north. The next peninsula has no coastal road, only dead-end tracks running northwards through it. That's no reason to not ride them. My road atlas shows them as F-roads.

Most roads in Iceland are numbered. The Ring Road around the country is Route One. Other roads are two- or three-digit numbers, where the first digit identifies the region. The road numbers generally increase in a clockwise direction from the 200s in the south, 300s to

Around Mývatn

the east of Reykjavík, 400s on the Reykjanes peninsula southwest of the capital, 500s on the Snæfellsnes peninsula in the west, the 600s cover the Westfjords, a remote region in the far northwest, then the 700s and 800s are in the north, and finally, the 900s mostly cover the lesser populated East Fjords and the southeast.

This system works exceptionally well for tourists when discussing routes and giving directions. However, if you mention a road number to an Icelander, don't be surprised by their puzzled or blank expression. Icelanders refer to the roads by their names. Being Icelandic words, though, they are incomprehensible to the newcomer. Deciphering what has been said and then locating it on a map is a double challenge.

As well as the Ring Road, two main routes across the interior are known to most by number and name: F26 is the Sprengisandur route and F35 the Kjölur route. Otherwise, roads are often called after the valley through which they ascend or the fjord from where they begin.

Road numbers prefixed with an 'F' have rivers to be forded and thereby require a 4x4 to navigate. They are often referred to as mountain roads since they're mostly, but not all, in the Highlands, the country's interior. Unpaved, the surface can vary from wide, graded gravel roads to rocky jeep tracks requiring a high clearance vehicle.

The prospect of riding rough tracks is exciting. I want a challenge and thrill, but my feverish anticipation is tempered by doubts and fears. Are my riding skills good enough? Am I brave enough?

I turn off the busy Ring Road onto a quiet graded dirt road. The wide Fnjóská River, with whooper swans floating on it, sparkles in the sunlight. The breeze has a faint smell of freshly cut grass from the hayfields beside the road.

I open up the throttle eagerly. But the bike defiantly cruises at the same speed. *That's odd.* I twist my right hand purposefully again. The engine revs. It's as though there is a disconnect between the throttle

ICELAND Serow Saga

and the drivetrain. The bike freewheels down the road as though it has a mind of its own and is content to just pootle along.

Something's wrong ...

7

Breakdown and Recovery
Akureyri

I brake gently, slowly grind to a halt and cut the engine. I can't think what the problem might be. I kick-start the bike and attempt to pull away in first gear. The engine revs; the bike refuses to move. *Shit*. I dismount.

The chain is hanging limply off the sprocket.

Oh, is that all!

Then I notice the sprocket wedged at an angle on the axle.

That's odd.

I crouch down to inspect it. The six bolts that secure the sprocket have sheared off at the hub. This is not a roadside repair. It's fortunate that I'm less than forty kilometres from Akureyri, Iceland's second-largest town. It's only a couple of kilometres back to the Ring Road where, hopefully, I can flag down a passing truck or pick-up to get a lift. I'm reluctant to push the bike that far if I don't have to, yet don't want to abandon it. I certainly don't want to leave my camping gear behind and be reliant on hotels and restaurants in town. I can't afford that.

I push the bike to a nearby farm and linger at the end of the driveway. As always, I baulk at the prospect of starting a conversation with a stranger and asking for help. A 4x4 approaches and slows down. The driver stares. I watch, neither signalling for help nor indicating that I'm OK. It doesn't stop. I stare at the bike, hoping some ingenious solution involving duct tape or cable ties will spring to mind. Unless six bolts and the tools for drilling out the holes in the rear hub appear from thin air, there is nothing I can think to do.

There's no answer when I knock at the farmhouse. I find a young man in the milking shed and explain my problem. He says they don't have the tools I need and suggests calling a vehicle recovery service. I find the number for a company in Akureyri online and call. The ringing goes to voicemail. It's Sunday. I return to the bike feeling dejected but soon focus on the task at hand. I will try my own emergency network, and if that fails, I'll start pushing the bike.

I message Högni. When I don't hear back immediately because he's at work, I contact Einar in Reykjavík, another biker. Högni had given me his number as a contact should I need help on the opposite side of the country. I don't expect either can help directly – I'm located midway between them – but they may know of someone closer. Then I write a post about my predicament on Facebook.

Two old men come down from the farm. They don't speak English. I point to the problem. They crouch by the rear wheel, talking to one another in Icelandic. I can't pick out a single vaguely recognisable word. I tried early on to learn a few words of Icelandic and quickly despaired. Languages are not my forte.

The two men point at the chain and hub and sprocket, talking as though trying to figure out the finer workings of a complicated piece of technology. I stare at the bike, wondering if I've missed something because the problem and solution seem obvious to me.

The 4x4 that passed earlier returns and stops. The driver, a big man with unkempt greying hair and a workman's shirt rolled up to his elbows exposing thick forearms, leans out of the wound-down window.

'Everything OK?' he asks. At least, I think that's what he's saying because he's speaking Icelandic. One of the old men explains at length.

The clean-cut passenger with short, dark hair, who I judge as slightly older than me, gets out and introduces himself in English. Jörvi tells me that he rides bikes too and is always happy to help a fellow biker. In his smart-casual jeans and trainers, he looks more like an off-duty manager than a manual labourer, but his friendly manner lacks any air of authority or superiority. Conversation comes

Akureyri

easily. As we talk, he looks at me directly in the eyes, which is rare for strangers and unusual even between friends. Unaware of his own charisma that would disarm anyone, he's instantly likeable.

I explain my problem; soon there are four of us gawking at the bike. The little Serow has never had so much attention paid to it. The consensus remains unchanged: I'll need to get it fixed in town.

'How long are you here for?' Jörvi asks.

'Until I can get a lift into town and get the bike fixed.'

'I mean in Iceland. How many days?'

'Oh, I thought you meant by this farm! For the summer.'

'Wow. You're very lucky. Most people only come for a week or two. You'll have time to see the whole country.'

'I will if I can fix my bike,' I joke.

'Don't worry, you'll get that fixed quickly. If you can wait here until this afternoon, we'll give you a lift into Akureyri. We have to work now but will be driving back later. We can put the bike on the trailer.' *Amazing.*

Then Einar calls. 'I got your message. I've been in touch with a colleague, Árni. He said if you can get the bike to him at the fire station in Akureyri, he'll be able to fix it. I'll send you his number; call him when you get there.'

How's that for a co-ordinated rescue effort? All organised within thirty minutes of breaking down. Once again, I've been blessed with the kindness of strangers and fellow bikers.

Left to my own devices for the meantime, I dig out my stove and brew a mug of tea. There is nothing to do but wait. It's a warm, sunny day that's perfect for lazing about outside when you can't be biking. I sit on the grass verge and watch snipe swoop overhead, listening to the distinctive sound of winnowing as the air flutters through their fanned-out tail feathers.

My phone beeps with several replies to my Facebook post: helpful suggestions and good wishes. There's a message from Constantinos, who I've not heard from or seen since the ferry. He's nearby and wants to know exactly where I am.

Thirty minutes later, two fully loaded motorcycles approach. Constantinos gives me a huge hug and introduces me to the Czech biker he's been riding with for the past week. We drink coffee and chat about our trips so far, laughing about the trials and tribulations of bike touring and how it's for these experiences that we do it. An hour passes in a flash. With only a few days of their trip left, we agree they should be exploring Iceland, not hanging around by the roadside keeping me company. Like a whirlwind, they're gone, leaving a lonely emptiness that wasn't here before.

I lie back on the grass, close my eyes and gradually the sound of the breeze rustling the grass and snipe in the distance filters through the silence. Smiling to myself, I contemplate my good fortune. Despite a broken bike – indeed, because of it – I've had a most enjoyable afternoon and entertaining day, and it's not over yet.

Shortly after three o'clock, my rescuers return. We push my bike onto the low loader next to a small digger and tie it down with the straps I use for my luggage and a large rope as thick as my wrist that was in the boot.

'A warning, though,' Jörvi says as he places his hands on the bike seat and gives a forceful shove to check it's secure. 'We take no responsibility.'

'No problem,' I reply. 'I'm sure the bike will be fine where it is. I'm just thankful you can help.'

I pile my bags onto the back seat of the 4x4 and jump in. We take the long way to Akureyri via the gravel road because it avoids the hill. They are concerned my bike could slide off the trailer.

Erik drives and Jörvi points out the turnings to the F-roads I wanted to ride and mentions other tracks that are fun on a motorbike. Then he talks about the geology and history of the area. I lean forward between the front seats and listen closely.

Akureyri

The situation reminds me of a similar time in Siberia when I was getting a lift. My bicycle was in another truck and Andrei was speeding along behind in the 4x4. Every now and then he'd slam on the brakes and pick up the vodka bottle by my feet and we'd toast to life and family, to good health and safe journeys. He talked about his country with affection and warmth that melted the thick ice until I could imagine how green and full of life it would be in the summer.

Now, mid-summer in Iceland, this valley with the deep-blue river, forest and mountains is as I had imagined Siberia beneath the snow. Jörvi talks fondly of his country. I detect a familiar sentiment as I had heard in the voices of many Siberians. Despite life being hard here in winter, he loves it. A country is not loved only for its beauty, but I think it's more beautiful because it's loved.

Jörvi reaches into the footwell for a large plastic bottle filled with a clear liquid. He pours generously into two plastic cups from the glove compartment. His actions so closely resemble Andrei's in Siberia, I assume the drink is vodka. *Have I misjudged these guys?* His words 'We take no responsibility,' replay in my mind.

'Would you like some?' He offers me the cup.

I turn down the offer. He passes the cup to Erik, who drinks it in one and hands it straight back. The cup gets refilled, downed and refilled twice more. I'm both impressed and horrified.

'It's only water,' he says straight-faced. 'Pure mountain water.'

Sure. So that's what Icelanders call vodka. Russian whisky, Icelandic water.

'We need to rehydrate. It was hot today,' Jörvi comments. 'We're ex-alcoholics,' he says.

I stifle a laugh; it erupts as a snort. There's nothing 'ex' about it.

'We used to do all kinds of stuff when we were younger, but not anymore. We don't drink. We're Responsible Family Men now,' Jörvi says seriously.

It *is* water. Mortified that they might think I'm laughing about them being alcoholics, I quickly tell them about my Siberian experience.

ICELAND Serow Saga

Jörvi's phone rings.

'Our friend's worried we're going to be late,' Jörvi explains after the call. 'We're going to a hot pool in the mountains tonight. We met at a group for recovering alcoholics. Going through the same difficulties, several of us became close. Everyone has moved on and has busy lives, but we never miss this annual get together.'

'Do you know about Icelandic hot pools?' Erik asks. 'You have to try them.' *Hmm, we'll see.*

'It's a real Icelandic sort of tradition,' Jörvi adds. 'A group of men sitting semi-naked in a hot tub, reminiscing and laughing a lot. Without drugs or alcohol, it's the most fun we can have these days.' We all chuckle.

Driving inland, Akureyri is spread out on the opposite side of the fjord. A large portion of the town is obscured by a cruise ship.

'You always see a big cruise ship moored at the harbour now. One stops every week. For a town with a population of about 18,500, the influx of visitors is noticeable. It's good for the economy, though. A lot of good cafes and restaurants have opened these last few years. It's a university town too. With plenty of students and visitors, it's thriving.'

I find it amazing that a town the size of Ely or Dorchester is the second biggest in Iceland.

'We like it here. It has everything the capital does, only in a much smaller space,' Erik adds.

'Yes, Reykjavík is like cities all over the world, too busy and full of strangers. I don't like it. Here you can walk downtown and recognise people. And we have time to make conversation. It's very friendly,' Jörvi says. 'There are lots of walking trails nearby. You can ski in the mountains behind the town in winter. They've recently opened routes for mountain-biking through the forest.'

It sounds like my kind of place.

'That's the main pedestrian shopping area down there,' Jörvi points to the left as we drive through town. 'And that's the harbour …'.

Akureyri

'This is the Viking brewery,' Erik says as we drive past a tall building. 'Do you drink beer?'

'Me? Yeah.'

'Viking is a good beer. You must try it while you're here.'

'You know beer was illegal until recently? Back in 1908, Icelanders had a referendum and voted for a ban on all alcoholic drinks. Since 1915, there was prohibition in Iceland. It wasn't until 1985 that you could buy a proper beer,' Jörvi tells me.

'Legally.' Erik adds.

'Seriously, why?' I ask.

'I think it was to stop everyone from becoming alcoholics,' Jörvi replies.

'As you can see, it didn't work!' Erik retorts. 'We drank the strong stuff like vodka and whisky or brewed our own instead.'

We pull into the fire station yard. Árni hasn't started his shift yet, so I leave the bike around the back. Then Erik and Jörvi give me a guided drive through town while debating the best route.

'Sorry, we're not very familiar with the campsite,' Erik says.

'We tend to leave our hometown when we go camping,' Jörvi adds. 'There's a lovely one just a few kilometres away, but I suppose it's more convenient for you to be in the centre.' I agree.

'Turn up here,' Jörvi directs Erik.

'That was the shopping mall and supermarket back there at the corner,' Jörvi informs me.

'It might be handy to know where to get essentials. You can't buy beer at the supermarket; you get it at Vínbúðin, the liquor store. Coming up on your left is the police station. Hopefully you won't need that. We spent many a night there in our youth, didn't we?' Jörvi looks to Erik.

'Yeah, it was like our campsite, home away from home!' Erik jokes and they laugh at their memories. 'Oh, those were the days!'

Erik's on the phone when we reach the campsite. I shake his hand through the driver's window and mouth, 'Thank you.' Once Jörvi and

ICELAND Serow Saga

I have dragged my gear from the back seat to the pavement, I give my hand and get a back-slapping hug in return.

'If you're in town for a few days, perhaps we'll see you in one of the coffee shops.'

'You never know,' I reply. *I hope so.*

Jörvi hops into the car, and they drive away. I regret not getting a contact number for them. Life is better with certain people in it. Jörvi and Erik were the best kind of company: easy to be honest with and laugh together. I'd known them for only an hour, yet it felt like we'd been friends for years.

I wander down to the fire station for the start of Árni's shift. It's raining, a steady drizzle that looks set to get worse. A guy pulls the sliding door open and beckons me in.

It's dimly lit inside and several men are sitting on low sofa chairs, all in dark blue uniform, all very quiet. Árni gets up to greet me.

'Follow me. We brought the bike in to keep it dry.' Momentarily, I wonder how that was possible with the bike locked. For a team of firemen, it's easy to lift. The bike looks tiny parked beside the fire engines.

All Árni says is, 'I can fix it, no problem.'

'Oh, OK. Do you need anything? What about new bolts?'

'No, I've got everything here. I am on duty now but will fix it when there's a quiet period. Hopefully, I can start once we've had our briefing.'

'There's no rush,' I reply.

'It will be done by tomorrow. I'll text you when it's ready. Then you can come and collect it.'

I head back out into the rain and trudge up the hill to the campsite. Less than two hours later, my phone beeps with a message to say that my bike is ready.

I walk back to the station. It's still raining.

'I had to use one longer bolt with a nut as the thread in the hub was damaged. Otherwise, it's all good. I've Loctited them, so they won't come loose. I've tightened up some of the spokes. The oil level is OK. You might want to tighten the chain. Otherwise, it's ready to go.'

'The chain should be fine once it's loaded up, but I'll check it.' I genuinely don't know what to say to convey my gratitude. 'Thank you so much.'

'It's nothing,' he replies casually. 'This is a good bike for Iceland. Too many come on these big tourers, but this is ideal for the Highlands. It's a large tank you've got on it, right?'

'Yeah, I can get anywhere between five and seven hundred kilometres before refuelling,' I explain. 'So, you're into bikes?'

'You could say that. I've got twenty.'

'Twenty!' I guess you can never have too many bikes.

'I've had more. I used to ride a lot, but there's not enough time these days. I have a family now. Too many kids. I had to sell some.'

Sell some bikes or some kids? I wonder, trying to keep a straight face. Árni seems a serious fellow. I'm not sure how he'd respond to my jokes. Just how many kids are too many, when twenty is an acceptable number of motorbikes?

Less than twenty-four hours after breaking down, thanks to all the help I received, I'm back on the bike. It rained through the night but now the sun is shining. My optimism for the day is gleaming.

I turn onto the dead-end F-road through Flateyjardalur, which I'd been heading towards the day before. I dismount to open a gate and push the bike through before closing it behind me. There's a yellow and red triangular warning sign. Below the heavy exclamation mark is a silhouette of a 4x4. Next to it, the image of a car has a red cross through it.

Let the fun and games begin.

8

Trails and Turf Houses
Flateyjardalur

I tug the luggage straps to check my bags are secure and speed off, weaving along the green hillside with snow-dipped peaks edging the valley. The track drops suddenly into a stream. I see the gully too late for stomping on the brakes to have a noticeable effect. The suspension bottoms out; the splash soaks my jeans and sprays water over my visor. *Easy now.*

It's hard to slow down because I'm having so much fun. Darting along the track, standing up on the foot-pegs and letting my legs absorb the ruts and bumps, the bike floats beneath me. My knees grip the sides of the tank to help lean the bike round the bends. My right hand twists the throttle when the trail straightens out, and I brake suddenly when sheep leap out in front of me.

More streams appear across the track. With each drenching and thud of the front wheel dropping into a carved gully, my colourful language soon turns to laughter. *This is what I've been waiting for.* The trail is everything I'd hoped for.

Then there's a river across the track that forces me to stop. It's not like the piddling streams I've been splashing through.

Is it too deep? What if I lose control and drop the bike?

I know it's important to keep the air intake and exhaust out of the water. It would be bad for water to get in the engine. I've no idea what to do if it does though. I'd better look that up online later. For now, it's simple: do not drop the bike.

Drowning in doubt, my confidence swept away with the water flowing past me, I'm on the verge of turning back.

I know little about Iceland's trails. Brief internet searches about recommended routes had returned a meaningless array of

Flateyjardalur

F-numbered roads. Guys on forums described trails in a sliding scale of nondescript words from fun to challenging. Only one thing was clear: the main obstacle to progress was always river crossings. The difficulty of the terrain or inclement weather, type of bike or how much luggage and what gear to carry were rarely worthy of mention.

I can't turn back at the first hint of a challenge. If I stay within my comfort zone, I've no chance of riding half the trails I'd like to later. I can't let my fears, doubts and insecurities immobilise me. I must listen to them and use them productively to assess and minimise the risks. Then, if it's safe to do so, just get on with the task at hand.

I walk across to gauge the depth. Water seeps over the tops of my boots and pools around my feet. My toes clench at the icy touch. The river is lower than the bike's air intake and exhaust. But is it too deep for me? I trawl my memories for similar scenarios: I crossed some rivers in Lesotho. I wasn't alone then. But one of the rivers was a raging torrent compared to what's in front of me now. *You can do this. You don't need anyone else. Trust in your abilities.*

I unstrap my luggage and carry it across. I know from experience that if I drop the bike, I can pick it up quickly by grabbing the rear rack and a handlebar. With bags attached, I struggle to get a hold. Then I get back on the bike and hesitate, doubts swirling in my mind. I must ignore them. Focussing on the far side, I take a deep breath and go for it. Low gear, high revs. Low confidence, racing heart.

I made it! *That wasn't so bad.*

Buoyed by this small success, I load up and ride on, faith in my abilities boosted. Contrary to what my map indicates, there are several more wide streams to cross, each one a little deeper, faster and scarier than the last. Each one extends my comfort zone.

Near the end of the trail, there's a small lagoon with a house perched at the foot of the hill behind it. I follow the trail over the narrow grey beach. These last metres are the most arduous of the day. I urge the bike on, paddling with my feet, the back wheel slipping and sliding in the sand. The trail ends at the foot of a hillock, the final obstacle before the open sea.

Dark red seaweed lines the bay at the high tide mark. Tall grassy tufts sprout up between the smooth rounded stones of the beach. I sit on a driftwood log that is bleached white like a bone, then light the stove for a cup of tea and drink in the view. I remove my boots, water pouring out as I upturn them. Then I wring out my socks and let them dry in the stiff breeze. My wrinkled feet dry out for the first time in hours. The cold wind numbs my toes.

A fine white mist now shrouds the valley and is floating towards me like an apparition. I drink the tea too quickly and burn my mouth. I want to be back on the bike before the rain reaches me. I don't know why; I've nowhere to go. I'll be as wet on the bike as on this log. For some reason, riding in the rain on dirt roads doesn't bother me as much.

Heading back across the sand, I see a track off to my left and decide to explore. It peters out at an exposed, flat grassy area. A small, triangular wooden construction raised off the ground turns out to house a toilet. The front of the shelter has sinks and taps with running water. The area is deserted. I could camp here.

I watch two red-necked phalaropes float past me on the river, fly upstream and float down past me again. They do this repeatedly, never tiring of their favourite fairground ride. Then I walk up the hillside. Wild ducks bob on the choppy water below.

The wind has picked up and now blasts through. I pull down my hat and make sure my gloves are stuffed deep in my pockets; I can't have them blowing away while taking photos. I try to make a short video on my GoPro but the howling wind steals my voice.

Down at the beach amongst the driftwood and seaweed debris, there's an old fire pit, a circle of rocks around a blackened hollow. There's another flat, grassy area with space for my tent and views of the bay. I crouch down. It's the most protected area, yet the wind

Flateyjardalur

forces its way in here too. It would be a restless night with the tent buffeting wildly.

On the lower slope are the remains of an old building, large stone piles. People moved out and the walls collapsed so long ago that nature has claimed them as her own. Soil has blown into the cracks and crevices between the rocks; grass and mosses have grown over them. In places, only an uneven ground hints at what lies below. There's nowhere to put a tent here.

Upstream, the flat ground is damp. My feet sink up to my ankles. I pick my way towards higher ground, then return to the bike through a wet pasture of cottongrass. Its wispy tips appear fragile yet remain steadfastly attached to their leaning stems, a hundred heads of white hair dancing wildly as though loving, maybe mocking, the Icelandic weather: *is that all you've got!* But their tiny, shrill laughs are lost in the wind. To accept your fragile appearance yet be strong in the core like the cottongrass seems a much better way to go through life than having a strong facade as I have tried. It's not easy to accept one's own vulnerability, but recognising our weaknesses will surely make us stronger.

The wind continues its attack, the assault unceasing. I barricade myself in the triangular shelter. I'm warm and dry but feel imprisoned. Sleeping next to the toilet wouldn't be so bad in an emergency, but I want to be camping in the open. I'll go find a more sheltered spot back up the valley. I can think of a couple of places I passed already.

The return ride is fast and fun and over in a flash. There's no need to stop at the rivers; I know how deep they are, know I can cross them. I don't stop to admire the view or take photos; the images of this beautiful valley are already imprinted on my mind. I simply enjoy the ride. There is only me, the bike and the trail ahead. I haven't seen another person or vehicle all day. It was fortunate I didn't break down in this valley yesterday.

I turn down a side trail. Like several others, it's marked with a blue metal sign towards an old homestead. In some places there is now

ICELAND Serow Saga

a modern summer house, for holidays and weekends away. In other places there is no evidence that a home once stood except for a flat area of grass beside a stream, which makes me think that's where I'd build a house.

People used to live here and in a hundred valleys like this. But the winters were long and hard. Cut off from the world for months at a time, a valley could feel like a prison with nothing to do except mark off the dark days until the first call of the plover signalled the arrival of spring, reminding Icelanders that the snow will not last forever. First, blade tips of grass will peek through the white until one day it is gone and they can step upon soft, spongy moss. Sunlight brings hope. The days will lengthen, the dark nights banished to a distant memory. Only the chill wind is a reminder that summer is a brief gasp of surprise before the freezing winter resumes its long, drawn-out sigh.

Most people prefer to live in Reykjavík now and visit the wilderness on summer weekends. They want a taste of simplicity and peace; to smell the fresh sea air and fish in the rivers, walk amongst the buttercups and over tussocky hills, listen to the plover call and the snipe winnow. Not willing to suffer the long hardship of winter for the fleeting reward of summer has made them tourists in their own country. There is no work here now anyway. Yet, the exodus from countryside to city is not unique to Icelanders, but common across the world.

Too much comfort, though, and people seek to break out of the mundane, repetitive existence of conformity and conventions. They crave adventure and challenge, entering races to push their bodies harder and faster, running away from their lives, to escape for a moment, knowing that once they cross the finish line the hardship ends. Life in an Icelandic valley was about persistent hard work for long term gain. Today we are mostly too lazy, the quick cheap thrill too alluring to pass up for something greater. It's easy to idealise the rural life of another age and say we would like a simpler life, yet we

Flateyjardalur

are not prepared to endure all the difficulties it entails, only revel in its wonders.

There is space for my tent beside the stream on a small bank. It's sheltered. I am alone. It's unlikely anyone else will come this way. With my jeans, boots and socks drying on rocks outside, I lie in my tent and listen to the constant, pacifying sound of water running over the stony stream bed. With the tent unzipped, the snow-sprinkled mountaintops fill my view. I am content here and don't want to leave, don't need to, so I stay another day. It's not so different from any other day when I'm travelling alone: I can do what I want, when I want.

As a child, I was always kept busy. If it was daytime and light outside, I should be awake; if I was awake, I should be doing something. This attitude is instilled in me. I usually feel guilty for having a lie-in even though there is no one telling me what to do. But now I can appreciate that not all important things in life are quantifiable or visible through productive action. I value times of inaction when there is, simply, time to think.

I wake early and doze, vaguely conscious of the warming effect when the sun reaches the valley bottom and shines on the tent. I boil water on the stove in the tent porch and laze in bed drinking tea with a book for company. Later I wander downstream and cross where it's wide and shallower, leaping from one exposed rock to another and plunging into the stream when my last long step fails to reach the far bank. The water trickles into my boot. I laugh because of the time and care I'd taken to avoid this happening, realising that it didn't matter because my boots will dry in the sun. With the surprise of it, my senses are instantly heightened. I notice the gentle breeze brushing over my bare arms and breathe in the fresh untainted air. The ripples on the water sparkle in the sunlight, wet rocks glistening; the mosses covering the ground suddenly appear a brighter, more vivid green. I spot bright yellow buttercups nestled in protected crevices.

ICELAND Serow Saga

I feel a part of this valley, no longer an invader, as though nature has spun an invisible thread around me, trapping me in a web of beauty. I don't struggle against it because I could happily stay here, in this moment, forever. I follow a track back up the valley and sit by a small stream listening to the soothing sounds as the crystal-clear water trickles down the mountainside. Then I return to my tent to write my journal and read for hours.

Icelanders have a strong literary tradition. It goes back to at least the thirteenth century when the majority of the sagas were committed to paper. The sagas of Icelanders are stories based on the historical events that mostly took place in Iceland from the ninth to early eleventh centuries. With a focus on family history, they detail the conflicts that arose between the early settlers. The genealogy and historical events that are recorded are generally considered accurate. However, given the time lapse between the events and the recording of them, the incidental details are as likely drawn from the writer's imagination based on oral versions passed down the generations. This is especially likely for the later sagas, which had more focus on style and storytelling. Realism discarded, exaggeration and a preference for the supernatural became more common. Embellishing a narrative for entertainment value is nothing new, although I prefer to tell it how it is.

By the late eighteenth century, when in England only around half the population could read, Iceland had almost universal literacy rates. Today, it is one of the most literate nations in the world. Not only does everyone read, but they are prolific writers too; there's a wealth of books from historical novels to crime fiction, only a fraction of which are translated for foreigners. Perhaps it is the long winter nights that encourage people to put pen to paper. Even when the world is in darkness, there is light burning inside each of us and untold stories crying to be heard.

I'm reading Halldór Laxness' *Independent People*. I can imagine Bjartur of Summerhouses eking out an existence on an isolated croft.

Flateyjardalur

Occasionally I look up from my book and stare out of the tent at the mountain view as though it were a masterpiece in a museum. It is a timeless work of art, as true today as any century preceding it.

This valley is not as remote as that where the fictional *Independent People* is set, but the nature is similar. Life for the average Icelandic farmer or fisherman in the early years of the twentieth century was little different to that of when the sagas were written seven centuries earlier. It is only in the last century that lifestyles have begun to change. But camping out here, unburdened by technology, I can easily imagine it.

Life centred around the home, simple buildings of low stone walls with driftwood used for roof construction, covered in a layer of turf. People crammed together as a family within a single smoke-filled room, eyes stinging from the burning peat fire. Reading and sewing were difficult in the dim light. A tiny window would let in some fresh air, although not enough to overcome the smell from the animals in the shelter below – the price paid for a little extra warmth from their body heat.

On my way to Akureyri the following day, I explore the turf house museum at Laufás. It's an exquisite example of a gabled farmhouse, much grander than that of Bjartur's croft or most Icelandic peasants of the time. The site of a wealthy chieftaincy and vicarage, Laufás has been occupied since the days of settlement. The buildings in their present form mostly date to 1866–1870 when Reverend Björn Halldórsson had the rectory enlarged and renovated.

The farm was ideally situated in the fertile valley of Eyjafjörður. The river provided salmon and trout; the sea gave halibut, cod and maybe the odd shark or seal. Driftwood washed ashore was used for house repairs and fuel. The birch forests had been depleted centuries earlier; so, if wood was in short supply, peat and manure were used. Occasionally a beached whale provided a major windfall, meat to feed many people. Whale oil was used for the lamps. Throughout the summer, people collected Iceland moss (*Cetraria islandica*), a lichen, which they'd carry in sacks back to the farm every couple of weeks. It was nutritious and used in soups, porridge and tea. Sometimes goats and cattle were also kept, the milk used to make butter, cheese and skyr.

Unnur had introduced me to skyr when I stayed at her home. A strained natural yoghurt, it tasted like and had the same thick, creamy consistency as Greek yoghurt, which I love. It remains an important Icelandic food, and today it is sold by the supermarkets in a variety of sweet flavours. It has already become a regular part of my breakfast diet, being delicious, nutritious and affordable. Finding anything affordable in Iceland is a challenge.

I wander through each of the farm's rooms, ducking through the doorways. A series of newer, small, wood-panelled bedrooms and a weaving room where the boys were schooled are at the back.

The large kitchen has exposed timber frames, the walls a herringbone pattern of cut turf bricks cemented with bare earth. One side has a low stone platform for a fire with chopped wood stacked in the corner. Smoked meat hangs from the rafters. A knife dangles on a string next to a leg of cured lamb. A note says to cut a slice off to try. It has a mildly smoky aftertaste but the meat is good, not too dry like shop-bought jerky or biltong.

The kitchen was also used for bathing. A sign informs me that people usually only washed twice a year: for Christmas and the first day of summer. That's staggeringly infrequent even by my standards of roughing it. I doubt the smoke from the fire was sufficient to overpower the smell of unwashed bodies in close confines, especially when twenty to thirty people crammed in during the winter months to escape the freezing cold. Just thinking about it is enough to quell any romantic notions of living a simple, traditional lifestyle. I'll take my tent and down sleeping bag any day.

Down from eider ducks was another valuable resource for the farm, used for filling duvets and pillows. Records show that in 1880, during the Reverend's tenure, 5,520 nests were counted and 180 pounds of

Flateyjardalur

eider down collected. Typically, 15–20 grams of down feathers were collected from each nest. To fill my lightweight sleeping bag, which is keeping me comfortably warm currently, I would have needed to raid about 25 nests.

The adjoining buildings were used as workshop, saddlery and storeroom. A small church was constructed in 1865. I wander around the stone-walled graveyard enjoying the fresh air and daylight after the confines of the dingy farm buildings. I look out across the fjord and see the snow-covered mountains beckoning me.

Although I've spent only a few hours in Akureyri and a couple of days in the area, I like it; I feel at home here. Yet I feel an urge to keep moving forward and see what treasures lie ahead while the weather is in my favour. I'm sure I'll be back, but for now, it's time to ride.

9

Coffee and Executions
Vatnsnes

As I ride across the Tröllaskagi peninsula. I notice that the bike's speedo cable has snapped. It's a minor inconvenience, not essential to continuing the journey. Speeding on an underpowered Serow is not something I often need to worry about. I haven't seen a speed camera or traffic policeman in Iceland yet. Though, I do use the trip odometer, resetting it each time I refuel and using it as a rough guide to fuel consumption. I can use an online route planner to work out my approximate daily distance as a record. I must remember to visually check the fuel level, although the tank has a reserve, so it's unlikely I'll run out completely.

I wonder what will break next. These things often seem to happen in threes. I mentally list everything else that could go wrong with the Serow, and whether I'm prepared to deal with it. Worn clutch plates seem the most likely problem. After the Serow's first ones wore out during the Africa trip and had to be replaced, I recommend everyone carries a spare set on a long trip to save the time and expense of having new ones couriered. Typically, I haven't followed my own advice.

The only other issue I foresee is that I might drop my bike in a river and have to drain the engine of water. *I must find out what to do.* I pull over and check my phone. There's a good 4G signal; I look online. I doubt I'm strong enough to lift the bike up alone should I need to drain water out of the exhaust. When needs must, I'll find a way or wait until someone else drives past. The rest sounds easy, although I'd prefer not to need to try: empty the air box by lying the bike on its side, squeeze out the air filter and let it dry while I remove

Vatnsnes

the spark plug, then, using the kick-start, turn over the engine until water stops coming out of the spark plug hole.

I ride to Reykir, little more than a farm at the end of the dirt road. If I'd known there was a small campsite here, I would have come last night rather than staying at the one in town. I'm sure there will be many places I miss by treating this journey as a serendipitous ride of discovery with a let's-see-where-I-end-up attitude rather than a well-planned and organised trip with every sight and feature bookmarked. On the other hand, I'll experience other things I might otherwise miss with a rigid schedule. I'm still under the illusion that three months is enough time to see everything at least twice.

On the small black beach, a swing constructed from driftwood and thick rope for securing boats stands alone, abandoned like a shipwreck, as sad as a toy that's never unboxed. I walk towards it, my boots making heavy going in the sand. Ultimately, I'm defeated in my quest to swing on it by the Arctic terns that swoop in, protecting their lair.

The flat-topped island of Drangey is like a giant's stepping-stone in the mouth of Skagafjörður. It doesn't look far from Reykir, but distances across calm, flat water as it is today are deceptive. Legend has it that two night-prowling trolls were crossing the fjord with their cow when they were caught unexpectedly by the rays of daybreak. It turned them to stone, as is wont to happen with trolls in sunlight. The island represents the cow, while the stack standing to the south is *Kerling*, the old hag. There was a similar stack to the north called *Karl*, although this has eroded and crumbled away. The scientific explanation is that the island is the remnant of a volcano.

Drangey's steep cliffs require ropes and ladders to ascend. The impenetrability of this fortress-like island made it an appealing refuge hundreds of years ago for the outlaw Grettir the Strong. This hero's story is told in *Grettir's saga*; written towards the end of the fourteenth century, it's one of the later sagas.

ICELAND Serow Saga

Grettir was brave and generous yet ill-tempered and prone to trouble. He was first outlawed for killing a man in a quarrel when only fourteen years old. Exiled for three years, he gained a reputation for many good, brave deeds whilst in Norway. On his return, Iceland was being ravaged by the *draugur* (an undead being like a ghost) of Glamur the shepherd. Grettir killed Glamur and earned a reputation as a monster-hunter. Unfortunately, he also set fire to a great hall, which killed many men, so was outlawed again.

On the run for almost twenty years, Grettir became the longest surviving outlaw in Iceland's history. It was on the island of Drangey that he hid out for the last years of his life, taking advantage of the high cliffs for protection from his enemies. Since the island was grazed by sheep and had plentiful birds' nests to raid, he was never short of food.

It was agreed that his banishment would be lifted once he had served his full sentence. At this news, Grettir's enemies made one final attempt to take his life using sorcery to aid them. A witch cast a spell on a piece of wood, which washed ashore on Drangey. When Grettir went to chop the wood for fuel, his axe glanced off it and struck his leg, cutting it down to the bone. His enemies then attacked and killed the injured Grettir, cutting off his head with his own sword.

While Grettir lived on Drangey, there was a time when his fire went out. He had friends here at Reykir who would give him more fire, so he swam the seven kilometres back to the mainland. It's not the distance, but the sea's temperature, which makes this feat sound unbelievable. In the height of summer, it averages around nine degrees Celsius. Since 1927 there have been twenty-four people achieve this feat, taking anywhere between two and five hours to complete it.

I was once enticed by a friend to swim off the North Norfolk coast in English wintertime when the sea temperatures were similar to Iceland's summer. I only managed forty minutes before I started shivering and my hands turned rigid like claws. I have no interest

Vatnsnes

in taking a prolonged swim today. I can't even be tempted to take a dip in the hot pool here. The effort of getting out of my bike clothes and rummaging through my bag to find my bikini and towel is discouragement enough.

I return along the track between the coast and mountains. Horses graze on either side. A black horse is galloping around one field with a grey. They turn abruptly and rear up at each other, front hoofs in combat, then kick and buck and gallop off again, muscles flexing, long manes flowing, tails floating behind.

They are small horses, stocky and deep-chested, muscular on the shoulder and flank. Long manes hide thick necks. Their forelocks hang low, parting when the wind catches them to reveal intelligent eyes. Their stature and build are similar to the Mongolian horse, and also the Yakut horses I saw in Siberia.

Another young grey, dark around the muzzle, stops grazing and walks over to me. The chestnut looks up with curiosity and comes trotting up behind. Soon they all decide I am worthy of investigation. Even the black one stops fighting and trots over to see what the fuss is about. I slowly raise my hand, palm down, towards the muzzle of the closest grey. He lowers his head until his rough lips graze my knuckles. He sniffs loudly and snorts with flared nostrils. The chestnut steps closer and pushes his nose against my hand, wondering if he's missing out on a handful of food. I turn my palm up and show he's not. With my other hand, I gently place the heel of my palm between the grey's eyes, where the hair radiates outwards in a whorl. He moves his head up and down, rubbing his face against my hand with the same kind of affection that a dog will nuzzle your hand or a cat will rub their body against your leg. Two more push closer, not wanting to be left out.

A vehicle stops suddenly behind me. The horses flinch at the sound of car doors slamming. The moment of intimacy between me and these wonderfully inquisitive creatures vanishes. I say hello to the group of people walking towards us wielding cameras and return to my bike. I never see anyone else photographing the horses by the roadside, except when I stop. A passing vehicle is then bound to pull over and disturb us.

Horses were originally brought to Iceland by Scandinavian settlers. The first known named horse, according to *Landnámabók*, was called Skalm. Its owner chose to settle where the horse lay down to rest with its pack on. There is as much sense to this as waiting for high seat posts to wash ashore having thrown them overboard from your sea-going vessel, the more common method. Later immigrants coming from Scotland and Ireland probably brought horses with them also, breeds that became known as Shetland, Highland and Connemara ponies in their places of origin.

Today's Icelandic horse has been purebred for one thousand years. In AD 982, a law was passed prohibiting the importation of horses to prevent cross-breeding. The ban continues today. If a horse is transported abroad, it can never be brought back to the country.

Unique in Europe, the Icelandic horse has five distinct natural gaits: walk, trot and canter/gallop (the Icelandic Horse Society considers gallop to be a faster version of the canter) plus the tölt and pace. The latter two were bred out of Europe's horses for military purposes so that soldiers with no experience could learn to ride quickly. The tölt is a four-beat running walk where the hoofs move in the same sequence as a normal walk and can be performed at any speed. It's a comfortable gliding motion where the body almost hangs suspended with the hind legs moving well underneath with the front end free and high stepping. At its slower speed, it looks remarkably similar to the extra gait of the Mongolian and Kyrgyz horses I have seen and ridden during previous travels.

I've been in touch with Einar since the breakdown; he's got time off work and can join me for a couple of days. We arrange to meet in Blönduós and ride around Vatnsnes peninsula.

Vatnsnes

I park by the supermarket and only have to wait a few minutes before Einar pulls in next to me on his clean, two-year-old bike. Tall and slim, he gracefully swings his long leg over the saddle. Once he's dismounted, I realise how big the new Africa Twin is. My battered Serow looks even smaller and more decrepit next to it. I wonder how I'm going to keep up. I still doubt my riding ability. Too often when in company, I shrivel in self-doubt. I try to appear confident, but it is a hollow shell that I spend too much energy maintaining and is easily shattered.

Einar suggests we first go for coffee. I'm happy for the delay. Besides, it's started raining again. I secure my helmet to the handlebars with a cable lock. Einar says there's no need. No one steals in Iceland; it's safe. He leaves his helmet without a lock. He's probably right, but I unzip my tank bag to take into the cafe with me anyway. It has everything I value: passport, camera, journal. Everything else on my bike can be easily replaced.

Ever since I arrived in Iceland, it's abundantly evident that coffee is an everyday essential for Icelanders; a strong coffee or espresso as important a daily ritual as brushing your teeth.

Riding through Europe I'd drunk instant coffee using three-in-one sachets, a cappuccino of convenience rather than good taste. There was no reason why the same shouldn't suffice for a few more months. It took until my second day on the Faroe Islands to realise the grave error I'd made in leaving my stovetop coffee maker at home. In the communal kitchen at Tórshavn campsite, I was offered a real cup of coffee by a fellow camper. The smell was intoxicating. Then I took a sip. The caffeine hit was mind-blowing. It smacked me round the face and shouted, *What the hell were you thinking, drinking that instant shit!* From that moment on, instant was out, the real thing in. I've been making camp coffee in my tent in the mornings ever since. It takes time for the coffee grounds to settle, and I must remember not to sip the dregs; otherwise, it's a definite improvement.

ICELAND Serow Saga

I have avoided the allure of Iceland's cafes because of the expense. I realise my mistake. Most cafes offer free coffee refills, transforming cafe stops from a luxury into an affordable extended break in the afternoon, especially when the weather is less conducive to riding.

In Europe, the first coffee houses beyond the Ottoman Empire opened in Venice in 1645 and gradually spread across the continent. The first record of coffee in Iceland is from 1703 when the scholar Árni Magnússon acquired a quarter pound from a friend. By around 1760 almost every Icelandic home roasted and ground their own coffee. By 1850, it was integral to everyday life and synonymous with hospitality, served as a treat for visitors, particularly the clergy.

Today, Icelanders are the fourth largest consumers of coffee per capita in the world. There are no Starbucks or Costa, but Kaffitár and Te & Kaffi each have several stores. Predominantly, though, the cafes are independently run and can be found in remote villages, which would be unsustainable for such a small local population in any other country.

It's a small cafe with little floor space and cramped seating, but it's warm and dry. We take up a disproportionate amount of room with our layers of waterproofs, jackets and armour draped over two extra chairs. Einar tells me about some of his travels here. Although he's only been riding a motorcycle for a couple of years, he's explored extensively on foot, by bicycle and 4x4. Like many Icelanders, he is passionate and knowledgeable about his country. Focussed on his stories, my coffee going cold, I try to store in my memory every fascinating fact and detail of the historical events, geological phenomena and other uniquely Icelandic cultural traits and traditions he describes. I could sit here all day listening to him.

After two coffees, Einar suggests we ride. There's no more delaying. We set off towards the small Vatnsnes peninsula, deep in Húnaflói bay between Skagaheiði to the east and the Westfjords. I follow Einar, who knows the area. My enthusiasm mirrors the gloomy weather. Einar is unperturbed by the rain and rides fast along the tarmac Ring

Vatnsnes

Road, the Africa Twin cruising. I follow with the Serow whining and hope some of his keenness rubs off on me.

We whizz past a collection of what look like giant molehills rising out of the flat valley floor, the grass-covered remains of a massive landslide. Three lie clustered together; Þrístapar, meaning 'Three Hummocks', is where the last execution in Iceland took place in 1830.

Agnes Magnúsdóttir, a 33-year-old woman, and teenager Friðrik Sigurðsson were sentenced to death for murder and beheaded. Their bodies were quickly buried in untreated board coffins without blessing, and their heads were placed on sticks as a warning to others, disposed of later at an undisclosed location.

One night two years earlier, Agnes had raised the alarm with a neighbour on the Vatnsnes peninsula that Natan Ketilsson's farm, where she worked, was ablaze. The fire was put out before everything was razed to the ground, but not soon enough to save Natan or a visitor. It didn't take an in-depth forensic examination of the charred bodies to realise that they had been stabbed to death first. The fire was an attempted cover-up.

Although the details have been lost through the passage of time, the mystery, passion, intrigue, jealousy and greed that surrounded this double murder combined with events leading to Iceland's last execution, of a woman no less, captured the public imagination. It is the name Agnes Magnúsdóttir that people remember when talking about Iceland's last execution, even though the role she played in the murders is questionable. A fear of rebellious servants may have been enough for the authorities to condemn her as an example to others.

Besides a white information board at the roadside, like those found throughout the country at tourist sites and parking bays, there's no other indication of what happened at Þrístapar. As we speed by, I try to imagine the scene on that historic day in 1830 with the executioner, Natan's brother, standing beside the wooden block waiting to perform his duty. The axe he held had been specially imported from Denmark. Friðrik was executed first. Agnes was kept at a distance so that she could not see the end that awaited her. Then it was her turn to put her head on the block. In the face of death, was she scared or calmly resigned to her fate having made peace with God? Did she cry or scream when the axe fell? Did the 150 onlooking men from the district's farms, who had been ordered to attend, consider it a gory spectacle of entertainment or did they watch in solemn disgust?

I'm pulled back to the present by the orange blinking light of Einar's bike indicating to turn right. We slow, lean around the corner and set off along a smaller road.

'Look at the state of you!' Einar remarks when we stop at a viewpoint. The wet, clay-like dirt has sprayed up from the tyres and now clings to my bike and bags in a grey film. I look as though I've been dunked helmet to boot into a mud pool. I'm not impressed. Einar appears to be shiny clean though, his waterproof overalls glistening in the rain.

From the clifftop, I look down to a rocky stack, supposedly another troll that turned to stone. This one lost track of time while throwing rocks at a nearby monastery and got caught by the sun. Apparently, trolls have a deep-founded hatred of anything with religious connections.

The stack is the favoured nesting spot for hundreds of seabirds. Isolated from the mainland, it is free from land-based predators. Called Hvítserkur, meaning 'White Shirt', it is covered in guano. For the protection of the birdlife, the rock base has been artificially reinforced with concrete to prevent the natural process of erosion and collapse.

A vertical slab of rock with two holes eroded through its base, it is one of Iceland's premier photographic landmarks. I leave my camera in the tank bag. There won't be any award-winning shots on this grey, wet day. I watch other tourists descend the steep, slippery path down the cliff in their bright waterproof jackets. The multi-coloured

Vatnsnes

specks spread out over the exposed beach like Smarties spilt from a tube.

Einar removes his thin-rimmed glasses, dries them with a cloth from his jacket and puts them back on. Water drips from the ends of his wavy hair. He looks and points inland, 'There are usually seals in the bay there.'

Holding my hand above my eyes to protect them from the rain, I scan the beach and water. 'Can't see any.'

'No, me neither. Do you want to take a walk down?'

Do I want to slide down the cliff, photograph a lump of rock, maybe see a distant speck that might be a seal but probably is just a rock, and then get hot and sweaty clambering back up the cliff? 'No,' I reply.

I feel sorry for Einar. He is a good guide, and I am being a terrible tourist.

We're about to set off when Einar shouts to me through his visor, 'You should turn your headlight back on.'

'It is,' I say.

It's not. The bulb has blown again. That's the third thing to break in four days. I hope that's my quota filled for this trip. I don't have any more spare bulbs. I'll pick one up in Reykjavik and meanwhile avoid riding in the dark, which is easy since the sun only sets momentarily.

We ride around the tip of the peninsula past the hamlet of Tjörn, where the heads of Agnes and Friðrik were eventually given a proper burial and laid to rest in the cemetery in 1934. How did the severed heads get to Tjörn a century after they were consigned to the ground at an undisclosed location near Þrístapar? The dead, beheaded Agnes spoke from her grave, of course. For a nation content with merging stories of trolls, giants and elves with historical facts in the sagas, it's not surprising the odd ghost enters the script occasionally.

Apparently, in 1932, a woman from Reykjavik claiming psychic abilities put forward a case that the spirit of dead Agnes had spoken to her, requesting that the heads of Agnes and Friðrik be buried at Tjörn church. With the woman's help, the heads were located, unearthed and reburied. The weather and riding may be sub-par today, but the stories surrounding Vatnsnes are fascinating.

At Illugastaðir farm on the western side of the peninsula, we wander on foot along a path to the shoreline shallows. The low tide exposes mudflats and a lingering stench of rotting seaweed. I watch two seals in the distance bobbing up and down in the water through misted binoculars from the small wooden hide on this miserable grey day.

What interests me more is that this is where Natan Ketilsson's farm stood in 1828. Scant details remain about the reasons for the crime and who was primarily to blame. Records attribute it to Friðrik's 'hatred of Natan, and a desire to steal', but that does not factor in Natan's womanising ways.

Agnes Magnúsdóttir was born poor and underprivileged. She was abandoned by her mother at a young age and spent her life toiling for others. She was, however, intelligent and craved more. She fell deeply in love with Natan, who encouraged her intellect and allowed her to dream beyond a life of poverty. Natan, however, was also having a long-term affair with a woman named Rósa. Then he became intimate with sixteen-year-old Sigríður, Friðrik's sister, who also worked for him.

Friðrik often lingered around the farm and was jealous of Natan. He knew Natan had money and was driven to get his hands on it. Was that reason enough to kill him? Did he find out about Natan and his sister? Or was Agnes distraught to find out that Natan had eyes for others and either scheme with or manipulate Friðrik to act? Whatever the inciting events, Natan and his guest were violently stabbed twelve times and bludgeoned with a hammer before being set on fire with shark oil.

With the dirt roads and puddles, I'm filthy. My hair is wet and plastered in mud. I look like the Himba tribespeople of Namibia, who cover their hair and bodies with ochre, except they do it for protection from the sun, which seems unnecessary in Iceland. I need a shower.

The last couple of hours riding on tarmac late into the evening are in the rain. This is not the shower I had in mind. Everything's damp; I'm chilled to the bone and can feel the cold biting at my chest. I'd barely ridden in the rain until now. I usually have a day off and hunker down in my tent rather than riding imperviously through it. I really ought to stop and put on more clothes, but I don't want to hold us up. I tense my arms and grip them closely to my body. *You'll regret not stopping.* It can't be much further. Eventually, we stop to camp at Borðeyri. There's no shower.

Einar informs me that Reykjavík is experiencing its wettest summer in a hundred years. I've been hearing this a lot. The dreary fact seems to cheer every Icelander and tourist I meet. People do love record-breakers; when you can't have the best, you might as well take consolation in having the worst.

During the following day's ride north up the east coast of the Westfjords, it stops raining briefly. My dour and lacklustre attitude continues until Hólmavík where a number of activities lift my spirits.

First, we eat pizza.

Then we soak in the hot pool.

And then we drink a beer.

Followed by another.

These are extravagances I wouldn't have sampled had I been alone. *Thank you, Einar.*

Did you notice how I casually slipped in the hot pool experience? I was coerced into my bikini and took a relaxing dip in the hot baths at the local swimming pool. It was wonderful. I think I might try one of the natural hot springs when I get the chance.

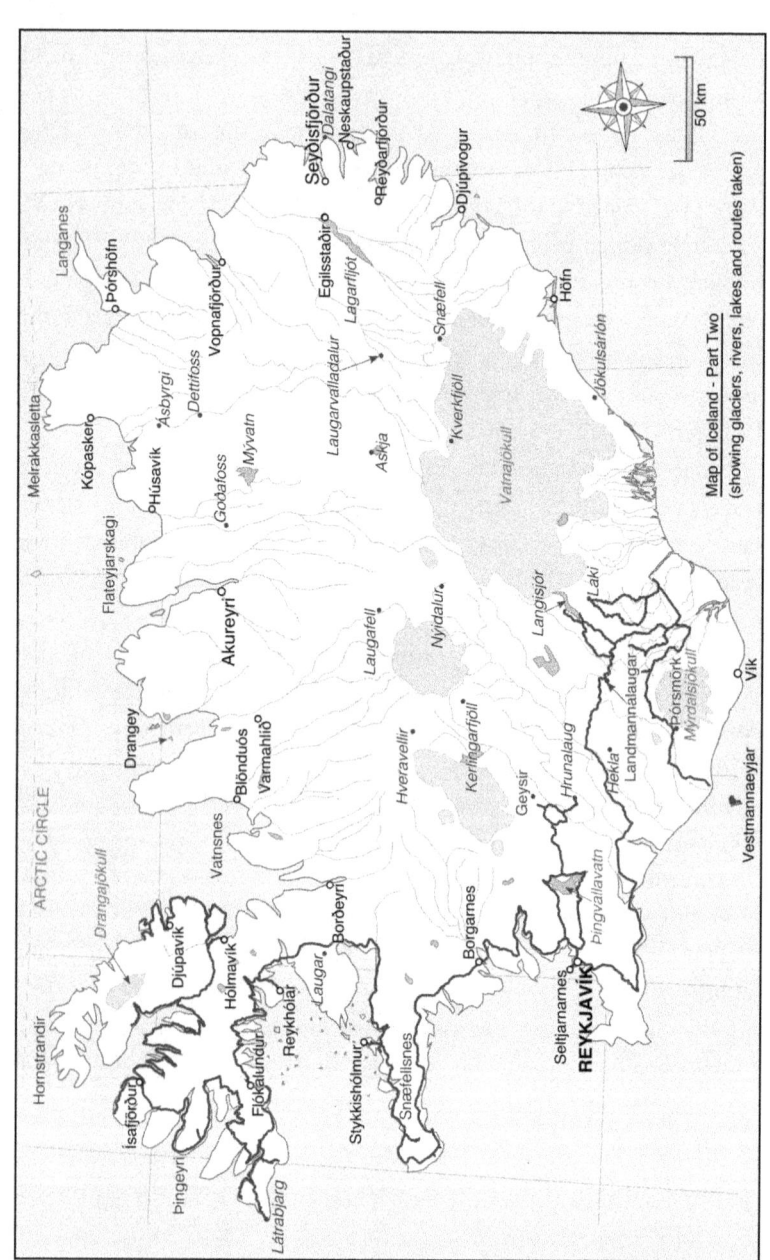

ICELAND
-
Part Two

View of the Laki craters from Mount Laki.

Rusting freight ship at Djúpavík.

10
Rough Tracks and a Herring Factory
Westfjords

My inflatable mattress keeps deflating, waking me up throughout the night, but the hypnotising pitter-patter of raindrops falling on the tent soon sends me back to sleep. It has eased to a drizzle by morning and stops completely when Einar leaves. I silently thank him for taking the rain back to Reykjavík.

I spend the day riding along the dark, rugged eastern coast of the Westfjords. Besides a gentle ripple near the shore, the sea is silky smooth today. A thin layer of cloud blends seamlessly with the water at the invisible horizon; I can't tell where the sea ends and the sky begins.

I pass through only a few settlements; not many people live in this region. The abandoned herring factory at Djúpavík is evidence that it wasn't always so. The largest concrete structure in Iceland when it was built in the mid-1930s and first fully-automated fish factory in Europe overshadows the few houses in the village by the bay. There was no road then; all material for the concrete structure and equipment, including boilers, engines, presses and grinders, had to be shipped into this remote location. The enterprise boomed for a decade. Failed attempts to diverge into the processing of other fish when herring stocks plummeted meant the industry was doomed. In 1954 the factory closed.

I park the bike near the remains of an old freight ship standing askew in the shallow water. Weathered and rusted, the metal hull has corroded holes, letting through streams of light. I wander around the factory on foot. The concrete is crumbling and has fallen off in huge chunks. There are broken gutters, boarded windows and external lights detached from the walls hanging by their wires. Large cogs, wheels and girders rust on the ground. The Arctic terns nesting on the roof of the large herring oil storage tank swoop in to attack me as I walk around its circumference.

In 1984 the grandson of a former resident of Djúpavík bought the old factory intending to repair it and establish a fish farm. Instead, he and his family, the only residents of the village, realising the tourism potential, converted the old women's dormitory into a small hotel. Over time, the masonry and factory roofing have been repaired and the windows replaced. The main storage area is now used for exhibitions and special events.

I love exploring these old, almost-forgotten places. Left to rot and decay under the relentless forces of nature, they evoke sadness and curiosity. Like Kolmanskop that sprang up during the rush for diamonds, now disappearing under the sands of the Namibian desert, and the Gulag remains buried under snow for half the year and deserted towns along the Siberian Road of Bones, they stand as a testament to the different ways of life that can spring up seemingly out of nowhere. They remind me of how quickly times can change, and that people and places must adapt to survive.

I turn onto a jeep track. Where it hugs the shoreline, I pass between derelict concrete buildings covered in graffiti. Metal scrap lies decaying in the elements. It's another factory built during the herring boom and abandoned in the bust. Three rusting ovens lined up in a row, facing out to the fjord, stand upright like headstones, memorials for a bygone era that's dead and buried.

I follow the trail to the end. The only way to continue further northwest is by boat or on foot. The Hornstrandir peninsula beyond is the preserve of nature. With no permanent settlements, wildlife has thrived. I'd like to hike here but plan to access it from the other side by taking a boat from the town of Ísafjörður, where I can stock up on supplies for a multi-day walk.

I wild camp by the water with whooper swans as neighbours. The next day I return along the coast, then head west across country to see

Westfjords

Drangajökull. Covering 160 square kilometres, it is the fifth-largest glacier in Iceland. Less accessible and only two per cent the size of the largest glacier Vatnajökull, which dominates the southeastern quarter of the country, it is often overlooked. The pure white layer of smooth ice that cuts a perfectly straight line across the skyline looks out of place amongst the gritty and imperfect rocky hillsides. The ice reaches down the valley like a giant's tongue licking the fjord.

The Westfjords are not like the verdant, fertile northern valleys. They look old, weathered and wise. It feels as though they have always been this way, with every crease in the turf and scar in the rock existing from the day they were created. Although, at fourteen million years old, the land is young in geological terms.

Iceland sits atop the mid-Atlantic ridge where the Eurasian and American continental plates meet. It is along this rift, which splits the country in a northeast-southwest direction like a slash, that most volcanic activity occurs. When molten magma is thrust up from the bowels of the earth to the surface, it solidifies in the cool air.

The terrain reminds me more of the East Fjords where Högni and Unnur live. When the island first formed, these regions lay adjacent to one another like conjoined twins. Over the course of millennia, separated by volcanic surgery, they have drifted apart as new land rose in between like a younger sibling craving the centre of attention.

The road follows the coast. It's like tracing a line around the fingers of a hand. Each headland is separated by a long narrow fjord, requiring fifty kilometres of riding to reach the other side of the water only a couple of kilometres across. I stop to camp. I would like to relax by the shore but am confined to my tent by swarms of black flies. Unexpectedly tired and with a sore throat, I fear I'm coming down with a cold. Best to nip it in the bud, rest up and keep warm. The next morning, I'm spurred into action by a lack of food in my bags and several days of rain forecast. I reach Ísafjörður before the threatening black clouds catch up with me.

ICELAND Serow Saga

Often the urban campsites are in the centre of town beside the swimming pool, located for convenience rather than beauty. Here, on the edge of town, I pitch my tent beside a stream to a backdrop of a waterfall streaming down the green hillside. The day disappears in showering, buying food, doing the laundry and attempting to dry my clothes between downpours. By the end of it, I'm exhausted.

The next morning I wake late and feel terrible. My nose is blocked, my throat so swollen and sore I can barely swallow, and my chest is drowning in mucus. *This the price you pay for not putting on more clothes when riding in the rain the other day.* I curl up in my sleeping bag and wallow in self-pity. I've only myself to blame.

The following day is worse. *Stop feeling sorry for yourself. It's just man-flu; get over it and get up!* I scrape together enough energy and motivation to get dressed, lace up my hiking boots and set off up a steep trail alongside the waterfall.

Every step is exhausting. *I shouldn't be this unfit.* I take a few steps and rest, a few more steps and stop again. I cough deeply and swallow down chunks of phlegm. I walk a little further. *Dammit, I'm gonna get to the top. I refuse to be defeated.* I cough again between laboured breaths. My heart is racing, my chest burning. After what feels like an eternity, I reach the top of the waterfall and collapse on a rock feeling dizzy and nauseous. There's no way I can make it over the hills into the next fjord as I'd hoped. Besides, I forgot to bring any water with me and my mind is already plagued by thirst. *I just want to curl up and die!*

Once over my moment of melodrama, I take the longer but less steep route back along the road, feeling unsteady on my feet. Halfway to the campsite, I throw up. With a parched mouth and lingering taste of bile, I disregard any concerns about pollution and drink from a trickle of water through the rocks and a pipe under the road. It seems incomprehensible that anything could make me feel worse. Back at the tent, I crawl back into my sleeping bag to fester.

After a couple more days, I feel significantly better. Although, I need longer to recover to be physically capable of hiking with a

Westfjords

loaded pack and enjoy it. There's more rain on the horizon. I've been saying to myself that I'll write when the weather is bad. But the more I learn about Iceland, the more I want to see and discover here, not spend time with my head caught up in past adventures elsewhere. My manuscript about Africa remains untouched. Besides, there's the Serow; I want to ride it. I decide to resume my methodical exploration of the country, one peninsula at a time, on my motorbike. I can always come back to hike.

The road south from Ísafjörður cuts through the mountains. I dislike tunnels and avoid them when there's an alternative route. What will I miss by travelling through this dark void? My reluctance today is significantly increased because the bike doesn't have a headlight, and it's a single lane tunnel with intermittent passing bays and no internal lighting. I fear, quite reasonably, that I could be mown down by an oncoming vehicle because it can't see me. I wait at the tunnel entrance for another vehicle. Then I follow, racing to keep close behind, using their lights to see and squeezing into the bays whenever they pull over. My heart's racing. Eventually, I emerge half-blinded into the light, as though regaining consciousness from a coma.

It's ideal riding weather: sunny and dry, the wind noticeable by its absence. The fjord's waters are completely still. The mountains and their mirror-image reflections are like sound waves resonating above and below the waterline.

There are not many F-roads or 4x4 tracks in the Westfjords, but I'm determined to attempt what's here. The thrill and enjoyment I got from riding the F-roads on the peninsula of Flateyjardalur hooked me. I've loved every dirt track I've taken since. I'm ready for another fix.

The northern half of the trail around the Þingeyri peninsula hugs the cliff. At the tip it passes a lighthouse and then weaves along the southern coast where blue-purple lupines and bright yellow buttercups cover the lower grassy slopes. The serrated knife-edge mountain tops tower above like an impenetrable fortress. Where the mountains reach down to the water in a vertical wall of black rock, I bump along over rounded rocks smoothed by the tides. Cold water drips onto me from the overhanging cliff. I ride in its shadow whilst the sun shines brilliantly across the sparkling waters.

I attempt to take a rough track up a valley and back to Þingeyri over a pass, but the trail disappears into snow. There are a couple of sheep tracks that skirt up and over it. No one has passed here. The risk of the bike sliding off the mountain is too great. The only way to proceed would be to dig a path, but I don't have anything in my luggage that could shovel snow in significant quantities. Reluctantly, I return down and continue along the coastline.

The 4x4 trail improves to a graded dirt road and then to tarmac. Having had the trail to myself, I'm surprised to arrive at a car park full of vehicles. I join the other people crawling about way-marked paths like ants to view Dynjandi waterfall, then continue my journey.

The Látrabjarg cliffs are another busy location. People are drawn here because it's the most westerly point in Iceland, and Europe if you forget the Azores in the mid-Atlantic. When you've made the effort to visit the Westfjords, you might as well go as far west as possible; it's no more time consuming than circumnavigating many of the deep fjords. Several species of seabird, including fulmar, guillemot and razorbill, nest among the cliffs. But it's the clown-faced puffins flying to and from their burrows near the clifftops that capture my interest.

The long road out of the Westfjords goes through Flókalundur, a hamlet named after Raven-Flóki (who gave Iceland its name) because he wintered here. I pull into a parking area and see a woman walking along the path in flip-flops and sarong with a towel wrapped around her head like a turban. The parking area is for a natural hot spring.

The dip in the pool at Hólmavík with Einar whetted my appetite. The hot pool, nestled in the rocks below the grassy bank, has wonderful views looking out towards the entrance of the fjord. *I could be tempted.* Then I see three white heads come into view and

Westfjords

look up at me, their bodies submerged in the dark water. A hot pool all to myself was marginally enticing; now, I feel a rising panic at the thought of being crammed in with strangers. I contemplate whether it's worth the hassle of finding my bikini and changing out of all my bike gear. I ought to try a natural hot pool at least once.

While I'm pondering, three vehicles arrive independently; two couples and parents with three excitable children. A twenty-something girl and her boyfriend wander past me and disappear down the steps. Moments later, the girl races back with a huge, uninhibited smile of joy like a kid at Christmas seeing her presents under the tree. She rushes to their hired camper van, then runs past me again with a towel in her hands. I wish I could get as enthusiastic.

There's a dotted line on my map indicating a jeep track that starts nearby. *I think I'll go find that jeep track.* I leave and immediately relax. Around the bay, the track is signposted as a footpath and disappears into the thicket of rowan and dwarf birch; though, my map indicates it's a legal road. I proceed slowly.

I stop where it ascends. It looks too steep, too rocky. Perhaps I should turn back. Once again I'm conflicted, consumed with self-doubt yet knowing that if I give up now, I'll never ride the tracks further inland that I want. It's easier when there's someone to follow; my theory is that if others can do it, so can I. Would other people ride this? Of course they would.

I imagine I'm trailing another biker and go for it. The bike bumps up the rocky terrain, loose stones slipping under the tyres, the wheel spinning in the dirt. I open the throttle, cruise over the rise and onto level ground. *Oh yeah, this is what I love!* Now I'm like a kid at Christmas. Not all girls love bikinis and hot tubs; some love dirt trails and motorbikes.

The trail is barely visible; grey rocks cover the ground like rubble. Tall cairns stand like sentries marking the way. The rough path continues along the course of a river. Water gushes between narrow rock canyons and cascades down a series of falls. Ahead, the sun breaks through the clouds in golden streams of light. A black brooding sky behind spurs me onward. I'm bursting with energy as though the storm is brewing within me, adrenalin pulsing through my veins like an electric current. On and on I go, a big grin spread across my face. I bump along, arms straining to control the bike, slowing over large rocks and accelerating on the smoother dirt. Past a small lake, up and up we go.

The scenery is grey and bleak and pitted white with snow that has stubbornly refused to melt. As I near the high plateau, the landscape is like an ugly quarry. The track follows giant pylons that run across the land like a scar. Still and unmoving, they are a modern version of petrified trolls. Where the ground begins to fall away on my right, distant sun-drenched hills and the sparkling sea are revealed. I look briefly, but my tired eyes take a fraction too long to refocus on the trail. I hit a rock and the back wheel slips sideways. I stick out my left leg to brace, feel the weight of the bike shoot through it, then accelerate away. *Easy now*. It's getting late; it's been a long day; I've not eaten; my body's tired. *You can't afford to make mistakes. Not here, not alone. Concentrate*.

There are two rivers to cross. Nervous and unsure about the first, I wade through to check the depth. It's rockier than anything I've attempted before, but not deep. Being prudent and lacking faith in my abilities, I unload and carry my bags over first, ignoring the inevitable wet feet. Then I ride the bike across. With each river I'm gaining confidence, expanding the range of what I am comfortable with. At the second river, I pause briefly to pick my route, then plunge in.

I can't stop smiling because I'm loving every moment riding this trail – the freedom, independence and responsibility for my own actions and their consequences, good and bad. I think back to how shackled I felt during my ride across Africa with company. The endless compromises I made now seem like concessions and sacrifices. I don't ever want to lose this feeling I have right now. I

Westfjords

know this free spirit within me is worth fighting for. I shan't give it up – give up on it – again.

I consider stopping to wild camp, but a storm is on the way. I don't want to be tent-bound on a mountainside or forced to ride through it because I've not enough supplies. I'm driven on, eager to stay ahead of the menacing sky behind.

Back on smooth tarmac, the bike glides as though floating on air, any unevenness in the terrain ironed out in the road's construction. I cruise around the fjords in the dusky twilight. The sun illuminates the clouds from underneath giving them a heavenly aura. The blue sky reflected in the water gives a metallic sheen. It reminds me of the serene autumn light and landscapes of the Scottish Highlands. All I want to do is ride perpetually in and out of a never-ending series of deep fjords, not having to stop to sleep or eat or refuel, or worry about what lies in the future.

With the sun dipped below the horizon after its long goodbye, the temperature drops. The wind chill freezes my toes. I wriggle them to get the blood flowing with little effect as the water squelches inside my sodden boots. I speed up to reach the next village quicker, to put my tent up and get warm. The faster I go, the colder I get.

I turn off the main road towards Reykhólar. A huge owl flies out in front of me, its broad wings moving with slow, powerful beats. It's ghostly pale in the muted light, as short-eared owls can appear. We're two creatures alone. I haven't seen another soul for hours. The night is ours until, towards the end of the road, a whimbrel chick, fluffy yellow and spotty brown, totters inelegantly across the road. A couple of redshanks join me on this last leg of the day, weaving in front of the bike, leading the way as they often do.

At the junction for the village, the illusion of solitude vanishes in an instant. I follow the campsite signs, then ride towards the tents I can see on the village green. There's a church on the hill, its spire stretching up to the heavens. The parking area is packed. I can't see any people, but it is nearly midnight. I find no signs for the reception, so I enter the nearest building. It looks like a school. About fifty people are sitting around tables listening to a speech. Occasionally a few people laugh. I have no idea what's going on. I go back out; I'll pay in the morning.

The tents are congregated along the edge of the parking area as though they've rolled off the hillside. I pitch mine at the end. I'm about to push my bike over when a balding man approaches me.

'You can't camp here,' he says sternly.

'Why?' I ask, perplexed.

'This is a private event, not a public campsite. You have to leave.' No wonder I couldn't locate the toilet or washing facilities.

'But …'. I haven't eaten dinner; this situation risks tipping me from hungry to angry. I'm too exhausted to charm my way into staying. Mildly disappointed in myself, I roll over like an obedient old dog. 'OK, I'll pack up now. Where's the actual campsite?'

'It's a few kilometres back the way you came.'

According to my map and also the signposts, there should be two campsites, one here in the middle of the village. My temper's rising. The five-year-old within me is throwing a tantrum, rolling around on the grass, kicking and screaming and refusing to move.

'So, why are there signposts leading here?' I ask, trying to stay outwardly calm.

'I don't know. I'm sorry.'

I take down the tent, thinking irritably that he could have spoken to me five minutes ago before I got unpacked. Or he could have let me stay.

As I'm putting on my helmet to leave, a young man walks over. 'Hi, is that your bike?'

Of course it is! I am not in the mood for this. I just want to eat and sleep. 'Hi!' I say cheerily. 'Sure is.'

'My name is Jón Stefánsson. Would you like a drink?'

'Yeah, sounds great,' I reply instinctively. *Why did I say that? I don't want a drink.* I want dinner and to be curled up in my tent with warm,

Westfjords

dry feet. A full belly and feeling in your toes are essential elements of happiness.

We sit on the collapsible chairs outside his trailer camper. 'We've run out of beer. Have you tried Icelandic vodka?'

This is not what I need right now. 'No.'

'Icelandic vodka is the best in the world.'

'Really?' I say with a liberal dose of scepticism.

'Yes. It's better – purer – than Russian vodka. It's very smooth and clear. It's all about the water. Ours comes from the glaciers. Of course, the wheat and barley are imported,' Jón Stefánsson explains.

'We've run out of coke. Do you want to try it with this?' He holds up a bottle of lemon-flavoured alcopop. 'It makes a good mixer.'

Not really. 'Sure,' I reply.

Jón Stefánsson talks passionately about his country, the words flooding out of him like a glacial river in spate. Gradually, his enthusiasm rubs off on me. I realise that I'm enjoying the evening or, more accurately, the morning.

'I lived in Austria for six years. I know what it's like to be a foreigner. I know that it's the kindness and hospitality of the people that make a place memorable, not the tourist site checklists.' He tells me that having seen all the motorcycles touring in the Alps, he'd been inspired to get his motorcycle licence. He's been riding a year now.

Jón Stefánsson is showing me Icelandic hospitality. It's a memory to take away with me from this journey. I am grateful. *But please, I'm tired and hungry, still need to find the real campsite, need to thaw my numb feet and drain these squelching boots.* I take another sip of lemon vodka, smile and listen on.

'Another vodka?' He asks.

'Er …'.

'For the road?'

'Oh, OK. Then I must go sleep.' It's one-thirty in the morning.

11

The Sagas
Snæfellsnes

Back down the hill, I see the campsite sign. I check the map on my phone and notice that the actual campsite is located a few metres down a small track opposite, out of sight. I realise my mistake; I'd seen the tents by the church and made an assumption.

The actual campsite is on a small plot by the swimming pool. A handful of vehicles are parked in a row looking out over the flats exposed at low tide. It's a beautiful, peaceful and sheltered location. It could be a good place to hide from the bad weather that's forecast for the next few days. It's still light, albeit that dull, shadowless light of overcast skies. Birds are calling from the long marsh grasses. I recall the dawn chorus of the garden birds at home. It seems the birds here are also confused by the eternal light of summer. My earlier annoyances float away with the breeze.

I quietly pitch my tent between a motorhome and a camper van, then add my wet jeans and socks to the collection of drying clothes laid over a wooden picnic bench. I cook noodles because it's quick, hoping the roaring stove doesn't wake the other campers.

Despite the late night, I'm up before anyone else. I go in search of a shower. There's a sign on the door to the swimming pool informing me that showers are in this building and cost extra. The building is closed until midday when the pool will open. There's also a piece of A4 paper pinned to the door informing me in small print that it is not recommended to drink the water without boiling it. The water has tested positive for E.coli. Iceland has pure mountain water in abundance; yet, I've found possibly the only place on the whole island where water should not be drunk straight from the tap (although I see many tourists carrying or buying bottled mineral water). *I hope this*

Snæfellsnes

isn't the water used for making Icelandic vodka. There's nowhere indoors to take shelter and no sockets to charge my laptop. Perhaps this is not such a good place to weather out the coming storm. I pack up and head off to the Snæfellsnes peninsula.

Riding south, I see a sign for the hot pools at Laugar and am tempted to stop. I still need a shower, but a desire to reach town before the weather deteriorates urges me to bypass it.

One of the most popular sagas, *Laxdæla saga*, is one of the family sagas written around 1230–1280. It relates the tragic story of a love triangle involving Guðrún, who was born at Laugar farm. The saga spans several generations and the tragic trio enter the story halfway through.

Guðrún is introduced as 'the most beautiful woman ever to have grown up in Iceland, and no less clever than she was good-looking'. She is also portrayed as a manipulator of men, a common characterisation of women in the sagas.

The author of the *Laxdæla saga*, as with most sagas, is unknown. However, there's speculation it was written by a woman. While most sagas celebrate the male warrior culture, *Laxdæla saga* is told from a woman's perspective, and strong women dominate the storylines. Using intelligence, wile, wit and sex to full effect, they do not need to fight with fist, sword or axe to show their power.

Dreams and prophecies were popular tools in telling the tales. When a chieftain visited Laugar, Guðrún asked for his interpretation of her dreams. He said she would marry four times: the first she would leave, the second would drown, the third would be slain, whilst the fourth would be the greatest nobleman of them all but would also drown.

Her first marriage was arranged by her father when she was fifteen. She did not love him. When she asked her husband to buy her a new treasure, he refused and slapped her, saying there was no limit to her demands. Since dressing as the opposite sex was valid grounds for divorce, Guðrún made him a shirt with a low-cut neckline and claimed he wore women's clothes. Then she married a man she'd become close to, but he drowned shortly after. When Guðrún met Kjartan, who regularly visited the hot pools at Laugar, they fell in love. Kjartan insisted that she wait to marry him, so he could go to Norway with Bolli his half-brother and friend.

Three years later, Bolli returned. Kjartan stayed behind, partly as a hostage to the king, who was hoping to force the Icelanders to convert to Christianity, but also because he had struck up a close friendship with the king's sister. Bolli was quick to tell Guðrún of this, then asked for her hand in marriage. Believing Kjartan had abandoned her, she accepted the proposal. A year later, Kjartan returned to Iceland, feeling betrayed and vengeful. This led to a series of increasingly severe acts of retaliation that resulted in Guðrún inciting her brothers and Bolli to attack Kjartan.

In Svínadalur (Pig valley), they ambushed Kjartan in a ravine while he was travelling with a few of his men. Kjartan was a good fighter and held off the attacks while throwing insults towards Bolli, who was reluctant to fight. When Bolli eventually drew his sword, Kjartan threw down his weapon, refusing to defend himself let alone attack his half-brother. Bolli killed him.

This happened in the same valley that I've been riding through. I stop at a waterfall beside the road. Standing in the rain, looking at the water gushing down a cleft in the rocks, I can imagine Kjartan and Bolli fighting here.

After Guðrún gave birth, she moved to Helgafell where she later married her fourth husband. He drowned at sea on his way back from Norway as the prophecy had foretold. The last words spoken by Guðrún in the saga are an enigmatic reply to her son, who asked about the greatest love of her life. She replied, 'I was worst to him I loved the best'. The reader is left to decide who she means. The Icelandic wording allows for it to be a general statement that she mistreated those she loved, a not uncommon paradox of love that is as true today as a millennium ago.

Snæfellsnes

Stykkishólmur is the main town on Snæfellsnes, a rugged peninsula that juts out from the west coast. I reach it as the rain begins, and hole up on the campsite next to the golf course.

Iceland has a lot of golf courses; surprising, given that for half the year, the fairways and putting greens must be hidden under a layer of snow. It seems odd that a sport where the wind is your foe is so popular in a country where that foe is so often present. It does give the Icelanders a chance to connect with their tough Viking heritage, each wielding their golf club like a modern-day Thor's hammer.

I pitch my tent in the most sheltered spot, tight in a corner between a raised rocky mound and a hedge. I'm surprised this pitch hasn't already been taken. It's only once I've crawled into my tent and unpacked half the contents of my bags that I notice a pungent smell of piss wafting to my nostrils. *Great.* This corner not only offers the best protection from the wind but also from public view, making it ideal when you need to pee in the middle of the night – a time when distances to toilet blocks inexplicably multiply ten-fold. I can't be bothered to move; I've done enough pitching and taking down my tent in the last twenty-four hours. I do up the zips and take off my three-day-old socks, which alters the aroma significantly. I still need a shower.

The campsite shower is in an outside cubicle with no roof. Having both cold rainwater and a stream of hot piped water shower down onto my goose-pimpled body is a uniquely Icelandic experience. I keep it brief because there's nowhere to put my towel and clothes out of the rain.

The reception is in the golf clubhouse, which campers are allowed to use. It has sofas below a big screen TV and additional seating at tables. There's a kiosk in the corner selling coffee, snacks and cans of beer. I sink into a sofa and watch the black sky outside. Rain lashes the windows, droplets smearing the glass like venomous spit. The wind has picked up, the yellow flag buffeting wildly in its hole and the pole bent close to breaking. I don't see any golfers. *I hope my tent isn't being ripped to shreds or blown away.* I'd better check.

I put on my jacket, pull my hat down over my ears and step out onto the clubhouse steps. The wind slams into me, a full-body assault. My tent is still pitched in Pee Corner, impervious to the gale. There's not a shudder on the guy ropes.

The cheap, four-man festival tents with flimsy poles pitched in the middle of the campground where the wind is blasting through like a freight train are not faring so well. A group of people rush about in brightly coloured waterproofs, battling to tame them as they are buffeted in every direction, flattened one moment, then at risk of taking off. Hands grapple with the guy ropes while others clutch at the fly sheets as though trying to catch a wild animal. Fortunately, the smaller tents, with lower profiles, are weathering the gale better.

I spend my days writing in the clubhouse and bakery cafe catching up on my journal. I have to make notes using old-fashioned pen and paper. My laptop keyboard has developed a fault: the space bar and two rows of letters don't work. I've accepted now that I won't be finishing my manuscript while in Iceland.

For a change from my instant noodles diet, I eat fish and chips from the van by the harbour. I huddle in my down jacket and waterproofs while sheltering from the rain. When the sun breaks through the clouds, the small boats sparkle on the dark water that mirrors the sky. Behind the harbour, a bright orange lighthouse is perched on top of a small rocky island, whose vertiginous cliffs shield the town from the open water.

During a break in the rain, I take a short ride out of town to Helgafell, meaning 'Holy Mountain'. A mere 73-metre rise, it's a grassy mole-hill of a mound where, according to tradition, if you walk up in silence without looking back, you will have three wishes granted. Apparently, your wish will only come true if you face east, tell no one what you wished for, and wish it from a good and true

Snæfellsnes

heart. I selflessly ask for Iceland to win their next round of the football World Cup being played later in the evening.

I guess my heart is not good or true enough. Iceland loses to Croatia.

According to the *Eyrbyggja saga*, Helgafell was named by Thórólfur Mostrarskeggi, who held it in such reverence that no one should look at it without having washed first. Luckily, I've showered already at the campsite.

The most memorable character of the *Eyrbyggja saga* was Mostrarskeggi's great-grandson, Snorri-goði (a *goði* was a priest-chieftain). Unusually for a saga hero, he did not earn his renown through Viking strength and force but sense and guile.

Snorri's father was the rightful heir to Helgafell, but when he married and moved away with his new wife, Helgafell passed to Snorri's uncle, Börkur. Snorri grew up at Helgafell under the foster-care of his uncle, whom he increasingly resented, regarding Helgafell as his birthright. At fourteen, he travelled to Norway to seek his fortune, then returned to claim ownership of Helgafell.

At the local Þing, Snorri formally requested a half-share in the estate as was his right. Börkur was not willing to form a partnership. Instead, Snorri proposed that one pay the other for his share and hence take full ownership. He suggested that Börkur set a fair price, then Snorri would either accept, pay and take ownership, or if he refused then Börkur would pay him. Snorri held the upper hand; he had kept secret his wealth obtained in Norway. Börkur insisted that the payment and exchange be done immediately and, believing Snorri to be without wealth, set a very low price so that he could get Helgafell for a bargain. Snorri gladly accepted the price and handed over the silver in his purse. At only sixteen years old, Snorri took full charge of Helgafell as well as the temple and chieftaincy that went with it.

In later years, Snorri was a kinsman and great friend of Guðrún, of the *Laxdæla saga* fame. After Bolli had been slain, Snorri went to

Guðrún to seek reconciliation for the killing, but she wasn't prepared to accept any payment. She would prefer to move so that she no longer had to be neighbours with her husband's killers. Snorri, amid an ongoing dispute with his neighbours, struck a deal to exchange homes and a year later, Guðrún moved to Helgafell with her young son. She lived there the remainder of her life. Today there is a small marker stone with Guðrún's name and the date 1008 engraved on it in the church graveyard.

After a four-day enforced retreat from the bad weather, I leave Stykkishólmur. I ride past Helgafell on my left and head anti-clockwise around the peninsula, first passing through the Berserkjahraun lava field, all mangled, contorted and moss-covered rock. The wily Snorri played a part in its story also.

Two brothers lived on neighbouring farms, separated by an impassable lava field. Vermundur, one of the brothers, was gifted two 'berserkers' by the King of Sweden whilst raiding in Norway. Berserkers were fighters prized for their ability to run wild during battle and their seeming immunity from pain. The old Icelandic word *berserkr* means 'bear-shirted', possibly due to them wearing bear pelts during battle, or perhaps a metaphor for their strength, ferocity and fearlessness.

The berserkers were too wild for Vermundur to control, so he gave them to his brother Víga-Styr to work as farmhands. Trouble started when one of the berserkers took a liking to Víga-Styr's daughter and asked for her hand in marriage. Unenthusiastic about the idea but not wanting to outright refuse for fear of inciting the berserker's wrath, Víga-Styr went to Snorri at Helgafell to ask for advice. Although Snorri was only twenty years old at the time, his reputation for cunning was already well known. He suggested that they walk up Helgafell to discuss, since 'plans devised there have seldom failed'. It may be this superstition of Snorri's that later led to the tradition of making wishes on the hilltop.

Snæfellsnes

They devised a plan that Víga-Styr would set the berserker an impossible challenge to show his worthiness for marriage in place of a dowry since he was penniless. The challenge was for the berserkers to make a road connecting the two brothers' farms through the lava field. To Víga-Styr's surprise, they completed the task.

To save his daughter from the marriage, Víga-Styr invited the berserkers to use the sunken sauna bath he had recently made. Once inside, Víga-Styr blocked off the trap-door entrance and poured scalding water through the skylight until the bathhouse was too hot to withstand. As the berserkers tried to escape, Víga-Styr dealt one a fatal blow and killed the other with his spear. Afterwards, he buried them in a deep hollow in the lava field. When Snorri heard the news of the berserkers' deaths, he went to collect his reward from Víga-Styr. They talked a lot and by the end of the day, Víga-Styr was so pleased with the outcome that even though the original plan had failed, he betrothed his daughter to Snorri.

Some consider Snæfellsnes to be Iceland in miniature. Examples of everything the country has to offer can be found on this one peninsula: black sand beaches, a dramatic coastline and cliffs full of nesting birds; lava fields, beautiful waterfalls, deep caves, distinctive conical mountains and a glacier; old fishing and trading towns, historical sites and saga settings. Today, it's all under a blanket of grey fog hanging low over the hills.

I ride the trail towards Snæfellsjökull, the glacier on the dormant volcano that features in Jules Verne's *Journey to the Centre of the Earth*. Up here, above the cloud, there's glorious sunshine. Snow blocking the roads makes continuing impossible. I return the way I came, then follow the main road around the peninsula in fog and rain.

It feels like I'm on a conveyor belt for tourists, making obligatory stops to take a photo of each differing landscape and then moving on. Finding little that grasps my interest on the southern coast of Snæfellsnes, I continue in the direction of Reykjavík. I stop halfway to buy lunch in the town of Borgarnes, wandering through a small park where an unusual cairn monument catches my attention.

The domed mound of rocks wrapped in chains marks one of the sites relating to *Egill's saga*. Egill Skallagrímsson was a well-known Viking warrior and accomplished poet, possibly Iceland's greatest literary hero. His father, one of Iceland's earliest settlers, built a farm, which he named Borg, just north of here.

It was at Borg that Egill was born and where Kjartan of *Laxdæla saga* is buried. Kjartan was Egill's grandson. Considering the small population during the settlement period, the number of locations and characters that overlap several sagas is unsurprising. Helgafell and Borg are central to several and remained places of importance. Ari Thorgilsson, the author of *Íslendingabók* and Guðrún's great-grandson, was also born at Helgafell.

Egill grew up to be an ugly hulk of a man, but strong and powerful like his father. Unfortunately, he could not control his temper or physical strength. An early starter, he composed his first skaldic verse at the age of three and was only seven when he committed his first murder, killing a boy with his axe who had outdone him in sport. By the age of twelve, few grown men could compete with him. He spent much of his life as a Viking warrior abroad.

Egill later settled at Borg. On hearing the news that a second son had perished in a shipwreck during a freak storm off Borgarnes, he rode down to the bay. He found his son's body and took it to be buried in his father's burial mound. I'm looking at a beautiful relief in the park of Egill on horseback with his dead son lying limp in his arms, legs dangling off the side of his horse. Egill composed a beautiful poem, *Sonatorrek*, to honour him. Full of agonised grief, Egill blames his pagan god Odin for the death of his son. It is considered Egill's best skaldic poem and one of the greatest in Norse literature.

It's the end of a long day; I am feeling immobilised by indecision and tiredness. I need a good kicking to spur me into action. I message Einar for suggestions of what to do. He invites me to stay, at least

Snæfellsnes

until the next forecast storm has passed through. The idea of having a warm dry place to retreat to this evening is too appealing. As it's not far to Reykjavik, I've time to ride a convoluted route and take a jeep trail across the mountains. Sure enough, the rocky tracks, rough terrain and far-reaching views out to the coast re-energise me.

12

Geysers and Greenhouses
Around Reykjavík

Einar lives in Seltjarnarnes, one of six towns, each with their own identity, making up the greater urban conurbation of the Reykjavík district. The towns may have been separate once, but urban sprawl means it's impossible to tell where one ends and another begins. It's a residential suburb on the peninsula northwest of Reykjavík with clean, tidy streets and modern apartment blocks in whites and pastel colours. With plenty of green space and footpath shortcuts, it's difficult to appreciate how close it is to the centre of the capital.

During the day, while Einar's working, I walk the promenade along the northern shore towards the lighthouse on Grótta Island at the tip of the peninsula. It's not permitted to walk right up to it even though it's low tide and the dark sand is exposed. According to the sign, it's breeding season for the ground-nesting birds in the area until 14 July. Today is the thirteenth. I don't expect the birds will still be busy procreating, yet stop tomorrow, and that by walking there now I'll have a detrimental effect on the long term health of the population. I comply nonetheless, aware that many Icelanders take rules relating to the environment very seriously, especially regarding where you must not walk or drive. Further along the shore, a couple of families are relaxing on the beach. The children, wrapped in hats and coats, are digging in the shallows with buckets and spades.

I continue along the paved walkway around a small lake. A woman is sitting on a wooden bench watching an Arctic tern swoop in, hover above the water and dive for fish. The whole area is bounded by tall grasses. It's unusual that such lush grass is not being grazed by sheep or horses. Besides the birds, the only animals I see in the city are cats, not strays but well-fed felines with glossy fur and sparkling collars.

Around Reykjavík

For a city population housed primarily in apartments, I'm surprised there are so many prowling the streets.

When Einar returns home, we head to the local swimming pool.

'There's no better way to relax after a long shift at work,' he says.

I take an obligatory butt-naked shower, making sure to wash every part of me including armpits, arse and feet like everyone else and as the signs indicate, then put on my bikini and walk outside. Einar is lounging in the main hot pool, temperature conditioned at 38 degrees Celsius. I get in quickly because it's cold in the open air at nine o'clock in the evening. I slouch back, submerged with only my head exposed.

This hot tub is almost full, unlike the smaller tubs, which at 40 and 42 degrees Celsius are too hot to stay in long; although, there's a cold pool to jump into between roasting dips. Only a couple of people are swimming lengths in the main swimming pool. It's more enjoyable than spending the night on the sofa watching TV or going for a strenuous workout in the gym.

We leave at closing time, exuding heat, and go get a takeout pizza, which we eat by the lighthouse at midnight. There are more people here now than during the day. It's as though the Icelanders want to taste every last drop of the summer daylight, knowing how scarce it is.

There is a perfect semi-circle rainbow of kaleidoscopic colour, vivid against the flat raincloud-grey sky. The distant horizon glows orange. As the sun makes its brief dip into the underworld, the clouds turn deep pink, the calm mirror of sea blushing crimson in reply. It's one of the most spectacular sunsets I've ever seen. Einar dismisses it in familiar contempt, beauty taken for granted.

Einar doesn't have to work the next day; he suggests we take the bikes out. I hope we can time it between rain showers.

We leave the city and follow the road that runs alongside the pipeline that transfers hot water from the Nesjavellir geothermal

ICELAND Serow Saga

power plant to Reykjavík. The plant serves the hot water and space heating needs of the capital. Around eighty-five per cent of Iceland's primary energy supply comes from renewable sources, mainly geothermal power and hydropower.

Later we stop for lunch at Friðheimar. The farm specialises in growing tomatoes inside giant greenhouses and has a dining area where buffet lunches of all-you-can-eat tomato soup are served. Sadly, we're too late but can buy a mug of soup and bread from the bar. There's a variety of foods and drinks on offer, all with tomatoes in the ingredients. I'm not sure about tomato-flavoured ice-cream.

Tidy rows of vines go on and on into a distant jungle, trained around wires that carry them several metres towards the roof. Bees imported from the Netherlands are used for pollination. There is a small viewing box where you can spot the queen bee, so much larger than the workers. Iceland has few pests due to its cool climate, so a lot of produce grown in the country is essentially organic. At this farm, biological controls are used for any pests that might be a problem.

Thanks to geothermal energy and climate-controlled greenhouses, tomatoes can be grown year-round, despite the long winters. Hot water is piped from a borehole only 200 metres away and enters the greenhouse at around ninety-five degrees Celsius. Cold water from the farm's supply is used for irrigation.

Locally produced fruit and vegetables were once limited to potatoes, turnips, carrots, cabbage, cauliflower and rhubarb. Iceland's greenhouses extend the growing season and add tomatoes, cucumbers, peppers and strawberries.

We ride on through green rolling countryside, past a small church and turn down a dirt track to a parking area, where Einar opens up his top box and pulls out a towel. He told me we were going to Hrunalaug, but the name meant nothing. If I knew some Icelandic, I'd have known we were coming to a hot spring; *laug* means warm pool. Who packs a bikini and towel for a bike ride?

Around Reykjavík

'Einar …' I say hesitantly, 'I didn't bring anything to wear.'

He replies, 'Well I only have a towel. I always pack it just in case. I'll just strip off. Even if there are other people here, it's not like I'll ever see them again.'

Firstly, if you always pack your towel just in case, why not pack your swimming trunks? Does he just like getting naked? Or is this a ruse to get me naked? Oh, sod it.

'OK,' I answer after a long pause, 'but you'll have to lend me your towel when we get out.' I can wear my underwear and ride back commando. Now that we're here, I'm not going to miss out.

I follow Einar along a trail that leads behind a small rise in the grassy hillside. Beyond, there's a small wooden hut with a turf roof and gable ends. A stream runs through it, then flows into a concrete pool that was once the sheep dip for a sheep-washing station. There's a bigger pool off to the side that has been dug out of the ground and lined with rocks. Einar seems surprised to find other people already bathing, piles of clothes dotted about on the grass. It's too late for him to back out of his skinny dip.

We strip off and clamber down into the pool, trying not to slip on the slimy rocks and submerge ourselves in the soothing, warm water. As people leave, we shuffle down to the deeper end where it's hotter. More people come to take a relaxing dip.

It's the perfect temperature to stay in forever. I'm reluctant to leave because it's started raining, and I don't want to ride back in the cold and wet. I'm only delaying the inevitable. Einar's towel is a pack towel not much larger than a credit card. It's not the size of towel you can wrap around your body as you dress to avoid exposing all. Then again, when you're already exposing all, it's rather irrelevant.

On the ride back, we stop at Geysir. The geothermal area is visible from a distance by the white steam plumes rising from the green valley. The Great Geysir, although currently inactive, is a fumarole that in 1845 spouted water in huge jets to a height of 170 metres. It gives its name to all geysers.

ICELAND Serow Saga

We wander across the bare orange earth with hot water running in rivulets across it and pass several pools of boiling water. Although Geysir may be sleeping again, its smaller neighbour called Strokkur is what most come to see. Spouting jets up to around thirty metres and doing so every six to ten minutes, you never need to wait long to see the show. We stand behind the cordon and wait with everyone else, cameras and phones raised in readiness, prepared and expectant. Nothing happens, the only disturbance a shuffling of feet. We stare at the pool of water and wait ... The surface ripples and then begins to bulge like a balloon. In the blink of an eye it collapses and, immediately, water surges upwards in a great white jet. As a steamy mist drifts downwind, the water falls back to earth, and the overflow trickles away over the rocks. The water is still again. It was all over so suddenly. I wait impatiently for six minutes, needing to see the explosion of activity again to truly believe what happened.

Shortly after leaving Geysir, it starts raining again, par for the course riding with Einar. Surrounded by a gloomy fog, we stop at the northern end of Þingvallavatn, a lake situated in the rift along the Mid-Atlantic Ridge where the continental tectonic plates of Eurasia and North America are gradually moving apart.

'That's Þingvellir,' Einar says, indicating the top of a wall of basalt columnar cliffs ahead of us. 'It means Assembly Plains and is where the Alþingi was held.'

The first general assembly was held here in AD 930. It's considered the oldest parliament in the world. Held for two weeks each summer, the assembly was mandatory for all chieftains; although, most people attended.

The broad, flat plains were an ideal location for a large encampment with grazing for the animals. The lake provided plentiful trout and Arctic char. Hundreds of people set up camp in tents to catch up, gossip, make new friends and no doubt enemies too, start relationships or perhaps get married, and watch the proceedings as general entertainment. It must have been like a modern-day summer

Around Reykjavík

music festival, a Glastonbury-style mud-fest considering the rain, minus the traffic jams.

In a sparsely populated country where neighbours might have been many kilometres distant, even uncontactable outside the summer months, this sort of annual gathering would have held extreme importance for binding society together. People from the East Fjords thought nothing of the seventeen-day journey on horseback. It reminded me of the barbecue I once happened upon in Solitaire, Namibia, where 'local' families had travelled up to 500 kilometres to attend their annual gathering. It was the only time they got to speak face-to-face with their neighbours.

The Alþingi had legislative and judicial functions. New laws were passed and old ones amended by public debate followed by the chieftains' vote. There were four courts, each with judges and a panel of jurors, who listened to the prosecution and defence of any case brought to them and then passed judgement. Verdicts were considered final and irrevocable. Enforcement of the judgements was the responsibility of the victims or their families.

No men were ever sentenced to death. Usually, the law specified a fine to be paid to the injured party. For men used to violence, and where honour was a highly regarded trait, financial compensation was a poor substitute for blood revenge. Sometimes, and when cases were unresolved, men took the law into their own hands or challenged the other to a duel. These duels were fought on an island in the Öxará River to the pleasure of the crowd. The drawing of first blood determined the winner rather than a fight to the death.

The alternative to a fine was outlawry. Outlaws were excluded from society and no longer protected by the law. They could, therefore, be killed by the injured party's family. The law forbade people to help, feed or harbour outlaws; although, this was often disregarded by kinsmen and others who might house and feed them in return for work or killing someone who posed a greater threat.

ICELAND Serow Saga

'Lesser outlawry' lasted three years, which the convicted usually spent in exile. 'Full outlawry' was permanent unless, as in some cases, the outlaw managed to kill three other outlaws. To be outlawed was near enough a death sentence, although some survived. Many outlaws were greatly feared because their deeds and crimes were of almost superhuman strength or evil. Outlaws that escaped capture or death became legends, like Grettir the Strong, alongside ghosts, trolls, giants and other feared creatures.

The Alþingi was a success and contributed to 200 years of peace and stability. By the thirteenth century, however, wealthy families began to seek more power and fought for overall control of the land, taking the law into their own hands in particularly violent ways. As the Alþingi became meaningless, people looked beyond their isle for justice and law. This culminated in a sworn allegiance to Norway in 1262, which effectively ended the Icelandic Commonwealth, although the Alþingi continued to be held annually until 1798.

The death penalty was introduced when Iceland came under Danish rule. When it adopted Lutheranism in 1565, the Alþingi passed new laws with harsher punishments, which were carried out at the assembly plains. Men were usually flogged, hanged or burned at the stake. Women were drowned in Drekkingarhylur, meaning 'Drowning Pool', just upstream on the Öxará River. Their crimes usually related to unfaithfulness or having children out of wedlock.

As I rode back to Reykjavík in the rain yesterday, several cars flashed their headlights at me. It reminded me I need to get a new bulb for the headlight.

Unfortunately, there is not one to be found in the capital. I've visited all the bike shops to no avail. An old man in the auto parts store commented, 'Oh, we ran out of those years ago. They're really old.'

Yes, so is the bike. I give up.

Around Reykjavík

I've had a parcel with a new speedo cable sent, addressed to Einar. It also has a replacement side casing for my GoPro camera, which had fallen off and got lost on the third day I used it. Without it, the camera isn't waterproof. Unfortunately, I dropped the GoPro on the pavement a couple of days ago, and the shattered screen means it still won't be waterproof even with the new part. At least it works, which is better than my laptop.

I go collect the parcel from the post office. I replace the broken speedo cable on my bike and ride up and down the street to test that it works. I top up the oil and check the chain is tensioned. The sun is out, beckoning me to play. I'm rested and the bike is now ready to go. But which way?

I've been happily riding the easy graded roads around the coast and could continue, but I want to explore the trails in the Highlands. The rough terrain and remoteness of the interior have me doubting my abilities, but the longer I delay, the more the interior grows into a terrifying beast, the trails morphing from an adventure rider's dream into impassable tracks that, on my little bike, I could never hope to conquer.

As though reading my mind, Einar asks, 'Have you decided where you're going next? It's a good day for riding in the Highlands. You'll love the adventure.'

He's right, I will. And before I know it, I blurt out that I'm going to head towards Landmannalaugar.

He looks at me bright-eyed. 'That's my favourite place in the whole country. I'm jealous; I have to work or I'd go as well.'

Einar recounts his fond memories of summers volunteering at one of the mountain huts near Landmannalaugar. My doubts are soon drowned out in a sea of his infectious enthusiasm.

He now works for Iceland's Search and Rescue Association. From their national command centre, he coordinates the emergency response teams for everything from natural disasters to tourists in trouble.

ICELAND Serow Saga

'There's a phone signal almost everywhere in the country now, even in the Highlands. Please, if you have any problems, call 112. That's what it's there for. We'll then decide what help is needed and send it. Or you can even just call me; you've got my number.

'If you haven't already, you should download the 112 app. If you do need to call the emergency services, the app will send a text message, which will often get through even when it looks as though there's no signal for a call. You can also check in to log your location. Then, if you don't check out by the time you specified, we assume you've got into trouble. If we are unable to make contact, we send a search team to locate you.'

I'm as prepared as I'll ever be. It's midday by the time I wave goodbye to Einar. We're hopeful our paths will cross again. *Now let's have some fun …*

13

Into the Highlands
Fjallabak

I ride out of the city and detour over the Reykjanes peninsula to the south coast. Then I turn inland and follow tarmac roads running through farmland. In the distance the ground begins to rise. Hekla, one of Iceland's most active volcanoes, dominates the skyline.

Hekla has erupted some twenty times since settlement. The largest eruption, in AD 1104, covered half of Iceland with tephra. Farms as far as seventy kilometres away were damaged and had to be abandoned. The ejected tephra, with high fluorine concentrations, poisoned livestock and people. Ash clouds affected climate and agriculture on the European continent. Sometimes, Hekla shoots lava bombs too. In the past, great chunks of lava rock measuring fifty square metres have landed a kilometre away on the slopes of the volcano; lava bombs weighing up to twenty kilograms hurtled thirty-two kilometres through the air before crashing down to earth.

During the Middle Ages, Hekla became known as the 'Gateway to Hell'. Viewed from afar by passing ships, the lava fountain and flows during a major eruption looked like the earth opening up to expose the underworld. The map from 1585, which I saw on the wall of the Húsavík Whale Museum, shows an erupting Hekla as the dominant feature of the Icelandic landscape, breathing orange and red flames above the southern glaciers of Mýrdalsjökull and Eyjafjallajökull. It was to be feared along with the sea monsters depicted around the island. The Latin text below the volcano translates as, 'Hekla, perpetually condemned to storms and snow, spews stones under terrible noise.'

ICELAND Serow Saga

Hekla's eruptions are irregular and often without warning. In general, the longer between eruptions, the more catastrophic the next. I hope it doesn't choose now to blow.

At the junction with Landmannaleið (F225), I stop to look at the route map on a large information board. There's a rumbling sound above the wind that gets louder. An overland tour truck approaches, its huge off-road tyres taller than my bike. Either it's overkill or the trail is extremely rough. I'm looking forward to finding out.

The trail weaves in long easy arcs around rocks and rises past Hekla, further into the mountains. On and on it goes, the barren ground becoming greener where a river flows. It's a fun trail; I lose track of time. I'm disappointed when I reach a junction with a well-maintained dirt road. I watch a camper van drive past, then a bus.

Near Landmannalaugar, the hillsides brighten. Vivid orange rhyolite rock and vibrant green moss contrast with the pockets of brilliant white snow glistening in the dips and sparkling blue water that reflects the sky. I understand now why Einar is so enamoured with this region.

I'm forced to stop by a substantial river rushing across the trail. Vehicles are parked, their drivers not prepared to attempt the crossing. There are only a handful of 4x4s across the river; I can't see a single motorbike. In the distance, hundreds of tents are packed together, a ramshackle multicoloured tent village. Some Icelanders call it a refugee camp, one that tourists pay to stay at.

Back in the eighties when there were half as many Icelanders, a small fraction of the tourists and roads in a much worse state of repair, you could have sought out solitude here. Now it is a major hotspot for lovers of the outdoors. I can't be bothered to haul my kit to the camp and suspect the hiking trails could be busy. I came to get away from the crowd. It's late, but there's plenty of daylight left. I'd rather ride.

The Fjallabaksleið Nyrðri (F208) passes small lakes and crosses rivers. The bigger ones I walk through first to test the depth, the water

Fjallabak

seeping into my boots and absorbed by my jeans. Only one, early on, causes me to hesitate and summon up courage before attempting it. After that, none are as deep and pose no concern. Whenever the trail rises over the hills, I stop, mesmerised by the extensive views. Dark hills with a greyish-green tint of moss roll on in waves and snow-covered mountains bound the horizon. In the wide valley bottoms, river lattices glisten when the sun breaks from behind a cloud.

I want to go everywhere and see everything on this beautiful evening, but the light is fading and I'm getting tired. The sun is a hair's breadth from where the mountains reach the sky. I'm chasing the glowing orb as though it were possible to catch and hold it close to me, feeling the warmth on my body.

At a junction with a trail heading up a valley, there's another large information board with a map. It shows 4x4, horse-riding and hiking trails throughout the park. It gives a good overview of the region and indicates routes that aren't marked in my road atlas. The trail (F235) goes to Lake Langisjór where there's a basic campsite. It's fortuitous to have a legal place to camp within reach.

I'm wary about wild camping with the motorbike. The Icelandic landscape is fragile. Vehicles damage the flora and leave tracks in the ground that remain visible scars even decades later. I follow the mantra of 'leave no trace', so I would have to leave the Serow on the trail and only camp where my footprints wouldn't remain.

It's forbidden to ride off legally-designated roads for this environmental reason. The Icelandic definition of 'road' includes the dirt trails and jeep tracks marked on my maps. As there's no shortage of these routes, which people used to riding in other countries would casually refer to as 'off-road', there is no need to ride or drive illegally for a sense of adventure in remote places. To do so is irresponsible and disrespectful.

I cross the stream and head up the valley. Colourful Landmannalaugar is a distant memory. Here, there's only wave after wave of desolation, a forsaken sea of brown-black sand. With the sun below the mountains, all traces of warmth have vanished like a dream upon waking. My toes are numb in my sodden boots. I tense the muscles in my stomach and shoulders, bracing against the chill. Overcome with tiredness, I want to stop. But this land is uninviting.

I feel uneasy, the isolation consuming me. I've never felt like this in the wilderness before. Perhaps it's because, unlike everywhere else I've been, nothing can grow or survive here. It's lifeless. Dead. The silvery-green hills ahead draw me onwards. Knowing there's a campsite at the end of the trail drives me on. It wasn't long ago I was racing to escape from people and civilisation; ironically, now I go in search of them.

Langisjór is a long, narrow lake flanked by hills. At the far end, there's nothing but the sky above, as though the water must flow off the edge of the world. I'm relieved to reach the campsite, basic though it is. A few vehicles overlook the lake and two tents are pitched near the toilet block to keep out of the wind. Underneath one 4x4 are two pairs of hiking boots left to dry. Otherwise, the place appears deserted. I check the time; it's past eleven o'clock. There's not a soul to be seen and not a whisper or snore to be heard.

I pitch my tent and cook a quick meal of noodles, acutely aware of every noise I create in this silent world. My last view before I zip up the tent is of the sky on fire, the clouds glowing like hot coals as the sun shines onto them from the underworld.

I sleep like the dead until sunlight on the tent wakes me. There's still no sign of another living person. I turn on the stove to brew a coffee to help banish the tiredness behind my wind-worn eyes. As I scrape the last morsels of muesli from the bowl, a couple of bodies emerge from one of the tents.

Soon I'm itching to hit the trails.

The sunshine has me bursting with energy.

There's only one way to pacify this feverish anticipation swelling within me:

Fjallabak

Ride.

Maps on the wooden building indicate that the faint trails I saw yesterday evening are suitable only for specially equipped or modified 4x4s. I take this as meaning they're suitable for motorcycles, despite the obvious flaw that they only have two wheels. I hope it's about needing high ground clearance for uneven terrain rather than deep, challenging river crossings.

A woman appears from her tent. She's from Reykjavík and travelling alone in her 4x4.

'Have you driven these tracks?' I ask, pointing to the dotted lines on the map.

'Not those, but I have driven other jeep tracks. I always try. If they are too tough, I turn back. I carry enough fuel so that I can do this.'

'Exactly, me too.' This philosophy has seen me safely through many adventures. Admitting defeat and turning back is often the hardest thing. Hearing this from another person gives me the confidence to continue with my approach.

'The main problem will be if there are deep rivers to cross,' she adds. 'The modified 4x4s can go much deeper than your bike, I think.'

'Sure, but if they're too deep, I'll just turn around.' I smile.

I'm no longer daunted by what the trails might throw at me, but excited to explore a new region. I decide, first, to ride halfway to the high point of Breiðbakur with the hope of good views.

The trail is hard-packed with rutted sections where water once coursed across the landscape but has now dried up, leaving only a spread of indented veins. The bike makes light work of the steep hill, but we're brought to a halt by snow. I switch off the put-put-putting engine, grateful it's got me this far, and walk the last 200 metres to the top of the highest peak in a range of black hills. Snow-capped mountains circle the horizon. Lake Langisjór stretches out far below me, a rich shade of turquoise that complements the blue sky. This is what I've been looking for: just me, the mountains and a silent tranquillity.

I ride back down the hill and turn onto the other trail. It should take me in a loop via a small lake to Faxasund. It's sandier here, reminding me of riding in Kaokoland in Northern Namibia. *Just ride carefully*. Over a rise, a small lake comes into view. I look up and down its length and stop concentrating on the track. As the trail contours around the hill, I over-correct; the bike topples over in the deep sand. Serves me right. I look at my bike splayed out like roadkill and laugh, then casually unclip the bags, lift it and reload it.

Fuel has leaked out of the filler cap, run down the side of the tank and pooled onto the ground, draining rapidly into the sand. The seal in the fuel cap is ineffective. This always happens when I drop the bike. If fuel can leak out, surely water could get in. That would be a problem if I dropped the bike in a river. I'd better buy or make a good seal when I can.

A river passes through a valley with a colourful array of yellow and green mosses. The trail follows its course, criss-crossing back and forth. The water splashes up, soaking my boots and bike jeans. Then it rises up over black sandhills and across large rocky slabs. Eventually, I join the main trail that leads to the Ring Road where I can refuel.

The fuel station is a car park of clean, white hire cars. For those making a tour of the Ring Road, this is the last chance for fuel before the long, barren stretch through the southeast. I refill with petrol and coffee, then escape to the hills again.

In the valley parallel to the one I took to Langisjór, I ride through a lava field of odd-shaped rocks, some of them taller than me and closely packed like a deformed city of twisted, distorted apartment blocks. The thick covering of pale-green, putty-grey moss softens the edges.

At the head of the trail, I park by the information building and change into my hiking gear. Bike clothing is unsuitable for anything

Fjallabak

more than short strolls and has me sweating uncomfortably even in Iceland. The place is deserted, so I spread my wet clothes out in the toilet block.

I walk to the top of Mount Laki. It feels good to stretch my legs. I'm only ten kilometres from where I woke up this morning, yet the scenery is markedly different. The mountain range between these neighbouring valleys has resulted in independent ecosystems. An enormous volcanic eruption over two hundred years ago here added to the difference.

The Laki Craters, a line of giant pockmarks run across the landscape in eerie contrast to the surrounding black sand of the Eldhraun lava field that spreads out towards the coast. The craters formed in 1783 when a fissure twenty-seven kilometres long erupted. Over eight months, basalt lava and poisonous gases spewed from the bowels of the earth. It is one of the most catastrophic volcanic eruptions in Iceland's recorded history.

The series of eruptions were called *Skaftáreldar*, meaning 'The Skaftá Fires', named after the river which filled with lava by the third day of activity. In all, there were around ten distinct cycles of volcanic activity during which a new fissure opened up northeast of the preceding one like a domino effect. Localised activity at several vents along each fissure resulted in the series of craters that I can see. There are 135 in total.

During the eruptions, lava spewed in fountains that reached 800–1400 metres high. The gas plumes reached thirteen kilometres in height and sent ejected gases into the stratosphere. Fissure eruptions like Laki are always basaltic, which produce volcanic gases high in sulphuric acid.

In Iceland, the consequences of the Laki eruption are known as the *Móðuharðindin* or 'Mist Hardships'. Low-level sulphur dioxide created acid rain that was strong enough to burn holes in leaves, kill trees and irritate the skin. Eight million tonnes of fluorine were released, which ruined grasses and crops, poisoned livestock and killed around twenty per cent of the Icelandic population in the ensuing famine.

Much of the 122 million tons of released sulphur dioxide entered the jet stream and circulated the northern hemisphere. Within a week, a thick haze covered Europe. It resulted in the hottest summer on record, with unusual weather patterns including thunderstorms and hail large enough to kill cattle. Crops were ruined; barley and the leaves of oats withered, and rye became mildewed. It's estimated that 23,000 people died in Great Britain due to the haze. The following winter was particularly severe and caused an additional 8,000 deaths.

Within a month, the gaseous fog had reached Russia and China. Benjamin Franklin mentioned it during a lecture in America. Global temperatures dropped 1.3 degrees Celsius, and the cold weather continued for three more years. Japan's rice crop failed due to cold and wet weather, resulting in the Great Famine. Entire communities died in Alaska. There is even a suggestion that the French Revolution was a consequence of the eruption causing extreme weather events in Europe. Surplus crops in 1785 in France caused poverty as prices fell. Then droughts and floods in the following years brought famine and the eventual uprising.

I return down the hill, cook a late dinner, then continue riding. I stop to take a short walk at one of the craters. Small and delicate white alpine rock cress dots the black sand landscape. The crater rims are lined in the pale green moss, and the turquoise blue lake within appears exquisite and in perfect harmony. That all this beauty came from something so dangerous is nature's deceit.

I'd like to ride late into the night, but my eyelids grow heavy, overcome with tiredness. I know this telltale feeling and must stop riding before I drift off to sleep. I don't want to disturb the pristine landscape either side of the trail, so when I see a small parking area amid the black hills where I can discreetly pitch my tent, I know the end of the day is close. The air is still and an all-consuming silence

Fjallabak

envelops this deserted landscape. It's both eerie and beautifully serene. Sleep comes easily.

Overnight, my boots and jeans dry out. Putting on dry clothing in the morning cannot be rated highly enough. I leave early and ride through the mangled lava fields until they fade into rolling hills and trickling streams. The white line of a glacier spreads across the horizon. My mind races ahead, wondering what the day will bring.

A wide languid river, slowly rolling south over the gravelly plain, breaks the trail. A hundred metres is very wide when you're contemplating getting a bike across it. I can barely make out the trail on the far side. The longer I look, the further away it appears.

There's only one way to check whether the water's too deep or not. I roll up my jeans and wade in. A quarter of the way across I decide there's nothing to worry about. It's not so deep, no big rocks. I should walk it all, but my feet are dry, and it'd be nice to keep them that way. I can already feel some water beginning to seep through the seams of the boots. I return quickly to the bike. *Let's go for it.*

The river looms large, a worthy opponent; I should not dismiss it so readily. I begin to have doubts; the longer I hesitate, the bigger they grow until there's a risk that fear will stop me succeeding, my mind a bigger obstacle to overcome than the river.

Once I start, there'll be no room for doubt or hesitation. There's no escape route and no turning back mid-stream. I psyche myself up to it. *You can do this.* I stare at the river, squinting to see each subtle change in the surface flow that tells me where there are rocks and where it's shallowest. I can feel my heart rate increasing. I take a deep breath. *This is the moment. Now go.*

I open the throttle and the front wheel enters the water. *Just ride slow and steady, lowest gear, high revs.* It's getting deeper ... I'm beyond where I'd walked to. Keep going, slowly slowly, halfway now. *Come on little bike, we've got the hang of this ... Er ...* It's getting a lot deeper. Bump. Rock. *Shit. Hold tight, can't stop now!* Water splashes up around my legs and sprays on my face, steam rising from the engine. I ignore my aching arms screaming for a rest and fight to keep the bike moving forward over the rocks.

Then I feel the bike speeding up; there's less resistance, the water's getting shallower. Suddenly that distant bank is right in front of me, and we pop out onto dry land. *Phew.* My heart pounds for minutes afterwards. I feel great, full of life. So much for dry boots and jeans; I'm drenched. I don't care and can't help laughing with relief.

Eventually, the adrenalin coursing through me subsides.

After refuelling, I return to the Highlands. It doesn't matter which way I go. I take the Álftavatnskrókur (F233) northwards until I reach a river that looks too deep and fast to cross. Having got more than I bargained for this morning, I don't want to tempt fate by attempting this one. I can turn around and try other routes. Scenery looks different from the other direction, and a trail is never the same ridden twice.

The Fjallabaksleið Syðri (F210), meaning 'Southern Back of the Mountains', goes west. I take it but am soon halted by another big river. *Dammit.* I park up, roll up my jeans and wade in. The strong current flows above my knees and soaks me to mid-thigh. It is deeper for longer, the flow faster than any I've crossed so far. Perhaps there's a better crossing further up or downstream.

I cross the damn river six times in different places, none of them much better or much worse. My only reward for this stubborn perseverance is numb toes. I'm certain it could be safely crossed with two people, one to ride and one to walk alongside offering a hand for support. But I'm alone. I've not seen another vehicle in hours.

I scour the map for an alternative route. There is one last trail to try. It's late afternoon. *Where has the day gone?*

The black sands are broken by gushing murky water and churning white waterfalls. Sheep graze on the red sorrel. At Öldufell I cross a river above a great waterfall. It's a lush green valley with crystal clear,

Fjallabak

ice-cold water running through it and a wide bank. It's the perfect place to camp.

An old German-registered Hilux with a camper conversion on the back arrives. It stops and shows no sign of continuing. My immediate reaction is to wish they would go away and let me enjoy the place in solitude. But then I chat to the driver, Norbert, who is in Iceland for several months. We realise we said hello to each other weeks ago and miles away in the Westfjords. He invites me to have dinner with him, his son and their friend. It's a cosy affair; I enjoy the evening far more than I would have on my own. Although we are travelling with different types of vehicles, we share the same approach to exploring the country. It's not often I meet people who are content to travel in a similarly slow fashion, preferring to explore a region in depth rather than rushing through it and barely skimming the surface.

Norbert has spent much time in Iceland and recommends several of his favourite places, which I would never have known about but now have a burning desire to visit. It's a one-way exchange of information because there is nowhere I've been in Iceland that he hasn't. All I can offer in return are tales of misadventure from other journeys and hope that in another month or two I shall be able to pass on my own tips and highlights to other people.

In the morning I'm invited back over to Norbert's camper for breakfast. Afterwards I wave goodbye and head north, leaving the green valley for black volcanic sand. The icy Mýrdalsjökull is always a couple of kilometres beyond reach as I ride towards the distinctive conical hill of Mælifell. Rising 200 metres out of the surrounding flat ground, the hardened ash and lava are covered with bright green Grimmia moss.

One trail goes to Strútur, where I stop for a second breakfast near the mountain hut. The small snack for dinner and light breakfast I ate with Norbert may be plenty when you sit in a 4x4 all day, but it's not enough to sustain a biker, not me at any rate. I rummage in my bags for my hiking gear to walk to a nearby hot spring, but I can't help

ICELAND Serow Saga

thinking that I'd rather be out riding more trails than having a bath so early in the day. A wooden signpost indicates several footpaths going in different directions. This would make a great basecamp; so, I'll ride today and can come back again armed with a week's worth of food and go on multiple day hikes. Although, I'm beginning to wonder whether it's an illusion that I'll have time to return to all these gems I'm discovering. And will I ever opt to hike when I've got my Serow and there are more trails to ride?

I re-join the Fjallabaksleið Syðri (F210) on the other side of the river that stopped me yesterday. The landscape changes from black sand sprinkled with tiny white flowers like confetti to a harsher, rocky grey landscape. Specks in the distance move across the land like ants. *What are they?* As I near them, they grow into people with large rucksacks and sturdy boots who are walking the four-to-five-day Laugavegur trail between Landmannalaugar and Þórsmörk. I stop to check my map; the hikers stare as they pass.

One young lady stops. 'I've seen plenty of 4x4s, but never a motorbike up here. How are you coping with the river crossings?'

'OK so far,' I reply about the main topic of conversation in the Highlands. 'If I'm uncertain, I don't attempt them and turn back.'

She points to the turbulent river with a footbridge over it. 'You see those three marker rocks? When only two are visible and then one, it is difficult to cross. When you can't see any, it's too deep. That's in a big 4x4, though. On a bike, I don't know what's possible.'

No, me neither.

The young lady offers to wait in case I need help. I politely refuse; I want to walk the route first, don't want to feel rushed and would prefer no audience. I don't want her getting drenched wading in to help or having to wait while I slowly drain water from the engine if I drop the bike. It's better if I only attempt rivers that I'm sure I can cross successfully alone. She wishes me good luck.

Wading through the river, I stumble into several submerged rocks that would stop the bike in its tracks if I hit them. I have to brace against the flow to stay upright. I don't think I could withstand it on the bike. If there were two of us, we could help one another and push the bikes across together. But I don't have a riding partner and don't want one. I turn the bike around and take the other trail. This is the sacrifice I make for the freedom of travelling alone.

Around the next bend ... *Not another river!*

I stop to assess it. It doesn't look so bad. It's the last route left to try. Remembering that Norbert successfully came this way gives me courage. There's no footbridge across this river; several hikers are in the process of removing their boots, wobbling on one leg or perching on rocks. As my boots are already waterlogged, I wade across with my bags without hesitating, dump them on the other side and return. Ignoring the hikers' watchful glares and before there's a chance to reconsider, I ride with gritted teeth and a tight grip on the handlebars, determined to make it through.

Phew! A couple of hikers give me a thumbs up as the bike lurches onto the dry trail. I reload my bags and ride off while they're still untying their shoelaces.

The track runs across a flat, stony plain. I'm glad to be covering the ground with a fun, fast ride on a bike. For me, the unchanging scenery would be monotonous and soul-destroying at walking pace with my feet aching from the continuous pounding on hard ground. Travelling slowly enables you to see all the intricate details of a landscape, but I've walked enough with a full pack to know that occasionally all you care about is crossing the terrain as quickly as possible. When the end point becomes the focus, it can blind you to the beauty of each step along the way.

When the trail diverges from the footpath, I regain a sense of solitude. I'd expected vast expanses of it in Iceland; instead, I find it in little pockets between interactions with other people, each looking for a piece of wilderness. My last chance to remain up in the Highlands is to take a small side trail north. The map indicates a large river system further along. I'm not optimistic about being able to cross it. *Is it worth bothering?* I wonder, despondent and downbeat about all the U-turns I've been making.

I take the trail because I've got all day and don't want to leave the Highlands yet. It contours around the hillside, then descends steeply down a badly eroded track. I halt to assess the route to be certain I can get back out if I have to retrace my steps, as I suspect I will.

Having to focus intently on the rutted track, it's not until I reach the bottom and stop to look around that I realise I'm in a narrow black-walled gorge, carved over millennia into beautiful curves and flowing shapes where the flow of water has cut into the black earth. If I get no further, I'm happy that I saw this. I criss-cross the shallow stream of crystal clear water lined with bright green moss. The canyon widens briefly before coming to a choke point. I inch past the massive boulders that almost block access.

Out of the gorge, I pick the least eroded sandy track up the hillside. The back wheel has poor traction and slips in the sand. The tread is already half worn despite being new for the trip. I urge the bike on and, as the trail steepens, I tap down into first gear and open the throttle. The engine whines under the strain as we get slower and slower. Suddenly the front wheel jerks sideways on some churned-up rocks; I can't stop the bike falling over. I unload the bags and try again, but the rear wheel spins, digging deeper into the sand. I dismount to lighten the load further and push alongside. It's futile.

Returning through the gorge, I wonder, *Should I have tried harder?* No, I don't have to prove myself to anyone. Back at the main trail, I sit down on the grass to rest at a viewpoint overlooking a river. There's a group of six Icelanders here too. As I drain the water from my boots, we all laugh. They tell me that I wouldn't have got much further along the trail I was attempting and confirm that over the hill I turned back on is a huge river impassable on a motorbike.

'Where are you going next?' one guy asks.

'I'm not sure.'

Fjallabak

He pauses in thought, then says, 'You should go to Vestmannaeyjar.'

'OK,' I reply and shrug my shoulders. I've no idea what or where Vestmannaeyjar is, having never heard of it until now.

'It shouldn't be too expensive with a motorbike.' He looks at his watch. 'I think there's a ferry you could catch around five o'clock, or a later one. They're frequent.'

I'm guessing it's not on the mainland if I need to take a ferry.

Soon I'm back down in a wide valley with water lazily meandering through the pale grey rocky riverbed west towards the ocean. Suddenly, my Highland adventure is over. With the rumbling of my stomach, I stop for a late lunch. I remove my boots and wring out my socks again, take off my jeans and hang them over the bike's handlebars to dry, then walk barefoot over the spongy moss-covered ground to sit on a rock. I inhale a sandwich of pre-sliced cheese shoved unceremoniously between two pieces of bread and repeat this magic disappearing food act with a second one.

A few buildings are pinned between the riverbed and last range of hills before the south coast. It's Þórsmörk, little more than a basecamp for hikers, but big enough to have a runway. I watch a small plane fly along the river, turn and make a landing.

The clouds are clearing, the sun shining through. I check the forecast online. The weather app predicts sun for the rest of the evening with cloud forming overnight and rain expected from mid-morning the next day. The longer-range forecast is not optimistic for any part of the country. The spell of dry weather I've been enjoying is coming to an end. But the evenings are long; I'm determined to make the most of this one.

I spread out my map on the ground. Vestmannaeyjar, the Westman Islands, off the south coast are little more than a speck on the map. I check the distance on Google Maps to Landeyjahöfn where the ferry departs: 44 kilometres. If there is a sailing around five o'clock, I might make it.

ICELAND Serow Saga

I leap into action. Jeans, socks and boots on, helmet and gloves too. Map back in the bag, swing my leg over the bike, jump on the kick-start and speed off down the gravel track. *Don't race recklessly.* I ease off the throttle a touch.

Once again, I revel in the freedom of travelling solo, with no one to make compromises or allowances for. I'm free to do as I please and change my mind on a whim, my path and future determined by the flip of a coin, as uncertain and changing as the fickle Icelandic weather (which I don't love so much).

14

Pirates and an Eruption
Westman Islands

The smooth asphalt across pancake-flat land at sea level is completely at odds with the rugged, mountainous Highlands that are the Iceland I identify with now; it feels as though I've already left Iceland's shores.

The large parking area at the harbour is filled with sparkling white camper vans facing the sea. I park outside the terminal building. At the counter, I ask for a return ticket and note that I arrived with five minutes to spare. I'm a strong believer that things happen for a reason; it appears that my visit to the Westman Islands is meant to be.

Feeling relaxed with a ticket in hand, I notice all the fresh-faced people in clean summer outfits, sandals and t-shirts. I become acutely self-conscious of my appearance: bulging in several layers and a waterproof jacket, my scruffy jeans rolled up to the knees as though I'm a rebellious teenager failing to set a new urban trend, and wet boots covered in dust. It's as if I've come to a dinner party in fancy dress when everyone else is wearing black-tie. I return to my bike where I feel less out of place.

I join the queue of vehicles as the ferry manoeuvres into the harbour. Minutes later the ramp lowers. I'm directed on board. From the upper deck, I watch the flat-topped Mýrdalsjökull glacier fade into the distance as the ferry dips and pitches with ease over the gentle swell of the ocean's waves. Ahead the islands are silhouetted in the evening sun. A juvenile gannet with mottled wings glides gracefully alongside the boat.

I brace against the waves, holding the rail for stability, loose hair waving wildly in the wind. Despite my inelegance, I feel at ease, equally at home on the waves as I had in the mountains. Possibly it's because, in both places, nature is a master that cannot be controlled. I admire and respect it, have no need or desire to tame it. I do not live in fear of it. We have become so used to being top of the food chain with the safety and security that it affords, it is difficult to accept that there are forces more powerful than us. Submitting to them can make us uncomfortable and uneasy, but it's liberating if you can. Perhaps that is what belief in a god feels like. Nature is my religion.

Half an hour later the ferry has crossed the four nautical miles from the mainland and is carefully manoeuvring through the narrow entrance to the harbour of Heimaey, the largest and only inhabited island of this archipelago. Fulmars bicker and squabble in their nests clinging precariously to narrow ledges on the towering cliffs, their cries filling the air.

Eager to explore the island under blue skies but overwhelmed by tiredness, I head to the campsite to cook dinner first, hoping that food will revive me. The site is in the base of a natural bowl called Herjólfsdalur where, according to *Landnámabók*, Herjólfur Bárðarson became the first person to settle on Heimaey around AD 900. Archaeological excavations, however, have revealed ruins of a settlement here almost one hundred years earlier. Unearthing the past often raises more questions than it answers, serving only to inform us of how little we know. I pitch my tent next to the two reconstructed Viking longhouses with low stone walls and turf roofs.

In the early days of settlement, while Ingólfur Arnarson was exploring the south coast of Iceland, his foster-brother Hjörleifur Hróðmarsson was murdered by his own Irish slaves. Before the discovery of Iceland, Ireland was the westernmost part of Europe; its people were known as West Men. When Ingólfur found out about his foster-brother's fate, he chased after the West Men slaves, who fled the mainland and escaped to Heimaey's hills for shelter. The settlers were brave and courageous people, but they were not innovative in naming places. So, it is these West Men slaves that the archipelago is named after, whilst Heimaey simply means 'Home Island'.

The island is barely five kilometres from end to end, small enough to walk around on foot, but I'm too tired. I hop on the bike and ride down to Skansinn, the old fort situated near the port.

Thick stone walls set into the hillside overlook the harbour and house a cannon. It was originally built in 1586 under the orders of King Frederick II to protect the Danish trade monopoly from English fishing efforts and other competition. It didn't, however, stop raiding slave hunters from the Ottoman-controlled Barbary coast of North Africa.

It's estimated that some 1–1.25 million Europeans were enslaved in the Maghreb from the sixteenth to eighteenth centuries. The turnover rate was high. To maintain a stable slave population in Algiers alone, around six thousand new slaves had to be brought to market each year. Hunger, disease, overwork and the occasional escape were all contributing factors. Also, it was possible to be released from slavery if a sufficiently large ransom could be paid to compensate the slave owner. Muslims could not be enslaved, so many captured at a young age converted to Islam. This was often encouraged, additions to the religious cause always applauded. Older slaves tended to remain loyal to their faith, the only connection remaining to their previous homes and lives.

Simplifying the situation along geographical and religious lines – Muslims from North Africa enslaving Christian Europeans – does not give a realistic impression. Algiers was a thriving, ethnically mixed city, where anyone regardless of background had the potential to progress upward in society if they had the right skills, intelligence, perseverance and luck. Murat Reis, who led the slave raids on the Westman Islands, was a Dutchman originally named Jan Janszoon van Haarlem, but who changed his name when he converted to Islam.

ICELAND Serow Saga

In 1627, a fleet of twelve ships sailed from North Africa to Iceland and split up along the south coast and in the southeast. The raiders attacked with ruthless and routine efficiency, looting and setting fire to farms and buildings. Those fleeing were forced towards the shore where they were sorted and loaded onto boats. A few people evaded capture by fleeing to the hills, but on Heimaey there was no safe retreat.

One corsair group of three boats set their sights on the Westman Islands. News of the raiders would have travelled fast, and the islanders would have been aware of the threat and begun fortifying their defensive position at the port.

The raiders had captured an English fishing vessel and promised the fishermen their freedom in return for showing the raiders an alternative entry point onto the island. One Icelander was among the English fishing crew. He directed the corsairs to Brimurð, a quiet bay that's now called Pirate Cove, in the south of Heimaey. With the islanders' attention focused northwards, they were oblivious to the threat from the other side of the island.

In what has become known as the 'Turkish Raid', some 300 corsairs landed and immediately split into three groups. The largest descended upon the Danish houses and took control of the harbour. Once they realised that the locals were unarmed, they split into smaller factions of four to ten men, moving from farm to farm, raping and pillaging as they went. They burned down the main church and both vicarages. Anyone resisting or too slow was beaten or hacked to death. One woman was cut in half, another thrown into a burning building along with her child. The corsairs used ropes to scale the cliffs to search the beaches and caves. After three days of scouring the island along the network of narrow trails, they left. In total, 242 people were captured on Heimaey, the majority of the population, and more than thirty killed. The corsairs' fleet set sail for Algiers with 380 Icelanders on board.

Westman Islands

Most Icelanders sold into slavery disappeared without a trace. One exception was Reverend Ólafur Egilsson, who lived to write a book about his remarkable travels from Algiers back to Iceland. Soon after arriving on the African continent, he was released to travel to Copenhagen from where he was to collect a ransom for the Icelanders' freedom. The journey took him six months, sailing first to Livorno in Italy. From there, he set out on foot to travel overland, but he failed and returned to Livorno. His second attempt by sea was successful, sailing to Genoa then Marseilles and on to Holland and finally Denmark. Despite finding an impoverished king there, he secured the freedom of thirty-four Icelanders, who eventually returned home.

Guðríður Símonardóttir, who became known as Turkish-Gudda, was one woman freed after a decade as a slave and concubine. Along with other slaves, she was first sent to Denmark for re-education, where she met Hallgrímur Pétursson, a theology student. They fell in love, moved back to Iceland and married when she found out her former husband had died. Hallgrímur became well known for his poetry, and Hallgrímskirkja, the main church in Reykjavík, is named after him.

I detour to Urðir lighthouse in the northeast. The rough landscape is littered with moss-covered lava rock and riddled with footpaths where people go for walks and numerous wildflowers grow. This part of the island formed recently.

In the middle of the night on 23 January 1973, residents woke to see the hillside east of town ablaze. A volcanic fissure two kilometres long had unexpectedly ripped open the earth, spewing fire and ash skyward. After a few hours, the activity had concentrated. When the eruption stopped 157 days later, there was a new hill overlooking the ash-covered town. Named Eldfell, meaning 'Hill of Fire', it sits next to pre-historic Helgafell, another cone-shaped volcanic hill.

I ride to the southern end of Heimaey. As the roads are tarmac and the distances small, I'm only wearing my hiking boots and trousers rather than full protective bike kit. With fewer layers on, the air blasts through the gaps in my jacket and chills me even though the sun is shining. It doesn't matter that I don't have any tools with me. If the bike breaks down or gets a flat tyre, I can walk back to the campsite and get what I need. Without the usual responsibilities required for travelling safely in remote locations, it's as though I can feel an actual weight has been lifted off my shoulders. It's a false impression; it's the bike that's lighter and more nimble without the luggage.

Past the two domed hills, out of town and beyond the turning for the small runway, the island narrows to an isthmus. It formed when Helgafell erupted around 5,000 years ago with the lava connecting two islands. The bay on the eastern side is Pirate Cove where the Algerian raiders landed. I park the bike at the end of the road near Stórhöfði lighthouse and meteorological station, then walk around the peninsula's grassy clifftops where a few puffins fly to and from their burrows.

Looking south, I can see the smaller islands that make up this archipelago. The furthest south and second largest in the chain, Surtsey, was born only fifty-five years ago when a submarine fissure on the mid-Atlantic ridge erupted. Several other smaller islands formed during the same volcanic explosion, but have since been eroded by the sea and wind. Unlike most of the islands, which are green on top with a short cropping of grass and moss, Surtsey is bald. It remains free from human habitation and is protected, thereby providing researchers with a live model of how new land is colonised by plant and animal species.

The next morning, bleary-eyed, I unzip the tent and peer out. *It's not raining yet!* I quickly dress and set out on foot. The tops of Helgafell and Eldfell are already shrouded in mist, but I'm going to make every waking minute of dry weather count. The streets are deserted, everybody else still asleep. Most Icelanders seem unaware that morning exists at this hour. Across town and up the steps, I walk through the new lava field and onto the green lower slopes. Partway

Westman Islands

up, the mound turns reddish-brown, the path skirting the crater rim until I reach the mist and the highest point.

I scoop out a small hole in the loose, gravelly rock with my hand and feel the heat in the ground. Because rocks have a low thermal conductivity, the inside of lava flows can remain heated to several hundred degrees for many years. This geothermal energy has been harnessed to supply hot water to most houses in the town.

The mist turns to rain on the way back, so I head to Eldheimar museum, a large, modern building of volcanic stone that encases a partially excavated house found buried under pumice and ash by the 1973 eruption. The contents that survived have been left exactly where they were found: scattered clothing on the floor, picture frames and a clock on the mantelpiece, lampshades fallen from the ceiling. People walked out of their homes with only the clothes they wore, their homes and belongings abandoned. Bewildered and in shock, they had no idea if they'd see them again. Lives and livelihoods were upturned in an instant.

Fortunately, stormy weather before the eruption meant the entire fishing fleet was in the harbour. The boats evacuated everyone safely to the mainland. The displaced population of around 5,000 went to live with friends and family or in temporary shelters. Only a few hundred – police, fire crew and rescue workers – stayed behind.

The main danger at that point was to the harbour, which risked being blocked by the advancing lava. This would have devastated the island's fishing industry, the primary economy. To stem the flow, water was used to cool the lava. It was an ambitious project, not attempted before on such a scale.

Seawater was sprayed onto the leading edge of the lava at a rate of up to 400 litres per second. A network of pipes distributed the water over an area of 12,000 square metres. While wooden and metal supports melted, the pipes remained intact because of the cool water inside them. Two months after the initial eruption, a fifth of the town was covered in lava. With thirty-two additional pumps flown in from the USA, each able to pump 1,000 litres per second, the flow was eventually halted around a hundred metres from the harbour. The new lava improved the port by narrowing the entrance to provide more protection.

Volunteers worked to save homes, shipping furniture to the mainland, clearing ash from the roofs to prevent collapse and blocking windows with iron plates to prevent lava fires. Even so, over 400 homes and businesses, a third of all property on Heimaey, were destroyed. The clean-up operation once the eruption ended took months of hard work. In photos from the aftermath, the houses look as though they are sinking in a sea of black ash. Those still standing had to be unearthed, whilst new homes were built. Within a year, most of the population had come back to the island. Some people never returned, the memories and losses too great to ever reconcile with.

I explore the island on foot during occasional dry spells. One day, I hike up and along the rim surrounding the campsite with views of the Atlantic one way and an aerial view of the town the other. The ordered streets are quiet; there's not much need for a car here. I descend from my viewpoint and wander through town. The pavements are clean, lined with modest houses, small shops and a few cafes.

On a whim, I enter the Slippurinn, which I'd overheard the lady at the campsite reception recommending to other visitors. After weeks of instant noodles and the occasional pizza, the rich smells of freshly cooked seafood coming from the next table are too tantalising to resist. Ignoring the prices, I order the pan-fried Arctic char and a beer.

I'm disappointed that the fish is served in the pan. This may be a novel experience for some restaurant-goers, but not me, who travels without a plate or dish to save weight and washing up. I've been eating every meal I cook straight from the pot. Here, at least, I have a range of cutlery to use and a table to sit at. As I eat the first piece

Westman Islands

of tender pink flakes of char with seasoned fried potatoes dripping in butter, my grumblings vanish. I take small bites and savour every delicious mouthful, trying to make the experience last longer. I shall feast on this meal in my mind for weeks to come.

To explore new places and meet people everyday expends a lot of energy, especially mentally. It's important to take time out to stop and relax when travelling for long periods, the downtime essential to avoid burnout. This compact island with the peaceful campsite surrounded by nature yet conveniently located within walking distance of all amenities a town offers is the perfect place to recharge my batteries.

Mostly when it rains, I drink endless coffee sitting contentedly next to a radiator in the communal room of the campsite and write. My laptop keyboard has mysteriously started working again on some of the occasions I turn it on. I have given up all pretence of working on the manuscript and focus on my journal about this trip instead. All tiredness recedes as I catch up on sleep; gradually, I am revived.

One day I open up my foldout map of Iceland on the table. My eyes are drawn to vast areas of the Highlands I've not yet explored.

I can't sit still any longer.

I must ride.

Explore.

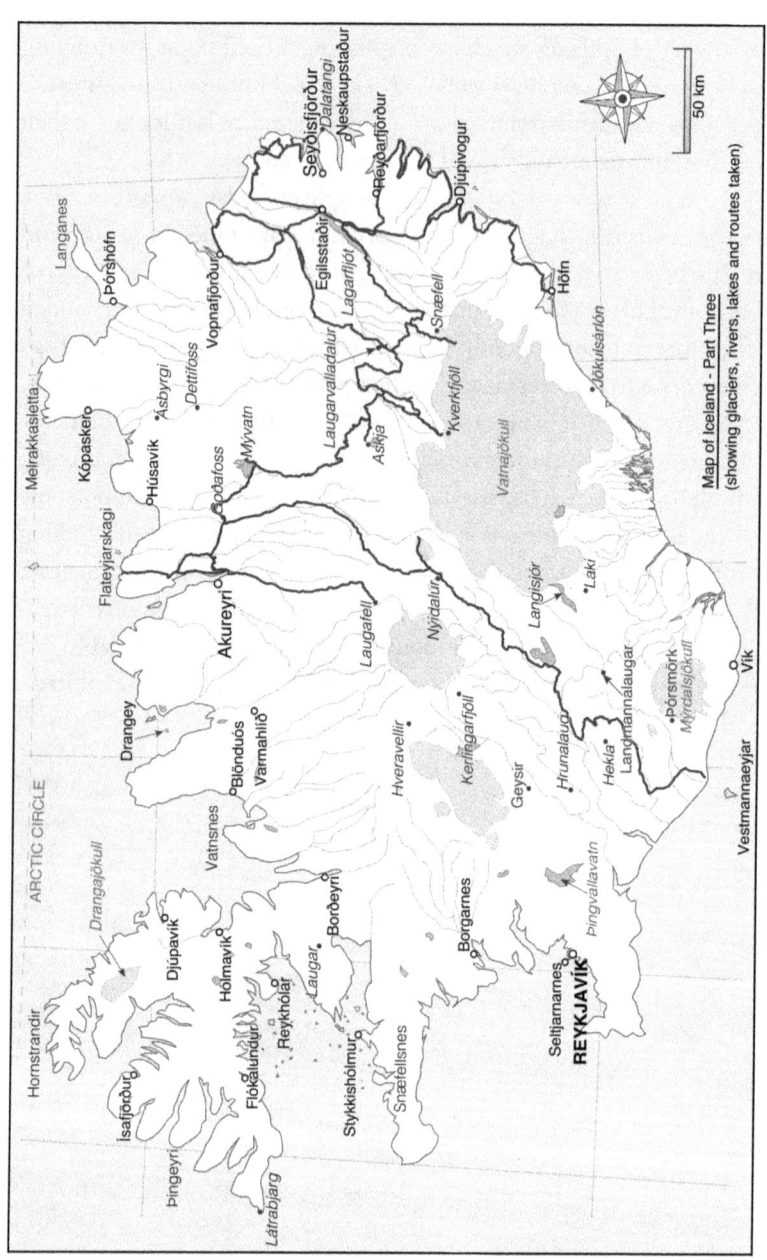

ICELAND

-

Part Three

Herðubreið, the 'Queen of the Mountains'.

Glacier at Kverkfjöll.

15
Highland Traverse
Sprengisandur

The Sprengisandur route (F26) is an ancient road across the country. It was travelled during the time of the Icelandic Free State, around AD 930–1265, to connect the remote north with the Alþingi.

Sprengisandur means 'Bursting Sand'. For hundreds of kilometres across the barren interior, there is no grazing for horses or shelter for humans. When horses were the main mode of transport, these journeys were arduous. People had to ride as fast as possible, pushing their animals to the brink of death, their bursting point, to make it successfully across.

Today, it's a mild adventure away from the asphalt Ring Road for anyone with a 4x4. The gravel road is well maintained with bridges over the major rivers. I hope to avoid it where possible in favour of smaller jeep tracks.

After disembarking the ferry onto the mainland, I head to the Ring Road, turn onto Fjallabaksleið Syðri (F210), then go north, skirting the eastern side of Hekla. There were clear views of the volcano the last time I passed. Today, as is common, it's veiled in cloud, which is what gives Hekla its name, meaning 'Hooded'. The surface of the trail changes from rough lava to hard-packed tephra. I increase my speed, still taking care around the bends where the sand is deeper. I let my mind drift. *How far will I get this evening? What obstacles will present themselves: fast-flowing rivers, steep tracks, deep sand?*

Snow.

A wide expanse of white fills the shallow valley and spills out over the trail. The snow in the main tracks has melted and frozen back into solid ice. *It must be better to follow one of the fainter trails.*

It's not.

ICELAND Serow Saga

The snow is slushy. The back wheel sinks up to the axle less than five metres in. I unload the bags, sling them over my shoulder and traipse through the snow. Icy water seeps through my boots and saturates my socks. *Sigh*. Twice more I get stuck in snow drifts. Other times I make it by skidding across the frozen tracks, my feet sliding along the surface as stabilisers.

I'd originally delayed venturing into the Highlands because summer is late to arrive this far north. Even in mid-June, several trails were impassable due to snow. I'd not expected this at the end of July.

It's cold riding in Iceland. The sun may shine but the wind is chilling when riding at speed on the tarmac. Even with the effort of manoeuvring the bike on rougher trails, I rarely get too warm. Typically, I wear six layers of tops: a vest, a thermal base layer, a mesh armoured jacket, a fleece, my old waterproof jacket that is no longer waterproof, and the new one I bought in Germany, which does keep the rain out. Exerting myself on foot, though, I can feel my body heat building. I'm soon sweating profusely. My toes, however, stubbornly remain cold, and the tips of my fingers are numb-white.

Past Hekla I join the familiar Landmannaleið (F225), then Landvegur (26). I speed along the smooth gravel, eager to get fuel at Hrauneyjar and put this flat, easy road behind me. I'm impatient to explore new trails despite the late hour of the evening.

The trail deteriorates, indicating the start of the Sprengisandur route (F26). Raindrops fall heavily at first, then settle into a soft fine smirr that very quickly drenches everything. I tire of repeatedly wiping my visor, so lift it and suffer the wind biting at my cheeks. I persevere through the narrow band of rain and am soon ahead of it, but it edges closer with every stop I make. Whenever I look behind, I see the menacing black clouds tormenting me to ride faster.

The road makes a ninety-degree turn, crosses a bridge over a large glacial river and winds through gently rolling hills. As I reach the highest point, the rain catches up with me. To the north, the river splits and weaves across the plain as ethereal silken threads. It

Sprengisandur

sparkles when the sun breaks through, revealing a gentler, lighter side to this harsh and forbidding environment. Spellbound by this magical sight, I'm lured on.

I descend until I reach a river, stop momentarily, and judging it neither too fast nor deep, ride on through, heedless of the water spraying up and drenching my boots. They couldn't get any wetter. There's a small parking area on the far side, perfect for pitching my tent. It's gone ten-thirty.

I wake to sunlight. The desolate black sands of last night have dried to dappled brown. I had thought this hostile landscape would be monotonous; instead, the wide expanse of undulating earth is like the ocean's swell and watching the shadows of the cumulus clouds rolling over it has a pacifying, hypnotising effect.

The land drops away gradually to the north; I can see for miles. There is no one in view, no living creature in this barren interior. I can think of nowhere else on earth so devoid of life; perhaps it's more like the surface of the moon.

I'm surprised to see buildings in this lunar land of nothingness. An Icelandic flag flutters in the wind from a tall flagpole. Nýidalur is one of the mountain huts where a rescue team is stationed. The huts look new, the whole place spotlessly tidy. There are some 4x4s with rooftop tents parked alongside. It breaks my illusion of travelling through a wilderness. I have no desire to stop.

Rangers on quad bikes set off across the river beyond the base. It looks deep, but they don't hesitate. I follow, happy to know the river is shallow enough to ford without having to wade through it and get wet feet. I'm happier still once the huts are no longer in view.

At the junction for Austurleið (F910), which skirts the northern perimeter of the Vatnajökull glacier, I turn off. A sign warns me that it's for 4x4s only, indicating rough terrain (exciting) and deep rivers (daunting). I ought to have asked at Nýidalur about the river conditions. I'm not going back now.

ICELAND Serow Saga

Perhaps I should have told the rangers that I was going to take this route.
Perhaps I shouldn't take this route.
I take the route.

The trail is fun, more so than the Sprengisandur route; the first river presents no difficulty. As the kilometres pass, I relax. There was nothing to worry about.

Then I'm confronted by a noisy torrent of murky water that drowns out my thoughts as it rushes past. I scout the river. Icy water gushes into my boots and drenches my rolled-up jeans with the first tentative steps. I flinch with surprise but must ignore my freezing toes. I brace against the flow and move slowly, pausing for balance between each step. Then my foot slips on a loose submerged rock. My ankle gives way, and I stumble to the other side. I walk up and down the bank assessing the water, then test where the stream splits into two channels. I'm very tempted to try this line. It's upstream slightly. Going against the current should have a stabilising effect. *Maybe I should try.*

The map indicates there are more rivers ahead. What will they be like? If I have to turn back, could I cross this river going with the current? As the day progresses it will get deeper, as the sun melts the glacier. *I probably shouldn't; be sensible.*

I really want to ride this trail. It's one of the longer dotted lines on my map and connects with other trails further east. If I cannot make it, this Highland exploration will be cut short. I think I can cross this river. If the ones further on are deeper, I can wait until the next morning for the river level to drop if necessary. I have enough supplies. *Go on, be a little reckless.*

If I drop the bike, there's a risk I could be trapped under it. *Don't do it. Be sensible.*

Although unlikely, the possibility that I could drown persuades me that it's not worth the risk. This river is my Schrödinger's Cat. There's always the possibility I would have made it, success and failure existing

Sprengisandur

simultaneously. To never know what the outcome would have been is the most frustrating part.

As I retrace my tracks and pick up the Sprengisandur route going north, the imposing glacier recedes from my rear view until I'm surrounded again by the endless volcanic sands.

Before people arrived a thousand years ago, it's thought that Iceland was mostly covered in forest. With the cutting down of trees for building and firewood, and clearing land for farming, the trees were soon gone. Sheep ate any seedlings that may have otherwise grown. Overgrazing damaged the ecosystem, leading to soil erosion and the inevitable desertification. The high winds that ravage this island whipped up great sandstorms of volcanic tephra, suffocating plant life where it settled.

Today seeds carried in the tyre treads of vehicles are unintentionally released in this foreign environment. Sometimes they sink into the tephra. Under the right conditions, some take hold and grow. I see a few stunted clumps of grass and plants along the track.

I ride the winding trail like molten lava; rising, falling and rolling inexorably onward with the natural contours of the land. It's an effortless ride. It doesn't require focus or concentration. My mind is free to wander unconstrained. I'd be happy riding through this desolate interior for eternity.

Then I see a blue expanse in the valley far ahead. The colour signifies a return to the fjords and coast. It had felt as though the desert would continue forever; now the bursting sands have ejected me. My blissful contentment vanishes. Suddenly I feel tired and lose momentum. Like cooling lava, I'll slow down and grind to a halt at the day's end, energy expended, immobilised by the cold chill of nightfall. A feeling of emptiness, which consumes me whenever I reach my destination, returns. For me, travelling is always about the journey.

But this day's exploring isn't over yet. There are waterfalls. I turn down a side-track, park the bike and set off on foot, stepping carefully from rock to rock in my bulky boots, encountering a group of hikers in shorts and t-shirts. It's turned into a glorious summer's day. I roll up my jacket sleeves and feel a glimmer of warmth on my skin. It's been hours since I waded through the last river. Having stopped several times to wring out every last drop of water from my socks, boots and jeans, they've finally dried. My feet are even *warm*.

The Skjálfandi River, spread out into many channels that meander lazily along a flat plain, converges here and plummets as white water over a vertical rock face. It's a powerful torrent of indefatigable might plunging into what appears like a massive sinkhole. The breeze carries a misty spray through the air. Droplets of water settle on the hairs of my arms. *Is it not possible to stay dry for five minutes in this country?*

I move away, clamber up some rocks to gain an elevated view from where to eat my lunch. Within moments, black flies come to torment me. I wave my hand about my head, yet they still manage to get in my eyes and caught in my hair. I'll get no peace here, so I return to the bike, scoffing a couple of biscuits on the way, then ride on to Aldeyjarfoss.

Columnar basalt rocks line the downstream gorge here, standing to attention with military straightness as the river parades by. I clamber down a rougher rocky section until face to face with the frothing white waterfall. It disappears into a cauldron, churning and bubbling with savage intensity.

Goðafoss is the last major waterfall along this river. The rising smoky plumes are visible as I ride the last few kilometres of trail to the Ring Road. The hundreds of people and overcrowded car park make me anticipate a natural wonder cheapened with walkways, cafe and souvenirs. I want to ride in the other direction.

I'd imagined the Sprengisandur route as a trail without end. But where one trail ends, another may begin. The longest trails nearby going north to the coast are on the peninsula of Flateyjardalur. With fond memories of the great riding, I'd be happy to go back. I had the

Sprengisandur

same feeling of contentment there as I had when riding alone across the open interior earlier today.

I turn off the Ring Road, take the gravel track along the Fnjóská River, pass the place where the rear sprocket sheared off exactly one month ago and see the farmhouse I stopped at to ask for help. The fields have all been cut, the hay wrapped and the marshmallow bales stacked by the side of the field. I ride towards Grenivík through the valley where Erik and Jörvi gave me a lift. Then I turn onto the F-road I didn't ride last time.

The countryside is red and orange earth, green grass and mosses, golden buttercups dazzling in the sun and dancing in the breeze that carries cotton wool clouds across the heavenly blue sky. The contrast with the barren, sepia-toned tephra of the Highlands is stark.

It's a fun ride, weaving along the narrow track, dipping into small streams and dodging the kamikaze sheep. There's even a bridge across the main river, so my feet remain dry. At the coast, the trail skirts the right-hand edge of a lake until it peters out on a rocky strip of beach that separates the lake from the bay. I ride along a faint trail until there's nowhere left to go. In less than twenty-four hours, I've crossed the country on my small Serow.

There's a smart-looking camper truck with German plates parked on the beach. Two people peer from the side door and wave. Professional engineers on a six-month sabbatical, they've had a taste of travelling and realise there's more to life than earning money. They have no intention of going back to work as they did before. Instead, they will do short-term consulting jobs between travels through Northern Europe. We talk as though we've known each other for years, with a familiarity only possible with like-minded people.

I'd thought I would camp here, but it was the prospect of having the place to myself that held the greatest appeal. The German couple came looking for the same thing, I'm sure. I leave and go pitch my tent on a grassy area beside a small bridge back up the trail. The valley is half in shade, the sun inches from the mountaintops, but it will still be light for hours.

I make a brew and begin to read, but the long day has taken its toll. I can't keep my eyes open. I lie down in my sleeping bag and stretch out. Relax. The tension in my back and shoulder blades seeps into the ground. *Ahh, that feels good.*

16

A Barbecue and Bike Problems
Akureyri

I've no intention of going anywhere today. The forecast is for rain. I feel no urge to move from this spot. With my down jacket and boots on over my thermals, I sit on the bridge with my legs dangling off the edge and drink coffee. The sound of the water running below me fills the air. It's overcast. Coastal fog is creeping up the valley, consuming everything in its path. When the flanking mountains have been devoured, I return to my sleeping bag, my whole world shrunk to the size of my tent. I brew another coffee and read.

Surprised that I haven't heard a drop of rain by mid-morning, I look outside. The fog has lifted. I go for a walk up the steep mountainside. It levels out and recedes into a sheltered amphitheatre of terracotta rock with a small stream running across a bright-green moss-carpet stage. It's as soft as sponge and sparkles in the light from thousands of water droplets trapped between the mossy fibres, like diamonds. It's as though I've discovered a secret garden known only to the handful of sheep.

Standing at the edge of the plateau where the water drops steeply down the hillside, I look out across the valley. Clouds are building around the hills; mushrooming, swirling, twisting, accumulating. I have a flashback to being upon a Spanish mountaintop years ago with storm clouds brewing like this. A near-miss lightning strike had my hair standing on end.

I put my camera away and return quickly down the hillside taking decisive strides, leaping from rock to rock and sliding on the scree, slowing only where the ground is loose and the footing unclear. By the time I reach the bridge, I'm out of breath and feel invigorated, hungrily eating up the fresh mountain air, huge lungfuls at a time.

ICELAND Serow Saga

I've missed the euphoria that comes from physical exertion; riding the motorbike requires little effort in comparison.

I spend a lazy afternoon reading, occasionally peering out of the tent to gauge the weather. The storm doesn't materialise; the clouds merely thicken into a blanket that wraps itself around the hills again.

There is one rock beside the trail where, if I stand patiently by it, my phone picks up a weak signal. Curious about what's going on in the rest of the world, I go to that rock. I have a message from an Icelandic biker:

> Hi, I noticed your post on the forum. It seems like you're on a great trip. I like riding too.
> I will be with my family in a summer house near Akureyri this weekend. If you are in the area, you are welcome for some barbecue. If you need a place to dry your gear or work on your bike, I can help. It would be fun to do some riding with you. Birgir

Sounds great! I'm close to Akureyri. We agree to meet and ride the following afternoon.

It's early evening, and the clouds have lifted. If I leave now, I can ride up to Laugafell hot pools in the Highlands, camp overnight, then ride back in the morning in time to meet Birgir. I like this idea. Having spent the day in aimless, time-wasting mode, I'm now on a mission. Within fifteen minutes, I've packed up the tent and loaded everything onto the bike.

I ride towards Akureyri and turn up Eyjafjörður valley in the dusky evening. The days of eternal light are beginning to fade. Daylight hours are getting shorter. I didn't notice it happening. I sleep with my neck-scarf pulled up around my eyes so that the world is blacked out. It stops me waking up in the middle of the night thinking it is morning.

Akureyri

Silver-white streams run down from the mist-covered hilltops as though the rock faces are crying. There is water everywhere; the rocks and grass are glistening, the air is full of it, I'm covered in it, and the trail is awash with it, making a second stream beside the gushing river. Ascending, I can soon see only a few metres ahead of me through the foggy twilight.

The trail is bumpy, rocky and steep until, after what feels like an eternity, I emerge on a tephra plain. It's a strange feeling to know without seeing that you are no longer hemmed in by mountains but on an open, exposed plateau. When the fog dissipates, I can see a little further, see the black sand rolling on and on until it vanishes in the white haze. I ride slowly, unable to see far ahead. Without a headlight on the bike, no one can see me coming; although, no one else is up here. This is the uninhabited Highlands at midnight. *Who goes out trail riding at this time?*

I'm riding across a dark land at night, although it's not completely black. There is a strange ethereal air from the diffused light of the moon through the fog. When I stop and switch off the engine, a complete and eerie silence pervades everything. It's as though I'm tiptoeing across the top of the world while it sleeps on unaware. Even the wind is dormant.

By the time I reach Laugafell, the mist has lifted and the wind awoken. It's cold. I rush to put up the tent, strip off my bike gear and hop into my bikini, then run across the tephra in my flip flops and take cautious steps down into the sunken hot pool. *Ahh!*

My frozen toes burn with the heat, but once I'm fully submerged, I realise the pool is not so hot, it's only that I was very cold. There are three others in the pool, huddled at one end where the hot water enters through the rock wall. We chat as the stars emerge above, the clouds clearing with the breeze. Eventually, the others leave for bed.

I float on my back and look up to nature's cinema, watching the orbiting satellites and shooting meteors flashing. The star-studded sky lights up the nearby land. The distant mountains are silhouetted as though the sky has been cut away leaving only the black underlay. Living through a summer of eternal light, I realise I've missed the night. I love knowing the hour by the position of the stars in the sky and the passing of the month by the waxing and waning of the moon.

I've lain in the water so long, I can see a hint of light on the horizon to the east where the sun will rise a few hours from now. If I'm to be up early to ride back to Akureyri and meet Birgir, I must get some sleep. Reluctantly, I get out, shivering as the cold air clasps its hands around my wet body. I quickly wrap up in my towel and run back to my tent. It's almost three o'clock.

I wake with the sun warming the tent at seven o'clock. There's one other early riser, a French lady slowly swimming up and down the length of the small pool. My tiredness vanishes in the fresh air and warm water; it's a wonderful combination made better by the strong coffee I brew. If only every day could start like this.

The return journey is like riding a different trail. Without clouds, I can see the distant mountains hemming in the world around me. With daylight, I can see the road ahead. I ride fast over the black sand plains, bump and jolt down the rocky valley and splash through the streams until, suddenly, I'm back on tarmac, the morning's adventure at an end. I'm sure the road was longer last night.

I meet Birgir at the fuel station in town. Well built and tall, he looks less like a lawyer and more like someone who could carry his motorbike out of the Highlands if it ever broke down. He introduces himself with a crushing handshake, his hand dwarfing mine even though I've got gloves on. But I can tell by the way he speaks, putting me at ease, that I'll be safe in his care.

Once he's got petrol for the bikes, he leads the way to their summer house. Along an unpaved road, it's not accessible in winter once the snow comes. The long, single-storey house on raised decking to level the sloping land has huge windows that provide a full view

Akureyri

of Akureyri across the fjord. Together with his wife Fjóla and their three children, it's a full house. I'm welcome to pitch my tent in the unfinished extension, which will at least be flat and protected from the elements.

There's time for a ride out before the barbecue. I have no idea about Birgir's riding experience, except that he's toured a lot in Iceland. I soon suspect that I've bitten off more than I can chew when I see him and his son kitting up in full enduro protective gear, then wheeling their KTMs out of the van. Birgir rides a 450 EXC; his eighteen-year-old son has a brand new 350 EXC.

'He's started going regularly to the gym and is getting very strong now. He rides faster than I can.' Birgir tells me.

Oh no, what have I agreed to?

We start up the bikes and let the engines warm up. Then, with nods to say we're all good to go, Birgir's son is off in a flash, dust kicking up behind him. *There's no way I can keep up with that!* I follow as fast as I can, faster than I've ridden trails before. We round a few bends then turn off the graded trail onto a steep, rutted track, the most technical I've ridden in Iceland.

I've never received any instruction on trail-riding techniques; instead, I've figured out my own way to get down a path. My style may be neither pretty nor conventional, but it works for me.

My confidence fades; I feel a fraud and out of my depth. I know Birgir isn't judging me; he's not the type to do so, but that doesn't stop the feeling that I'm being watched. Distracted, I lose concentration and veer onto a sheep track. Realising my mistake, I try to get back onto the better trail, but struggling to get the bike out of the deep rut, it topples over. *As if they need more proof that I'm not good enough.*

Birgir rides past on the right track and stops to wait further down the hill, whilst I fumble to lift the bike from the awkward angle it landed. I curse and swear under my breath. *Why the hell isn't he coming to help! Can't he see I'm struggling?*

ICELAND Serow Saga

But then I realise the reason Birgir hasn't come to my aid. He knows I'm capable of picking up my bike, even if I had forgotten. Besides, even the most experienced riders drop their bike sometimes; no one is immune from making mistakes. I need to stop putting myself down, give myself some credit. The Serow, after all, doesn't have great suspension or brakes, and the tyres don't have deep enough tread for these trails.

'Are you OK?' Birgir asks when I pull up behind him.

'Yeah fine,' I reply.

'Look, don't rush yourself. There's no need to try and keep up with us. Ride at the pace you feel comfortable. We'll wait; we're not in any rush. Besides, you need to look after your bike; you've got a long journey ahead. Our bikes only need to last the day, then they'll be loaded in the van until next time.'

'OK, you're right,' I agree. 'But let me ride at the back. I'll feel less pressured there.'

With no one behind to watch, I begin to relax as we wind through an overgrown, wooded hillside. As I relax, the riding becomes easier; my confidence returns. Soon the only thing preventing me from keeping up is the Serow's underpowered engine.

We stop at a farm to ask the route over the next range of hills. It's a while since Birgir came this way. We race fast along the valley floor; I drop back despite riding on full throttle. I can't stop grinning. Then we make a sharp turn up a barren, rocky side valley and follow the giant pylons across the land. I'd never have known about these trails with only a map as my guide. I'm glad Birgir invited me along.

Eventually, we reach the next valley and a proper road. Birgir's son wants to ride more, but Birgir suggests we head back to the summer house. I'm happy to oblige, having already ridden a long way this morning.

While Fjóla prepares the salads, Birgir lights up the barbecue outside. Then with beers in hand, we chat. Birgir keeps an attentive watch over the marinated leg of Icelandic lamb that's slowly cooking

Akureyri

and wafting a mouth-watering aroma my way. Besides a hotdog of questionable origins from a stand in Reykjavík and the pepperoni topping on the pizza I had with Einar, it's the first meat I've eaten since leaving the UK. Then, when it's cooked, we feast. It's delicious, and we all have second helpings.

Once satiated, we clear the table and spread out a map of the Highlands. Birgir traces the dotted lines with his finger, suggesting various routes, describing the trails and highlighting those that avoid major river crossings. His favourite trail in Iceland goes from Mývatn south to Askja, a large crater, visible on the topographic map as a circular ridge. There are no other landmarks nearby. We agree that it'll be a good route for me to take from here.

'Be careful; it's rough, remote terrain for over a hundred kilometres. I've never seen anyone else on that trail,' he warns. I struggle to hide my excitement. It sounds amazing. I know little about Askja, but suspect it'll be worth going for the ride alone.

I thought I'd have time to go everywhere and see everything. People on weeklong holidays wondered how many laps of the Ring Road I'd make. I'd methodically ride all the trails on each peninsula and then the Highlands. It had quickly become clear that my route would be more haphazard, dependent upon the weather. I considered my journey so far as a reconnaissance ride to scout out the places I wanted to revisit and spend more time later in the summer. Now I realise that three months is not enough. The volcanic sands of time have slipped inexorably through my fingers. With each fjord I ride and mountain I pass, I'm given a key that opens my eyes to another realm, each one revealing more detail to be explored. It's futile rushing around, trying to see and do it all like a dog chasing its tail; I'll never catch it. This summer ride is now a recce for another season.

With this realisation, I no longer feel the urge to rush about. Why not sit and relax in the sun when it shines? Birgir and Fjóla offer me the use of their summer house this week while they're working in Reykjavík. I don't hesitate to say yes.

'We'll leave the leftovers for you,' Fjóla says. 'Eat it all. It won't keep.'

There's still half a cooked lamb in the fridge.

Sleeping in a bed makes a comfortable change from my punctured inflatable mattress. It's wonderful to be warm and dry, not caring about the weather. When it rains, I look out the window and watch the light changing throughout the day, the sea fog creeping inland and marvel at the rainbow appearing in the fine mist below the clouds that glow a soft pink. When it's warm enough, I sit on the summer house decking with a large glass of red wine in the evening and look across the fjord to Akureyri and the mountain backdrop. The snow that was on the hills the last time I passed has all melted.

I use the time and space to sort through my gear, wash clothes and attempt to repair my inflatable mattress. It always seems to have one more hole. It's the same formula for the number of bikes you want being always one more than the number you own.

I top up the oil in the bike, as I do almost every other day. I can't smell oil burning when the bike's running. None is leaking from any gasket. I can't work out where it's all going. The air filter is oily again, but that doesn't account for all that I've been adding. Since I cannot replace worn piston rings here, I must do whatever I can to coax the little bike through the next few weeks.

As I'm tightening the chain, I notice how worn the rear sprocket is. It should have lasted for the duration of the trip, but will need replacing. I run my fingers over the worn teeth as though it's a wounded animal I'm caring for. Like the ponies who were ridden to exhaustion to make the Sprengisandur crossing before dying from lack of food or dehydration, this Iceland trip is pushing the Serow to its bursting point.

I order a new chain and sprockets and get them couriered to Unnur and Högni in the East Fjords. The direction I go from here is now

Akureyri

determined by the bike's needs. To prolong the life of the sprocket, I'll have to ride easy. If I'm to venture back into the Highlands on remote trails, I'll need to keep a close eye on it. I can't afford for it to wear so much that the chain slips when needing to give the bike throttle to make forward progress over rough terrain.

Then I notice a broken spoke. *Great.* At least I brought a couple of spares.

I scan my eyes over the hub; there are three broken spokes. I'll have to find replacements. The motorcycle repair shop in Akureyri doesn't have any spares; although, the mechanic says I can work on my bike there. I phone the Yamaha dealer and two other bike stores in Reykjavík to no avail.

Out of desperation, I visit the bicycle shop. It's hidden away in an industrial area, a large, dimly lit place with lots of secondhand bikes. An old guy, who I'm sure could out-cycle me any day despite a slow, stooped walk, is in charge. I follow him into the workshop where he picks out a spoke from a tray of them on the table. Amazingly, it's the same thickness, only marginally different in shape and a fraction longer. I can work with this.

'I'll buy two,' I blurt out, as though there's a risk someone will jump in front of me and buy all the stock.

I return to the motorcycle repair shop and, using their bike stand, remove the rear wheel. I'm surprised at the slick operation despite drops of blood congealing on the rim from where I cut my knuckle when removing the rear sprocket. The jeans I cleaned yesterday are soon streaked with grease, my hands black.

I bend the ill-fitting spoke using Mole grips to increase the angle where the spoke threads through the hub flange, then use a circular saw to cut the spoke to length and file the end so it threads easily into the nipple. I tighten the loose spokes and true both wheels. Hopefully, it will resolve the front-end wobble I felt when riding into town.

ICELAND Serow Saga

I visit the motorcycle museum. Dedicated to one hundred years of motorcycles in Iceland, there is everything from an old Henderson, Nortons and Triumphs, vintage mopeds and trail bikes, to a Yamaha XT660R with its panniers covered in stickers, which was donated to the museum by one of two brothers who were the first Icelanders to bike around the world.

In the same time that I will have spent exploring Iceland, the brothers circumnavigated the globe. I can only think of all the things that must be missed by travelling so far, so fast. I prefer to go slow on my little bike.

I wonder if I could sneakily swap my Serow for one of the enduro bikes that look in better condition. Judging by the oil in the trays strategically placed beneath some of the engines, my bike isn't leaking enough oil yet to justify a place here.

17

Lunar Landscapes
To Askja

It's a lovely, dry, cloud-speckled blue-sky day. I turn off the main road at Mývatn, excited about the trail ahead and with only a slight nervous apprehension about whether the bike's worn sprocket will hold out. *As long as the chain doesn't start slipping on it.*

There is one tiny raincloud in the distance, water streaming in a shower to the earth – a signpost from heaven indicating my direction of travel because, of course, the trail to Askja that Birgir recommended goes directly beneath it. *Sigh.* I put on my waterproofs. Again.

Beyond Grænavatn lake, the grassland and sandy soil fade. The track is barely visible over the lava rocks. I can only see the faint imprint of tyre tracks where sand has blown over and mosses taken hold. At a junction with a small handwritten sign, I dismount and pull a straggly bush to one side to see which way I should go. In places the only evidence that I'm on a trail is the regularly spaced wooden marker posts. I ride slowly, scanning for the next marker and watching the uneven ground. Anyway, I must ride gently to preserve what's left of the rear sprocket.

The lava disappears into an ocean of sand spreading out to the south and east. Where clumps of pale grasses grow, dunes with wind-carved ripples have formed. Mountains peak over the horizon in the distance.

I'm enjoying the ride so much, I speed right past another junction. I brake and turn suddenly, almost dropping the bike as the wheel jams in the sand. The sign is for Vikrafellsleið, the route Birgir recommended I take.

ICELAND Serow Saga

The trail turns north, skirting low rises like giant dunes. I think I'm going the wrong way. I stop twice to consider going back. Perhaps I misunderstood Birgir's directions. Doubts plague me. *I'll just continue a few kilometres more.* And I say this over and over in my head like a stuck record because I don't want to go back; the further I proceed, the less appealing the retreat.

Eventually, the trail turns eastward and south, and my faith that I'll emerge near Askja returns. I gauge my direction of travel by where Herðubreið, the 'Queen of the Mountains', sits on the horizon. It is a flat-topped steep-sided tuya, which formed when lava erupted through an ice sheet or glacier that has since melted. Now it stands proud, raised above the rest of the land like a top hat beacon. I feel drawn to it like a moth to light.

The sand plains become a lunar landscape of mangled lava. On and on the trail continues, marker posts showing the way less frequently spaced. I must stay alert. The trail turns unexpectedly on itself over and over like an unravelled ball of wool. I must avoid the protruding rocks that appear suddenly. I swear that the ground is alive with devilish intent, waiting for the moment when I become complacent or distracted to eject pieces of lava into my tracks. I could swear that they weren't there when I looked a moment ago, but now it's too late to avoid and the front wheel crunches into them and the forks cry tears of oil in pain and the handlebars shudder in my grip and I worry that the bike is going to fall apart beneath me.

The most fun trails do not always make the most interesting read; don't doubt, I am having one of my best days of riding since I was in Namibia and Angola over two years ago.

It's nearing the end of the day when I merge onto the main route to Askja from the east. There's blue sky on every horizon, yet rain falls on me from the one raincloud I saw earlier. *Typical.*

I park at the trailhead to Askja and change into hiking trousers and shoes for a walk to the crater that's indicated on the information board. Halfway there, I realise I'm already inside the pre-historic

To Askja

outer caldera. The view in all directions is bounded by its low rim. It's as though the world has been flattened and shrunk to a fifty-square-kilometre disc. Inside, it's a level plain formed over millennia as ash and dust settled to form the base.

I walk towards Öskjuvatn. This lake fills a smaller caldera, which formed during an eruption in 1875, sending tephra on the winds to settle over Norway, Sweden, Germany and Poland. The substantial ash fall over the eastern fjords of Iceland poisoned the land, killed livestock and initiated a wave of emigration as people left for a new life in Canada.

Old photographs online show Icelanders in departing boats, men in bowler hats and double-breasted jackets, women with tartan blankets wrapped over their shoulders like shawls, each wearing a stern, serious expression, a reluctant acceptance of their fate. It is one thing to move abroad with dreams of a better life and quite another to be forced from your home due to unexplainable events beyond your control, to begin again in a foreign country you know nothing about with only what you can carry in your hands.

Whilst Öskjuvatn is cold and frozen over for much of the year, the milky blue water pooled at the bottom of Víti (Hell), the explosion crater next to the lake, is warm enough to bathe in if you're willing to scramble down the steep and slippery crater edge and don't mind stinking of sulphur afterwards. I content myself with dipping a finger in the tepid water. Small bubbles rise from the bottom and pop on the surface. Why anyone would want to jump into this toxic-looking murk, I've no idea.

When there is not a cloud in the sky and the air is still, a calmness descends upon the Highlands. It is as though time stands still in an ageless land. I exist only in the present, with no haunting past or uncertain future. There is only what my eye can see. There is nothing. And that is everything.

ICELAND Serow Saga

Despite ample rainfall, Iceland's interior is like a desert in every other respect: desolate, sandy, sparsely vegetated, uninhabited and starkly beautiful. Deserts are special places, harsh and unforgiving; but, for those who are willing to suffer the difficulties of travel here, they offer a priceless reward: simply, to be.

There is something more to these Highlands. There is no one around yet I am not alone. It is as though the land is a living creature, a dragon's body gradually rising and falling with each long, slow, steady breath measured over years. I can sense its heartbeat, an almost imperceptible pulse. I do not wish to disturb this sleeping beast. I am riding the long calm before it awakens, breathing flames and erupting with a fierce and violent rage.

As I lean left then right, I am one with the bike, no longer controlling it, merely an extension like a limb. Feeling each subtle change in the environment through the rubber tyres, it is as though I am connected to everything. I ride across the black sands, the trail weaving gently like a lazy river through a valley, rocks scattered across the open plain like fallen leaves in autumn. Low-profile, gently sloping shield volcanoes shape the horizon. The last remnants of snow remain in crevices even though the summer is waning.

With enough fuel, I turn south towards Kverkfjöll, the mountain range on the northern edge of Iceland's largest glacier, Vatnajökull. I have a strong desire to ride as many trails as possible. Partly, it's for the excitement of the ride. I can't get enough of the feeling of freedom that riding my bike gives. The rougher and remoter the trail, the bigger the high. It's also because I want to maximise my time in the interior. The Highlands are the part of Iceland I love the most. Least touched by man, it's where I feel most closely connected to nature. It's here that I come alive and feel most at ease with myself and my surroundings. Like a drug, I'm addicted and crave more.

The wide plain narrows until I'm riding between high-sided walls and then opens out again. Here the trail is a light sandy colour, etched into the dark surrounding surface, which is scattered with red rocks

To Askja

like spilt sugar. I ride past mangled lumps of lava, up and over a rise and on towards a hikers' hut. Beyond, the trail is rocky. I bump along until it peters out and I can go no further.

Vatnajökull rises in front of me. It's not the pristine, gleaming white icing I'd seen from a distance. It has a blueish tinge. Where sand and ash have blown over it and the ice has melted, dark stains stream down. The cracks and fissures are blackened into harsh, gritty scars where the tephra is trapped, frozen in time.

The ice is hollowed out into a cave where a river of murky grey water gushes out. The noise, like the white static of an old TV, drowns out all other sounds. The water will flow across the Highlands and join up with more glacial streams to form the mighty, frothing Jökulsá á Fjöllum, which creates the Dettifoss waterfalls and flows by Ásbyrgi before opening out into the delta at Öxarfjörður on the north coast, 206 kilometres downstream.

Rather than retracing my steps, I take the only other trail from here, the Hvannalindavegur (F903) back to Austurleið (F910). At the first river I come to, several Land Rovers with British plates are parked.

'You're on your own?' the tour leader asks.

'Yes.' *Obviously.* He gives one of those approving nods with raised eyebrows, which could be interpreted as incredulity or respect.

'Do you ride?' I ask, guessing that he does. Most people who strike up conversation when I'm in my bike gear are bikers too.

'I've got a Versys 1000. I keep thinking about how great it would be to ride here. But what about the rivers?'

Ah yes, the question I'm always asked. 'I cross them. Or I don't.'

'What about the ones on this road?'

'I'm about to find out. You tell me. How deep is this one?'

'Quite deep. Almost up to the wheel arch.'

'Hmm …'. Standing beside the 4x4, that means it's above my knee. 'I'll have to see how rocky and fast-flowing it is.'

'We've got to get moving, but we'll wait to see you safely over the other side,' he tells me. *Great.* I hate having an audience.

Having learnt through trial and error, the wet boots and cold feet way, I know that the shallowest point with access is always at the way-marked crossing. I've noticed, though, that the water is usually deeper where the tyres of heavy 4x4s have carved up the riverbed and shallower on the downstream side of them, where the disturbed sand and rocks settle in an arc spanning the river.

I follow this line shaped like a drawn bow, marked by a subtle change in the surface of the river as it ripples over the raised bed. It's not deep at all, no cause for concern. My confidence is boosted and, feeling a little smug, I turn and wave as I accelerate away on the far side.

When cycling, I take advice from drivers regarding how hilly the terrain is with extreme scepticism. When you only require a slight increase in pressure on the accelerator, you don't pay attention to small changes in incline, which are very noticeable when pedalling under your own power. Now, riding my motorbike, I treat the advice regarding river crossings similarly, assuming that 4x4 drivers have most likely paid little heed to the depth and simply followed the main track blindly across.

I stop at a junction I wasn't expecting and look at my map. A 4x4 approaches.

'Are you OK?' the driver asks.

'Yeah. I'm figuring out which way.' I point in the direction they've just come from, 'Where does that track go?'

'To this place where an outlaw hid to evade capture.'

'You mean Eyvindur?' I ask, hoping I've pronounced it correctly.

'I don't know. I can't understand any of these Icelandic names,' the woman replies seriously.

I smile, remembering the countless times I've had similar discussions with other non-Icelandic speakers.

To Askja

I take the side trail, park and walk along the hillside to reach a lava field. I cross wooden planks bridging a stream with angelica growing along its edges. A shallow mud-ringed watering hole makes a bright oasis. On the edge of the lava, I can see a shelter built of lava rock, where Eyvindur the outlaw hid during the eighteenth century. It's recessed into the lava field, now overgrown with dwarf willow. The beauty of the outlook makes it hard to imagine how difficult survival would have been.

Fjalla-Eyvindur (Mountain-Eyvindur), as he was known, has become a popular figure. The playwright Jóhann Sigurjónsson wrote a play in 1912, which was later turned into a film, based on the personable Eyvindur and his unpleasant wife Halla.

Eyvindur had a normal upbringing and became a well-mannered, strong and athletic man. His life changed when, falling upon hard times, he was caught stealing some bread and cheese by a homeless woman. She said she was a sorceress and put a curse upon him, condemning him to a life as a fugitive. His life and story may be from the eighteenth century, but the characters could be straight from the sagas written five centuries earlier.

He then travelled to the Westfjords, where he met Halla. Despite her being ugly, cold and ruthless, he fell deeply in love and married her in 1741. Halla's life of crime began with petty theft but escalated to her drowning a young farmhand. The couple were forced to flee. Supposedly, Halla wanted to burn the farm down with her children in it before escaping, but Eyvindur convinced her to abandon them and let them live.

Halla is remembered as a heartless, murderous bitch. She killed most of their subsequent offspring at birth under the pretence that their crying might alert someone to their whereabouts. There was only one child who survived until the age of two. When they were caught by surprise by people who had been tracking them, Halla decided that the child would slow them down and threw her daughter over a waterfall. It's hard to imagine how he could have loved such a woman.

During their twenty years on the run, they were seen all over Iceland. Sometimes they were helped; other times they fled to the mountains. Eyvindur put his practical skills and ingenuity to good use, which enabled their survival in prolonged harsh conditions. To avoid being found at Hvannalindir, Eyvindur constructed a sheep pen out of the lava to conceal the animals he had to steal to survive. According to legend, Eyvindur only stole sheep from people who had wronged him when he was a free man.

Walking over the mangled protrusions, I follow a faint trail where the rocks have been worn or crushed by heavy feet. I come across a small enclosure, the walls built up by piled rocks and a slab of lava that acts as a partial roof. The small stream next to it would have provided water without having to let the animals roam free, which might have compromised the hideout.

Back on the main trail, 4x4s going to and from Askja travel at high speed. It feels like rush hour in the Highlands. Instead, I take Birgir's suggested alternative route without river crossings. It's a bleak, open valley of dark sand and few rough stones. Vehicle tracks are faintly visible, the way easier to identify from the spaced wooden markers, although several have been knocked down. I expect most were flattened by the wind, but some that are split were probably hit or driven over, impressive when you consider there is nothing else here. Perhaps it is like riding a bike, where you will go in the direction you are looking, so if there is a rock you want to avoid the worst thing you can do is look at it, which is the instinctive reaction.

The trail descends to the Hálslón Reservoir. I follow the edge of it and cross below the dam. After a brief exploration of Hafrahvammagljúfur (try saying that!), a narrow gorge with vertiginous cliffs looming close to one another as though about to clamp together and squash everything inside, I go in search of the nearby Laugarvalladalur hot spring.

18
A Hot Pool and Rum
Laugarvalladalur

Voices are coming from a small wooden turf-roof hut partially dug into the hillside. I walk by and follow the path along a stream until it plunges off the hillside into a pool. Two people are bathing. No one sits that contentedly in cold water.

I put my bag down on an old sheep trail carved into the hillside so it won't roll away, strip off my bike gear until I'm barefoot with only my towel wrapped around me, then wriggle into my bikini. I cover all my gear with my waterproof jacket, in case it starts raining.

I walk-run on my toes like a cartoon burglar because the soft, bare earth along the trail is cold on my feet and I don't want to get them too dirty. At the edge of the pool, I whip off my towel and gasp – ooh! – as the frigid air hits my exposed body. As quickly as I dare without slipping on the algae-covered rocks, I step into the water before my skin erupts in goose-pimples. I grab my hair and tie it up so it stays dry, then sink until only my shoulders are exposed and exhale – aah! – as the warm water envelops me.

I sit near the edge, facing the hillside of slanting, layered rock like runny icing that's about to slide off the top of a cake. Water runs over it, then drops several metres into the pool. Behind, the water has eroded a small cave with an overhang as though someone has scooped it out with a giant spoon. The water flows out and down into another, smaller pool before trickling into the main river of icy, clear water into the bottom of the valley.

The water is tepid, but with my legs stretched out in front of me I can feel the soothing heat from the waterfall on my feet. I step towards it, my toes sinking into the loose, pebbly earth, and reach out my hand to feel the hot droplets splash over my arm. As much as I'd love to stand beneath it like a shower, I know my long hair will never dry tonight. I'll be cold in my tent.

More people come and go. I can't bring myself to leave. The pool may not be warm enough for prolonged bathing, but I'm warmer here than fully clothed on my bike. I psyche myself up and, quickly, before I change my mind again, stand up straight, clamber out of the pool, grab my towel and bag, then struggle to dress as my clothes stick to my damp body. In those few minutes, my toes have gone numb again. I race up the hill to warm up. Unfit after months of sitting on the bike with little other exercise, I'm soon puffing and panting and have to slow to a brisk walk.

'If you go in the hut, you'll get some rum,' a woman says, passing me on her way to the hot pool.

Intriguing. Rum, indoors: the appeal is enough to overcome my shyness.

I knock and say hello loudly as I slowly push the creaking door ajar.

'Come in!' a voice bellows.

As my eyes adjust to the dim room, I see two men sitting on opposite sides of a small wooden table in the centre of the hut. Around the edges are wooden bed frames and bunks in varying states of disrepair and collapse.

'Have you been to the hot pool?'

'Yeah, it's lovely.'

'You look like you need a rum.' The older man says as he unscrews a bottle. He fills the cap with the dark amber liquid and passes it to me. I raise it to my lips, toss my head back swallowing the small shot in one and wince at the burning sensation in my throat.

'Is that your Land Cruiser outside?' he asks as I pass the bottle cap back.

'No.'

'How did you get here?'

'Motorbike.'

Laugarvalladalur

'Oh, excellent. In that case, you need another drink.'

I take the refilled cap and drink it down. It's surprising how dehydrated you get spending an hour or two in a hot pool, especially after a day on the trails. I need water, not rum.

'Come, sit down. We'd like to hear about your trip and what you think of Iceland. I'm Ásgeir, and this is Felix.'

We shake hands. I take a seat on the slatted lower bunk near the door and begin my story. It's interrupted by countless questions, but I don't mind.

Then it's my turn to ask. 'What brings you here?'

'Hiking,' Ásgeir replies. 'We're going to drive towards Snæfell tomorrow and hike from there to another mountain hut, stay overnight, then hike back.'

I'd intended to do lots of hiking too. The one book I brought with me was on walking and trekking in Iceland. I've not used it. The desire to bike whenever the weather is favourable is too strong. If it's too cold, wet and windy for biking, I prefer to stay in my tent. I'm a fair-weather outdoors person by choice, which again begs the question, *why did I come to Iceland?*

'If I was to come back and hike, where would you recommend?' I ask.

'Landmannalaugar is beautiful. There are lots of fantastic hikes there like the Laugavegur trek.'

I interrupt. 'I went through that area on my bike. It was too busy for me. Laugavegur was like a human highway and Landmannalaugar was a crowded refugee camp.' Ásgeir laughs at my use of the Icelanders' metaphor; even quiet Felix can't help but smile. 'I enjoy the wilderness precisely because there are few people in it.'

'You're right, it's very popular now. I haven't been for years. You used to be able to go and be alone.'

'If you could guarantee the weather and had unlimited time, where would *you* go for a long hike?'

ICELAND Serow Saga

'I'd hike on Hornstrandir,' Felix speaks up. 'It's very remote, in the far corner of the Westfjords. There's no one there, just lots of wildlife. I've been many times. The problem is it rains a lot.'

I had hoped to hike there, but that was when I was ill in Ísafjörður. And it was raining a lot.

'My favourite place in the whole of Iceland is Lónsöræfi,' Ásgeir adds.

My ears prick up at the unfamiliar name. It may be that I don't recognise the Icelandic way of saying it, where the word gets lost in the mouth and swallowed. Ásgeir points out the region on the map.

'The scenery is very colourful. The rocks are bright orange and red like at Landmannalaugar. You won't see anyone else there. It's not easy to get to. You have to walk in the way we're going tomorrow. There's also a 4x4 track from the southeastern part of the Ring Road. It goes almost to the first hut, but you need a good vehicle for that. It's very rough and the river can be very deep.'

The combination of rough access tracks and unspoilt wilderness has me wishfully dreaming. If I've time towards the end of my trip, I could make a detour on my way round the last section of the Ring Road.

Listening to Ásgeir and Felix, and having followed Leo's journey on foot across Iceland through his Instagram photos, I realise there are still plenty of beautiful parts of the country I've not explored. It will have to wait until next time. I'm sure there will be another time, although perhaps not for a few years. Certainly, it'll be after I've forgotten about the cold, the rain and the wind. The mind is adept at remembering the good and forgetting the bad.

I've created a map in my mind of Iceland's natural highlights that I want to visit or return to. These are the less well known but no less wonderful places that appeal to me: the in-between places frequently ignored, the end-of-the-road spots too distant to be bothered with by many. They're those favourite back-door walks from home whose paths you'll walk day after day, revelling in the familiar details and

Laugarvalladalur

subtle changes each season brings; and your favourite locations you'll return to again and again because of the feelings they invoke. It's the album played over and over that never loses its charm, not a one-time hit wonder soon forgotten.

'Where are you staying tonight?' Ásgeir asks. I'd not thought that far ahead. 'You're welcome to stay here. There's space. That's if you don't mind sharing a hut with two old blokes. I don't know what your thoughts are on sharing with strange men.'

The hut is like a Scottish bothy. The idea of not having to put up my tent is immensely appealing. Besides, it's getting late.

'Yeah, I'll stay.'

'You sure?'

'As long as you don't mind, of course.'

'Absolutely not! It will be lovely to have some different company for a change. We've been doing this for twenty years. It'll be refreshing to hear some new stories.' Ásgeir beams.

'And it's Ásgeir's birthday today,' Felix adds.

'Really?'

'Sixty years old. An old man,' Ásgeir jokes. 'I thought it was going to be a lonely passing with just this old bugger for company,' he says, pointing to Felix. 'Now, it'll be a party.'

They seem an unlikely pair. Ásgeir is a man who enjoys life, well prepared with an ample supply of quality food and alcohol, a good man to have on an expedition crew. Felix, tanned with chiselled features, lean and fit, is more careful about his health. He's quiet under Ásgeir's shadow, but they make a good team.

'We've got lots of wine. Would you like some?'

'Sure,' I reply. Wine is preferable to rum.

'We've eaten, but I can cook you some sausages on the barbecue.'

'Oh, it's fine. I've got plenty of food with me.' I don't mention that I haven't eaten yet and can't be bothered to. I don't have the same obsession with calorie consumption on the motorbike as when long-distance cycling. If I'd been on a bicycle all day, I'd have taken up his offer of sausages, cooked my own dinner too and would have still been hungry.

'So, tell me, aren't you concerned for your safety, travelling alone, sharing huts with strangers?'

'No, I reckon I'm safe with you. I think I'm a reasonable judge of character; I've had a lot of practice. You seem harmless,' I reply, then added jokingly, 'Or should I be worried?'

We ask about each other's lives. When Ásgeir asks where I live in England, I tell him I've no fixed abode, that I live in my van and love it.

'But you have to settle some time, put down roots somewhere,' Ásgeir tells me with an air of authority that comes with age and experience.

I disagree. There was a time when living in a community was essential to survival, but that is not true today. With modern transport making long journeys not only possible but quick and easy, the community has expanded. The internet has improved communications and created jobs and livelihoods not constrained by location. My roots are spread across the globe.

When I cycled through Africa a decade ago, I was repeatedly asked, 'What are you searching for?' I found freedom and happiness in travelling, seeing the world and living simply one day to the next. In the years since that revelation, I have found that living in a van offers me these things even when I'm constrained by work in England.

It would be nice to have a base to which I can return whenever I want, but if owning a home requires a mortgage, I would become tied to it. Living in a van is a compromise, but I choose my freedom above being a slave to debt. This is not a situation I have fallen into or endure because I have no alternative; it was a conscious decision made after much consideration. I have looked at how others live and decided what I do and don't want. There is no need to go along with the convention of getting married and buying a house and having

Laugarvalladalur

children to know it is not what I want. I am lucky to have these choices. Ásgeir and Felix probably didn't have this luxury.

My van may not be a house, but it is my home. My lifestyle may not be conventional, but it is my life to spend how I choose. And it is this low-cost lifestyle that allows me to spend my summer biking in Iceland, to spend this evening talking with Ásgeir and Felix.

Ásgeir does not agree with my ramblings on this topic; although, when it comes to nature and the outdoors we have similar interests and ideas. I change the subject. I have given up trying to make people understand. Despite our differences of opinion, I'm enjoying their company and could talk and listen and debate all night.

The wine flows; my mug never dries up. Like the hot pool, it's continuously topped up despite a steady outpouring down my throat. And words tumble through the air, thoughts and ideas building in momentum, new topics blend with the current and become a blur of white water gushing past me until Ásgeir announces that it's late and they ought to get some sleep before their early start in the morning.

19
Bike Repairs
East Fjords

After an early coffee, Ásgeir and Felix pack up. I set off on the bike, heading north towards the Ring Road to refuel. It's marginal whether I've got sufficient fuel for a more prolonged ride in the Highlands. Besides, the bike surely can't go much further in this state. The rear sprocket is noticeably more worn than before yesterday's ride, the rate of wear increased.

When I get a phone signal, I message Unnur to ask about my package of replacement parts for the bike. She replies instantly; using the tracking number, Pósturinn the Icelandic postal service confirmed that they are in the country but haven't cleared customs yet. She expects I'll have to wait a few days; it's nearly the weekend, and Monday is a national holiday.

Wondering where to go in the meantime, I try to block out the possibility of any more jeep tracks until I've replaced the chain and sprockets. However, the map reveals two dotted lines of 4x4 trails that I've not ridden in the area. One crosses the mountains and re-joins the Ring Road near Vopnafjörður on the north coast.

I can't resist. *I'll take it gently.*

It looks as though the trail goes between some outbuildings. I see a man standing outside the farmhouse front door. As it would feel like trespassing to continue, I stop and enquire about the route, pointing up the hill behind.

'Oh,' he says with concern, his dark eyebrows furrowing over his ice-blue eyes. 'I think it's very rough up there.'

I grin uncontrollably, my concerns about the bike forgotten.

'Let me check with the old man who's lived here all his life,' he says, seeing my eager expression.

East Fjords

He enters the house and disappears into the shadows of the hallway. I follow as far as the front door and hover, waiting for him to return or invite me in. I can hear voices, an unintelligible jumble of words that I can now identify as Icelandic even though I don't understand a single word.

While I'm waiting, his teenage daughter, with the same dark hair as her father, the colour of rain-soaked volcanic ash, comes and talks with me in perfect English. I explain where I want to go.

'I didn't know there was a track up there. I've been coming here for sixteen years.'

'In some ways I know Iceland better than Norfolk, the county where I grew up,' I say, partly in jest.

It was when I returned from my cycle trip through Africa that I realised how little I knew of my home country. Since then I have made an effort to explore closer to home; I always discover somewhere new.

The man returns and leans on the doorframe.

'The old man says you'll be fine, said he drove it in his car once. There's a river, but it shouldn't be too deep. He says it's beautiful up there.' There's no longer concern in his voice, only a hint of envy. 'Makes me wish I had time to go up there now,' he adds, 'but we're about to leave. If you ride around the back of that building and through the gate, you'll see the trail going up beside the waterfall.'

I presume the old man's definition of 'car' was lost in translation. It's too steep and rocky for anything other than a 4x4 or motorbike. Still, I like to imagine him with grey hair, wrinkled hands gripping a leather steering wheel, head peeping over it to see out of the windscreen, offering grunts of encouragement to his little car rattling, groaning, bumping, jolting and jerking its way up the mountain.

The dotted lines in the road atlas always look innocuous, the twists and turns of reality lost in the lack of detail, the rough ground and steep gradients impossible to ascertain from a map that lacks contours or shaded relief. I had not given it much thought, knowing

ICELAND Serow Saga

that I had enough food and water for several days, but I guessed the trail would take an hour or two.

It takes most of the day to climb up alongside the waterfall, traverse the plateau, continue past a small mountain hut and descend the rockier, more barren west-facing mountainside. There's little left of the teeth on the rear sprocket by the time I reach the main road; the chain slipped once.

I follow the Ring Road east to Egilsstaðir. It's raining again, like the last time I visited, and it's set to continue. According to the forecast, the southeast is the only region that will be dry and might see the sun this weekend. I daren't push my luck riding more trails with the worn sprocket, so head south on the tarmac Ring Road in search of sunshine with as much speed as the Serow can muster.

It rains fiercely throughout the East Fjords and eases only when I reach Höfn (which sounds like 'hupf', a noise you might emit when lifting a heavy motorbike that's fallen over). The campsite in town should make a good base for a few days.

The next day I ride to the seafront to get views inland of the glacier rising up behind the town. On a park bench by the sea, I read my guidebook to see what there is to do nearby, trying to summon enthusiasm for anything other than trail-riding. It's frustrating that, now I've gained confidence in my abilities to ride any trail, my desire to ride as many trails as possible whilst in Iceland is being thwarted by the bike's deteriorating condition.

Unnur messages me. She's got my parcel of parts earlier than expected. All I want is to replace the chain and sprockets and ride back into the Highlands.

I pack up and ride back the way I'd just come through the rain. Inconceivably, the weather gets worse. I think the East Fjords lie under a perpetual raincloud. The wind gusts through the mountains down to the coast, threatening to de-road me and the bike into the soggy verge, off a cliff or under a car.

East Fjords

I pass a young guy putting up a small one-man tent on the grassy verge. His bicycle and panniers lie on the ground next to it. He's lost the battle against the wind, I think. At least he'll be dry once he's got his tent up, although I doubt he'll get much sleep with the flysheet flapping wildly.

At least I'm not on a bicycle. It's a phrase I've repeated frequently here.

Over the years, I have concluded that cycling is the best form of travel; although, with age and laziness, the motorbike is beginning to take preference: pure fun without the hard graft.

Cycling could be a good way to explore remote trails in the Highlands. It's not overly hilly once you're up there. A fat bike with oversize tyres could handle the rocky terrain and sandy sections. A significant advantage would be that a bicycle can be carried. Rivers would not pose the same difficulties or prevent progress as they do with a motorbike. However, most cyclists I've seen are riding long sections of the Ring Road. I cannot think of anything worse than, day after day, battling the strong winds that pummel the coast and contending with the dubious driving skills of many a tourist in a rented vehicle speeding along the tarmac.

I'm determined to reach Högni and Unnur's place today, driven on by the idea of not having to camp. With sodden gloves and boots, my hands and feet are painfully freezing, my tears indistinguishable from the rain running down my red cheeks. I force myself to ride past Djúpivogur where I know there are warm cafes to retreat into. Sitting indoors with coffee and cake when it's raining is like being in a hot pool when it's freezing outside. It takes a monumental strength of will to leave.

It also takes monumental powers to resist.

I don't possess them.

I stop in the next village. A pool of water forms around me on the front door mat of the cafe as I remove my waterproofs. I squelch my way to the counter, order cappuccino and a massive slice of chocolate brownie. I don't even flinch at the price, which could have got me roast dinner and a pint in a pub back home. I'm beyond caring about anything other than getting warm and dry and filling my stomach.

The rain shows no sign of easing. After much procrastination, I finally drag my sorry self out of the cafe to endure the last fifty kilometres. I turn up at the house dripping and bedraggled.

Unnur tells me that while Reykjavík has been suffering its wettest summer in a hundred years, the East Fjords have been revelling in a relatively sunny period. I find this hard to believe. Every time I come here, the weather is atrocious.

When it is wet and cold in the west, the east often enjoys glorious sunshine and vice versa. This summer, the East Fjords enjoyed a tourist boom as Icelanders living in Reykjavík followed the forecast and came here in search of sun. Any that have come today must be sorely disappointed.

The bike repairs and maintenance are a three-day battle. With the rear wheel removed, whilst my back is turned and I'm crouched down looking for a ten-millimetre spanner in my tool kit, the Serow takes the opportunity to leap off the bike stand and body-slam me like a pro-wrestler. I crawl out from underneath with a scratch and bruised shoulder. I put the bike back in its place and tie it up with rope from the girder.

I replace the broken spokes on the rear wheel, deflating the tyre first to ease slotting the new spokes into the existing nipples in the rim. Then I fit the new rear sprocket, replace the wheel on the bike, fit the new front sprocket and chain, then tension the spokes. Replacing the blown headlight bulb is quick and easy.

A lot of the front wheel's spokes are also loose and need tightening. Whilst I'm raising the front end to lift the tyre clear of the ground, the bike haemorrhages oil onto the floor. I quickly grab a rag and stuff it below the airbox to stem the bleed, then mop up the mess.

East Fjords

So that's where the oil has been going! It's worthy of a place at Akureyri's motorcycle museum now.

Remembering I'd deflated the rear tyre, I begin pumping it up, a laborious process with a bicycle pump. It's taking longer than usual. I check the pressure; the gauge tells me it's not inflating. *Damn you.*

Must be a puncture. *How is that even possible?*

It's not a puncture.

The valve has detached from the inner tube. Fortunately, I've got spare tubes. I sometimes wonder whether it's worth carrying all the tools and replacement parts; they take up a lot of space and weight. But I'd rather carry them and not to need them than the other way around. My load is now one inner tube lighter. I can't get the tyre seated on the rim properly but should be able to by using an air compressor at the local garage. The last thing I do is an oil and filter change.

Finally, the bike is good to go – as good as it's going to get. The slightly loose steering due to worn headset bearings and the oil leak due to a worn piston ring are getting worse. The tyres are beginning to look very worn. With only three weeks left, we'll soldier on. There's plenty of time to make a shortened loop via Kjölur in the Highlands and return along the southeast coast, both regions I've not yet explored.

It's still raining, the hills obscured in low fog. The weather app, though, tells me the whole of Iceland is bathing in sunshine and will be for forty-eight hours. I need to get out of this fjord. Sure enough, there's blue sky in the Highlands.

I ride towards Snæfell, make a loop around the western side, then take the dead-end trail past the snowy peak to the edge of the glacier. The trails are fun, the scenery stunning. It's nothing new; I've been spoilt by having spent the summer in the country. I ride fast; the bike can handle it now.

ICELAND Serow Saga

Driven by the desire to ride as many Highland trails as possible, I want to attempt the jeep track that skirts the northern edge of Vatnajökull tomorrow. I suspect it'll be a long day. The closer I can get this evening, the better. I aim for the campsite at Askja, which is en route, judging that I should get there before dark if I don't hang about.

The sun begins to set, with Herðubreið silhouetted against the orange sky. Standing isolated, she is like a guardian protecting all those venturing into the Highlands. She beckons me, Ride!

As the light fades, I tire. My eyes strain to make out the bumps and rocks in the road. I'm mesmerised by the twinkling stars in the sky. They are like a million friends, always with me on my travels, keeping watch through the night.

At the last junction, I lose concentration and don't straighten the bike in time. The front end jams against a chunk of lava and the wheel beds into the sand. The bike topples over. It's no big deal. I pick it up and ride on. Not far to go now.

There are plenty of tents at the campsite but not a soul stirs. Only the stars in the night sky see me arrive. After a midnight dinner of noodles, I crawl into my sleeping bag wearing several layers. It's much colder now, mid-August.

I'm reading *Letters from Iceland* by W. H. Auden. In it, he says that his excitement at trying new things tended to make him think he was better at them than he actually was.

Having ridden with so few people, I have few comparisons by which to gauge my riding abilities. The side of me that's easily swamped by self-doubt questions whether I'm making this ride into something more than it is. In my limited experience of trail riding and river crossings, this trip has been a bigger adventure in my head than the reality. I'm not conquering a mountain, real or metaphorical, nor breaking any records. A more experienced rider may not have paused for thought along any of the routes I've taken. But that is not the point. Adventure is not absolute.

East Fjords

I've been pushing my boundaries; what matters is where they lie relative to my comfort zone, which has expanded with each river I've crossed that was deeper or faster flowing than the last and each trail that's been rougher than those before it. One person's walk in the park is another's great exploration. No experience is more or less valid than another. What's important is what we learn from it and what we can pass on to others.

On the whole, this is not a perilous journey, merely one long holiday. That's OK. I no longer feel any need to prove myself. I've tested my limits of endurance, both mental and physical, in the past. As I grow older, the risks I'm prepared to take have reduced. Adventure and danger, though, have a way of appearing when it's least expected …

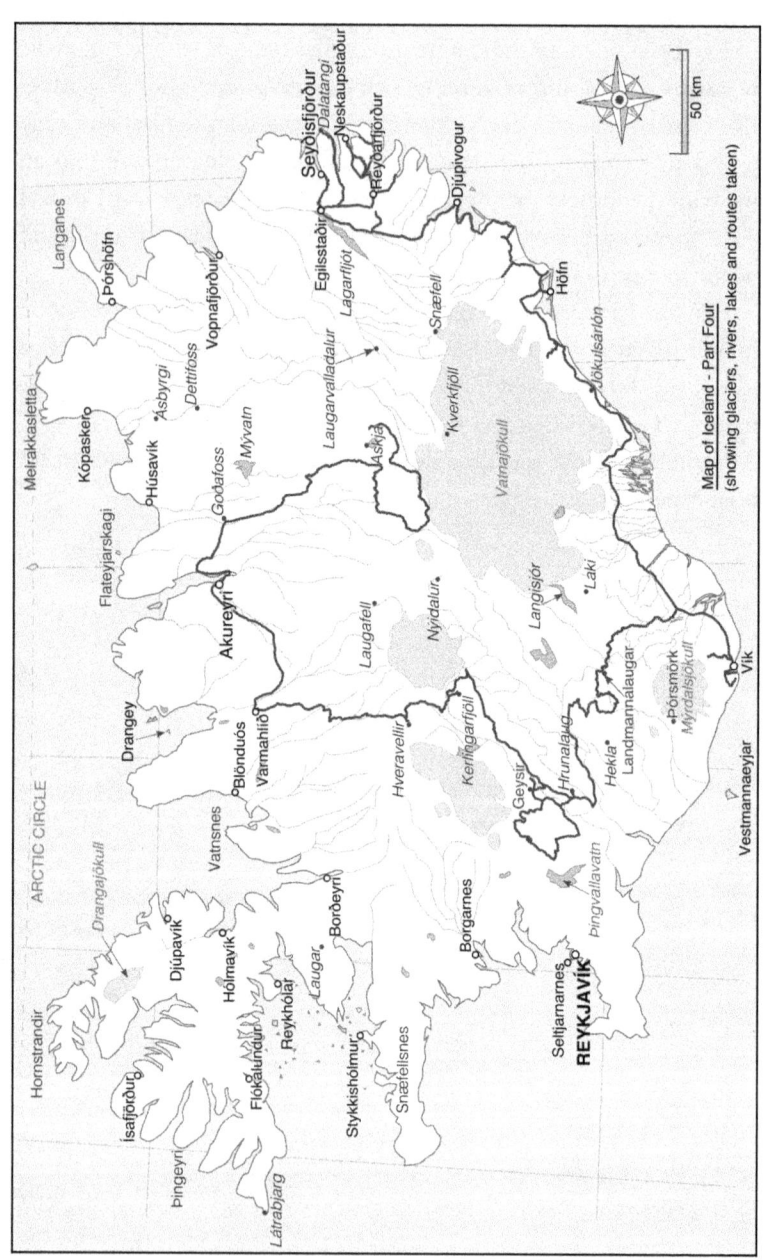

ICELAND
-
Part Four

Hini, his DRZ400 and my Serow.

Jökulsárlón glacial lagoon.

20

In Deep Water
Highlands

The pages I've torn out of the road atlas are spread out over the picnic bench. They're well-worn and crumpled with watermarks around the edges from the rain running into my tank bag where the plastic cover has split. I'm drinking my morning coffee, perusing the map, when a ranger approaches. I know the routine, having stayed here before. He asks me where I'm going. I show him my planned route for the day.

'That southern route nearest the glacier is very rough,' he informs me.

I feel confident enough in my abilities now and, most importantly, my judgement. No routes are too intimidating.

'That's what I'm looking for,' I reply with a grin.

I detect a brief flash behind his eyes. I can't tell whether it's a conspiratorial acknowledgement or a seen-it-all-before look because he thinks I'm a foolhardy tourist with big ideas and no clue of the dangers.

'You won't have any major rivers to cross, but there's a very sandy section here …'. The ranger points on the map to Austurleið (F910), south of Askja.

I'm undeterred. My only concern is that I could burn out the clutch. It's one of the few things that hasn't been a problem. The original clutch plates wore out at 50,000 kilometres. By that gauge, this current set should be fine, but Iceland is proving tough on the little bike. *Please hold out.*

'That track parallel to the Sprengisandur route is not well-marked or patrolled. You would be better to take the road past Askja towards Mývatn.'

ICELAND Serow Saga

'I rode a lot of that the other day, although I turned onto Vikrafellsleið.'

'Really?'

'Yeah, it was awesome,' I reply enthusiastically.

'What, this track?' he asks with disbelief, again pointing to the map.

'Yeah!'

'In that case, you should be fine,' he replies. 'I'm sure you're aware of not driving off-road.'

Of course I am. Just as every tourist you pass in the Highlands will enquire how deep the rivers are, so every Icelander will mention that driving off-road is illegal and unacceptable, because the land is extremely fragile. Whilst a tourist may only pass through momentarily, their footprints last a lifetime. We're on the same side when it comes to protecting the environment.

'Yes,' I reply.

'In case you're not completely clear about what off-road driving means …'. The ranger pulls out a laminated sheet of paper with diagrams on. It reminds me of when I first learnt to drive a car and my instructor showed me a step-by-step guide to parallel parking.

'I'm very clear,' I interrupt.

'Nonetheless, just to be sure …'.

I listen patiently as the ranger points at each diagram of a car, with tracks and arrows showing where the car must not go as though the big red crosses need translating. I had thought that volunteering as a ranger must be a fantastic way to spend the summer surrounded by nature. All jobs have a less desirable aspect; I guess this is it.

'As you're with a motorcycle, make sure you stay in one of the tracks. Don't ride between them or take the harder ground on either side; that's off-road and not allowed.'

'OK,' I reply, although I'm uncertain how he expects vehicles coming from opposite directions to pass if they aren't legally allowed out of the single-lane tracks. I keep quiet.

Highlands

'If you're interested, there's a free guided tour at the Holuhraun lava field at ten o'clock.'

'Um ... Er ...' I stutter. I'm lost for words, confused by the concept of time. It's irrelevant to me out here. I have no idea of the date or day of the week.

My day is not split into clockwork hours but divided unevenly from sunrise to sunset by when I wake, eat and sleep. Even this vague routine has vanished in Iceland where, until recently, there had been almost continual daylight. Instead, my days are dictated by wind and rain. The weather forecast is my clock.

Einar had mentioned this lava field, although I can't remember why it was of special interest. Not one to miss out on a freebie and always interested to learn about something new, I'd like to go.

'What time is it now? And where is Holuhraun?' I ask, attempting the correct pronunciation, but no doubt failing with the H's jammed in the back of my throat.

'It's nine now. It begins at a parking area on your route about thirty minutes away.'

I hate commitment. Besides, I'm enjoying my coffee in the sun and don't want to rush. If I happen to pass at the right time, I'll stop. The ranger leaves me to give his pep talk to the next group of campers.

I gulp the last of my camp coffee. The instant my mug touches the wooden bench, I'm ripped from my steady state of relaxed contentment and calm to running in top gear with not a moment to lose while the sun is shining.

I wash me, wash up, pack away the tent and quickly load my bags onto the bike. Then I ride out of the camp and onto new trails. I'm carefree and happy and living right in the moment, looking forward only as far as the trail I can see. Two 4x4s in the distance are visible by the dust clouds they are kicking up. Sand.

I expect the worst. I expect to be slipping and sliding, inching along in first gear, rear wheel spinning, clutch burning. But the feeling of

ICELAND Serow Saga

exhausted elation when I make it through means I'd do it all again in an instant. Those are the days I live for, when I feel truly alive with my senses sharpened to a knifepoint.

I race along, catch up the 4x4s and overtake when they pull over. The trail changes direction to head west with the sun on my back and Askja's crater edge filling the horizon on my right. I'm in the left-hand rut of the track with no option but to go where it does.

I've no idea what the best technique is for riding in sand except to go fast. But my Serow doesn't go fast. I'm not sure I have the nerve anyway. I brace, gripping the sides of the bike with my knees. With stomach muscles tensed and white knuckles, my arms strain to keep the front end going forward. When the burning in my arms is too much to bear, I ease off and stop where the track is firmer.

The 4x4s are far behind, struggling or driving more cautiously than me. After a few more kilometres, I reach the parking bay, which is marked out with lava rocks to prevent people from driving beyond. It's five to ten, perfect timing for the ranger's talk.

One couple is already waiting. They're from Australia, retired and spend half the year travelling at home and half the year touring in Europe in their 4x4 camper. Once their children left home, there was nothing to tie them to where they lived; now they travel and love it. Their faces have a weathered look, their bodies tanned from years of sun exposure, which they obviously didn't get in Iceland. The guy has a straggly beard. The woman's long, wavy grey hair has not been cut for years and is tied back in a ponytail. They look amazing and have a zest for life that is infectious. I hope to be like that when I reach their age. You don't have to settle down and make roots, not these days, they tell me. We are kindred spirits. I wish Ásgeir could hear their views. We debate over who last bought new clothes. They can't remember when they last went shopping for anything other than groceries.

Highlands

Once the other vehicles arrive, the ranger gives an introductory speech and leads us into the lava field following a line of marker posts.

On 29 August 2014, a vein of lava began to flow north towards Askja from the Bárðarbunga volcano, which lies under Vatnajökull. There were fears that an eruption would occur below the glacier, resulting in ash clouds like those from Eyjafjallajökull that disrupted air travel in 2010. Instead, a fissure opened through the surface of the Holuhraun lava field, which was created during an eruption in 1787. Within three months, the amount of new lava covering the old was greater than that released during the devastating Laki eruption. The lava flow ended in 2015 with no human deaths, mainly due to the remote location.

At the edge of the lava field, marker posts protrude a few inches out of the sand; further in where the lava is still exposed, they stand well above knee height.

'The posts were all put in at the same time to a similar height,' the ranger explains. 'Those short ones show how much sand has covered the ground in the subsequent three years. The area beyond the road, although it's barely visible beneath the sand, is also part of the original lava field. Eventually, this new lava we're standing on will also be covered.'

I remember the harmattan winds in Mali that create a smog each year, the Saharan sand getting lifted into the stratosphere, carried halfway around the world and dumped as far away as North America. This land is not static, but constantly reshaping and re-forming, fluid like a river rather than one solid piece of earth.

After the tour, the 4x4s return towards Askja, and I continue. The bike floats across the hard-packed sand as effortlessly as a cloud in the sky. Silvery veins of glacial water spread out across it. At this time of the day, it's little more than surface water. I slow momentarily at each series of channels, assess that they are safe to cross and speed up through them.

Then the trail rises over undulating land of rough lava rocks. Where lava flowed from a shield volcano, it has cooled into a smoother layer of concertinaed ripples like the surface of a beaten egg white. The route is identifiable only by marker posts.

I descend into the next wide open, black sand plain. The water streaming across it resembles a delta at the mouth of a river, not what would be expected near the source. As I near the water, I ease off, kick down a gear, then give some gas and ride on through. The next liquid web is bigger, the water murkier and flowing faster as the midday sun continues to melt the ice with relentless vigour. Still, these are tiny compared to the rivers I've crossed before. Importantly, I can see the sandy bottom. They're not deep. *Nothing to worry about.*

I enter the widest stream and aim for where the trail emerges onto dry land. Suddenly the bike plunges into a pit of quicksand, dropping like a cartoon character off a cliff.

The engine cuts out.

Shit!

Steam rises with a hiss as the cold water hits the engine. I pull out the kick-start lever and stamp down. It fires up the first time. The wheels have sunk enough into the sand that standing flatfooted I'm clear of the saddle. I keep my weight off the bike and inch along in first gear, the engine squealing, back tyre spinning. Then the front wheel jams against a submerged bank. The back wheel spins and digs deeper into the loose sand.

Quick, cut the engine!

There are bare millimetres of clearance between the water level and both the air intake and exhaust. I urgently need to lift it before the bike sinks or the water level rises. I unstrap the bags and carry them to dry land, stumbling as I step from the compacted bed into another pit of quicksand. Then I plunge back into the water and,

Highlands

with all my strength, I pull and yank at the rear rack until the sand loosens its vice-like grip and releases the rear wheel.

In first gear, I push alongside the bike. Slowly, we move forward. *Gently does it ...*

Oh Shit!

The bike topples onto me as my legs sink, trapping them at an angle. I brace against the bike to keep my upper body above water. My heart is racing uncontrollably, pounding with fear at the sudden danger I'm in.

A thousand thoughts rush through my head. Might we sink further into the sand until swallowed whole? *Can that actually happen or is it just in the movies?!* How fast and far will the water level rise? *I suspect not much.* When will another vehicle come this way for help? *That could be hours or days away. You're on your own. You have to get yourself out.* How long can I hold the bike up and keep my body out of the water? *Not that long and, yes, that means you could drown. Then get your legs free.*

I manage to drag my left foot out onto the firmer bed so that I'm in a stable position without risk of being submerged. With my right leg still stuck under the bike, I can't get the leverage to lift it off me. I ignore my instinct to pull myself out first. I must try not to let the bike fall into the water. I'm not sure I have the strength to push or drag it through sand without the aid of the engine.

This whole stream crossing had seemed so trivial, I hadn't even bothered to put my camera in its waterproof bag within the tank bag. If I drop the bike now, my camera gear and phone will also be destroyed, the photos lost. And there's an open packet of chocolate Hobnobs that'll be ruined. No, I have to keep the bike out of the water.

I twist my body around until it feels as though my knee joint is going to snap. The muscles in my back strain as I stretch them further than they've ever gone before. I fumble for a secure grip on the rack, then push hard. The bike rises a couple of inches. I want to let go.

ICELAND Serow Saga

The burning muscles and my knee are screaming at me to stop. But every attempt will make me weaker. It's now or never.

With every ounce of energy and strength, I push, ignoring my screaming body. Gradually the bike rises, the centre of gravity shifts. It's no longer weighing me down. I push it upright, then get my other leg free from the sand.

Catastrophe averted, my bike now stands like a faithful dog at heel, not the bastard that just tried to drown me.

With the next push, I get the bike onto solid, dry land. There's no lasting damage. I'm not injured, only drenched from the crotch down with boots and jeans covered in fine, ash-like sand, dripping like a half-drowned rat. But the sun's out. I'll dry.

As the adrenalin subsides, I become acutely aware of how hungry I am. I've not eaten since breakfast. I unzip the tank bag, quickly check the camera is not wet, then grab the pack of chocolate biscuits. I'm usually able to devour one after the other without pausing for breath, but with the first bite, a sickly feeling in my stomach replaces the gnawing hunger. I chew laboriously and swallow.

It's my subconscious: *You were damn lucky.* As though I were not already well aware. Had it not been for my drive to save the Hobnobs from drowning, I might still be trapped. Fortunately, my bike's not heavy or the outcome could have been different.

I need to put some distance between me and the river. Riding is a good way to clear thoughts. Having the trail, which is now arid and rocky, to concentrate on is the best thing for me. I see a speck moving in the distance. It's a hiker. Surprised to see anyone out here, let alone someone travelling on foot, I stop. Perhaps I wouldn't have had to wait so long for help after all.

The first thing he asks is, 'Is there water nearby?'

I stifle a laugh. 'Very close.'

He follows my gaze as I look down at my jeans, which are dripping. Pools of water squelch in my boots whenever I wriggle my toes.

'Oh,' he says.

Highlands

I stop further on where pillars of lava tower up from the high ground. I strip off and wring out my socks and jeans, then hang them to dry. The Highland plain is spread out below me to the horizon like a sea. It appears flat from a distance, but the lava terrain is like choppy water breaking the surface. This beautiful vista is much easier to take in than the cheese sandwich I force down.

I'm not far from where I had turned off the Sprengisandur route (F26) a couple of weeks before and tried to take Austurleið (F910) from the opposite direction. I made the right choice to turn back at the river crossing then. Out here I've only myself to rely on. There's no phone signal to call for rescue. I know the risks and consequences. Complacency was my near downfall today.

I hit my regular post-lunch afternoon low. At the junction for the remote trail north, I'm overcome with tiredness, unable to think clearly and make decisions. Should I attempt this trail, which the ranger advised against, or take the regular route to Mývatn?

A Land Cruiser trundles towards me. The German driver tells me it took him five hours to travel a hundred kilometres. The trail was often impossible to see. He spent much time walking to a high point to scout out the route. He met no one. The question is, do I try it in my tired state?

Tiredness is as dangerous as complacency. It also drains me of energy and my appetite for adventure. After my earlier river escapade, I'm more risk-averse than usual. My heart isn't in it. Although I don't need to, I start arming myself with excuses for taking the easy trail out. I take a cursory look at the rear wheel, as I do repeatedly each day, to check that the spokes are intact.

Not again! A broken spoke.

I take it as a sign. *Don't push your luck.*

The road back is great fun. The lava formations and rock protrusions in the landscape look like a scene from a Wild West movie. I'm riding through the badlands, wary of bandits or an ambush. I've nothing to fear on this trail except another broken spoke. At the western edge of the Dyngjufjöll mountains, I turn north. Behind me, the snow-covered Queen of the Mountains is shining brilliantly, keeping watch.

At sunset I put up my tent beside the track in fertile grasslands before reaching the first farms near the Ring Road. I can feel the drag of civilisation pulling me in. I want to turn around and escape again. If I replace the broken spoke here, I won't need to go into town.

I decide to do the repairs in the morning. I have my walking pole that doubles as a bike stand to lift the wheel off the ground. It's not very secure but will work if needed. I can use the ring spanner end of the tyre lever for extra torque with my small socket wrench to remove the sprocket bolts, and I have a small unopened tube of Loctite for replacing them afterwards. I crouch down at the rear wheel as I ponder my plan of action.

Oh no! Two broken spokes.

The black flies that plague Mývatn appear, making straight for my eyes and getting caught in my hair. I wave my hand across my face in irritation and retreat into the tent. My resolve wavers. If I go to Akureyri tomorrow, I can replace the spokes at the workshop like last time and pick up more spares from the cycle shop too. At this rate, I'll be needing them.

This will be my third visit to Akureyri. Each time, I've had to make repairs to the bike and order parts: sheared bolts, broken spokes, new chain and sprocket, now more broken spokes. It's as though the town is cursed. I like Akureyri, but I hope I don't have to visit again after this.

The tracks through the grassy plains join up with a good, graded road. I cruise at eighty kilometres per hour; it feels like I'm flying. I slow down only when I see horses trotting along the verge, rounded up to be taken back to the farm. Safe in their herd, none pay me any attention or shy at the noise of the bike.

Highlands

I see a 4x4 parked at the roadside. Two young Asian women with mobile phones in their hands stand watching a guy who's crouched down, attacking the front near-side wheel with a large socket wrench. The tyre is shredded. I stop to ask if they need help. There's not much I can do except ride to Goðafoss on the Ring Road to summon help. Besides, there's a phone signal here, and they have a spare tyre anyway. From Hong Kong, they are on holiday for a week and are on their way to Akureyri too. The town *is* cursed.

21

Company on the Trails
Kjölur

'How many do you want?' the old man asks in the cycle shop.

'Four, I guess.' I pick up the tied bundle of spokes and pull out a couple, checking them against the length of one of my spares. I'll have to bend, cut and file them again.

'Actually, make that eight.' Eight might be excessive, but I don't want to have to return to Akureyri *again*. The old man looks at me in surprised silence.

Then I go to the supermarket and stock up on food. I don't want any reason to linger in town once I've fixed the bike. When I return to the car park, I notice a pool of liquid on the ground by the front wheel. Oil.

What is it with my bike and this town!

The minor leak from the left front fork seal has turned into a torrent. There can't be any oil left to leak. From the stains around the right fork, it's going the same way. I call a couple of bike shops, then the Yamaha dealer for spare seals. It would take a week to get the parts and would mean detouring to Reykjavík. With only a couple of weeks left of the trip; it doesn't seem worth it. We'll limp on.

For now, I need to get out of Akureyri. It has mystical powers that cause my bike to fall apart while in its forcefield. Although, by this point, there's not much intact bike remaining to break.

I've become very efficient at removing the rear wheel and sprocket, replacing spokes and refitting it all together again. I'm soon on my way, riding the busy Ring Road west towards the start of the Kjölur route (F35), another ancient road roughly parallel to the Sprengisandur route (F26).

Kjölur

The clouds are building, the sun disappearing, my motivation waning and petrol running low. I pull over at the fuel station in Varmahlíð. There are several bikes parked in the forecourt, a couple of cruisers with polished chrome next to a line of big BMW GS1200 bikes with German plates. Most bikes I have seen have been parked up at fuel stations and supermarket car parks. I've only come across a handful of motorbikes on trails or in the Highlands.

I park in a space next to the one bike that looks different from the rest. I nod a greeting to the guy rummaging around in his tank bag. He pulls out a map and looks up, casually brushing his sun-bleached hair out of his eyes.

'Which way are you going?' I ask with feigned confidence, ignoring the thought that this tall, fit guy with a surfer's look is too cool to be bothered talking with me.

'I will take the F35,' he replies. 'And you?'

'I think I'll go a similar direction, but take a different trail. I think the Kjölur route, the F35, has been improved and is an easy ride now.'

'Perhaps we can ride together for one or two days,' he suggests. *Steady on; I don't know you.*

'My name's Hinrich.' He adds, as though hearing my thought. 'Call me Hini. Sorry, my English is not good; I'm from Germany. Nice to meet you.'

'Helen. You too.'

I have become appreciative of the freedom to stop whenever I want and ride as long into the evening as the sunlight allows. I have accepted my and the bike's limitations and adapted accordingly. There are rivers I won't attempt to cross alone; occasionally, there's a hill too steep and rough to ascend. Whereas I'd initially been worried about riding alone in the Highlands, I'm now confident enough to enjoy the responsibility of it. This is how I travelled in the past, whether back-packing, hiking or cycling alone. Being on a motorbike shouldn't change my fundamental approach. It has just taken a while to remember since being single again.

But, for me, travelling is not only about the countries I visit, their histories and landscapes. It's about the people I meet, locals and tourists alike. I'd get bored of travelling if my routine were the same every day. Whereas I might start the day expecting one thing, it can turn into something different, usually better, following a chance encounter with someone. Sometimes an experience is not so wonderful, but that is the risk you take for a life full of great memories.

A conversation I had with Unnur two days ago pops into my head. I'd been telling her about Birgir's invitation to a barbecue and subsequent offer to stay at their summer house.

'You always say yes, don't you?' Unnur commented.

'I guess so,' I replied after a moment of thought, remembering the many people I'd met and rich tales I'd heard as a result of accepting an offer during my travels.

'It's good,' Unnur added with a far-off stare. I imagined she was recalling stories from her own travels. I spent hours chatting with Unnur. It was refreshing to talk with someone who contemplated life and tried to make sense of their experiences, not simply rush from one moment to the next without thought. She's right, it is good to say yes.

If I ride on alone this evening, I can predict now how the next few days will pan out. They'll be fun, but more of the same. On the other hand, if I ride with Hini, I've no idea what might happen. Perhaps, I think selfishly, I'll be able to ride some routes I would not otherwise. With each other for backup, we can attempt rivers I wouldn't dare alone; although, if he doesn't have any off-road experience this probably isn't sensible.

I look him up and down, trying to make a quick judgement on the type of rider and traveller he is. His matching bike gear looks new. He has a DRZ400, a dual sport bike similar to but more powerful

Kjölur

than my Serow. It's clean. The chunky off-road tyres have little wear. My initial impression is that he is a nice guy, but not much of a biker. Perhaps he's ridden for years, but only on sunny Sundays to a cafe or beach down the road and has seen something in a magazine or on TV luring him to Iceland.

My assumptions are, of course, completely baseless. After all, I know nothing about him except his name. I ask about his trip. He's got two weeks. He lays out his map over his bike and points out the route he took to get here from the East Fjords. He rode through the Highlands via Askja. It seems I might have been wrong.

There is nothing in his outward appearance or the short conversation we've had to suggest he's a murderous psychopath, narcissistic bore, or has any other less severe but unappealing personality traits. He seems like a nice guy. I reckon I can trust him. Better still, he has a sense of humour and a happy outlook on life.

I show him the tracks I'm thinking of taking.

'If you still want, let's ride together,' I say. There is no good reason not to. If it doesn't work out, we can go our separate ways; neither of us is under any obligation to the other. In the worst case, I can ditch him, pack and ride off in the middle of the night while he sleeps. That would be a coward's way out, but it's always good to have an escape plan.

'I think the weather's going to turn after today, so I was going to ride until late this evening,' I say.

'That's fine by me,' Hini replies. 'I'll follow you.'

Ugh, do I have to lead? Suddenly I'm filled with doubts about my abilities. *What if he's a professional motocross rider? What if I'm too slow?* Perhaps he's filled with the same insecurities as me.

Once we're ready to leave, Hini says, 'Can you give me a push to bump start my bike? I think I've drained the battery by leaving the GPS on.'

Oh no, this is not a good start. 'Sure,' I reply with a smile.

ICELAND Serow Saga

He wheels the bike to the highest point on the forecourt. I give him a running push. The engine thumps into action. He heads towards the exit and grins back at me. *I hope that's not the reason he wanted to ride with me!*

I hop on my bike and kick-start it, thankful I have that option. We set off inland on rural farm roads between golden fields. Gradually we rise towards a distinctive cone-shaped hill. It's bathed in a soft glow that warms me on the inside. *I'm so lucky to be here, riding on this lovely evening* ... Suddenly I notice that the road ahead makes an abrupt ninety-degree turn. I slam on the brakes and grind to a halt, not daring to take the bend with the loose surface dirt. It would be rather embarrassing to crash into the hedge.

Hini takes the corner, slowing to check I'm OK, then accelerates away. I set off again, following him. The road narrows as it turns up the valley. When the sheep hear the bikes, they stop grazing and dart and leap in front of us as we approach. I'm beginning to think they are homicidal rather than suicidal. I'm more used to Welsh sheep grazing the verges, oblivious to traffic. They usually stay where they are.

The trail plateaus out. We stop to negotiate a gate, then continue riding. My long shadow ripples over the tussocky land. It isn't far to Hveravellir, the hot pools where the outlaw Eyvindur spent time hiding out. The prospect of a midnight soak after another long day is appealing.

We come to a glacial river, the milky grey waters flowing fast over the rocky bed. Hini walks across first. I don't want to attempt this river without having tested the route on foot for large rocks; so, I roll up my jeans and wade in too. It's deep; water pours over the tops of my boots. Having dry feet was too good to be true. Like the sun, it's a rare phenomenon in Iceland. I never expect either to last long.

'I think we should camp here. It's not a good idea trying to cross now in case we have a problem. It's late already; the daylight is going,' Hini comments.

Kjölur

'Agreed.' I thought the same thing once I let sense and reason take over from my disappointment that we won't reach the hot pool tonight. 'The river ought to be shallower in the morning.'

Having had ample practice, my tent is up and gear organised inside well before his. Hini extolls the virtues of his various pieces of equipment while unpacking. He works at a motorcycle store and has clothing and gear from them in return for providing reviews and an article for their magazine. As with Leo the hiker, I am envious of Hini's kit and amazed by the sheer quantity he has on his bike. It looks like he's travelling light, but he takes out one thing after another. Then, like a magician pulling a rabbit out of a hat, he makes a chair appear.

'Where the hell did that come from?' I exclaim.

'Here, you use it,' Hini offers as he clicks the foldable legs into place and attaches the canvas seat.

'Oh, no, I can't possibly. You need it,' I say. 'Besides, I have my seat here.' I wander over to a flattish rock beside my tent and perch my backside on it. 'It's amazing really, I always find my seat waiting for me at the next campsite. It's even better than yours; I don't have to carry mine with me.'

Hini laughs. 'When you get to my age, you need something softer.'

Hini is not old, although older than I realise. But age is immaterial; it's only a number. Some days my body aches like an old woman and yet my mind is as youthful as a teenager. What matters is that we're both here, riding bikes in Iceland and sleeping on the floor in tents beside the river. I'd say that puts us at about the same age.

We sit on our respective chairs and cook dinner. Hini is saving space and weight on his food. He has small packets of instant noodles for dinner and instant porridge for breakfast. I'm carrying enough fresh fruit and vegetables to eat well for at least five days. I didn't want to come into the Highlands and be forced to leave because I was low on food. I offer Hini some of my supplies, but he only takes a square of chocolate.

The river is lower in the morning. We're both confident that we can cross it now. Erring on the side of caution, we unload our bags.

'I will take off my trousers and boots and wear my kayaking shoes I brought with me to carry my bags over. I'll take yours too. That way everyone stays dry.'

It would be quicker if I portage the gear over. I needn't bother undressing; my boots are still soaking from yesterday. But Hini insists. I concede; it matters little. If he wants to strip down to his boxers and show off his legs, that's fine by me.

Less than two kilometres further down the trail, there is a much wider, deeper, faster-flowing river. We might have to backtrack after all. We stop to open the post and wire gate at the top of the riverbank.

With fortuitous timing, a black Hummer approaches the river from the far side, pauses momentarily, then delves in, water splashing up the doors and body swaying from side to side as the wheels lurch over submerged obstacles, axles rolling independently.

Oh, that looks too deep. We look at each other, silently communicating our fear but not daring to say it out loud.

'One way to find out,' I say.

We ride down to the river to check the depth on foot. Hini loses no time in changing into his kayaking shoes and stripping down to his boxers again. Thankfully, he doesn't prefer a tight budgie-smuggler thong.

The driver and his friend say they'll wait until we're safe on the other side. I think it's a genuine offer, rather than wanting to check out Hini's muscular thighs.

'You stay here and keep your feet dry,' Hini orders. I think my comment that my feet can't get any wetter has been lost in translation.

Kjölur

He scouts the best route. 'What do you think?' Hini asks when he returns. 'The first part is the worst.'

Neither of us is confident; we both waver with uncertainty like fully fledged chicks contemplating our maiden flight. If I were alone, I wouldn't attempt it. With two, we can help each other, and the consequences of dropping the bike are less concerning. I want to try, but I don't want to be to blamed for the decision if it goes wrong.

'I'll cross it if you do. I'll take this bike anywhere if I've seen another one go first. The decision's yours,' I say helpfully.

It's clear by now that Hini is a far better rider than me and more experienced; I consider it reasonable, unfairly perhaps, that he goes first.

'Thanks,' Hini replies with a smile oozing sarcasm. 'So it's up to me?'

'Yep,' I beam back, almost as amused as if he had been wearing a thong.

I can see my fears about blame mirrored in Hini's eyes, although I can't imagine him ever blaming me. He's not that kind of guy.

'If you're happy to try, we can unload the bags, and I'll walk alongside you. We'll do it together,' I suggest. We are in this together.

I've got my thermal leggings on, so take off my jeans, which are more or less dry. With bags unloaded, Hini walks with his bike in first gear. I go on the other side, one hand at the rear to steady it if needed. It's much deeper than I expected, but we get across.

With his bike safely on the far side, we return for mine. I prefer to sit on the Serow and ride. With its low seat height, I can easily put my feet down for balance if the bike hits any rocks. I fight against the current pushing hard into the bike in the deepest section. There's a brief respite in the middle where the water is shallower over a gravel bank. The second half is easier. Soon I'm on the other side. *We made it!*

ICELAND Serow Saga

We're both grinning uncontrollably. In the spur of the moment, we high-five and are so happy we don't care that no one, except children and Americans, ever does that.

The hummer driver had offered to bring our bags and helmets over. He delivers them, the hummer making light work of the river.

I drain the water from my boots. Again. My jeans might be dry but my thermals are dripping.

We ride on. Five minutes later it starts raining. *Oh, come off it!*

After another fifteen minutes, we arrive at Hveravellir. Finally, we can take a dip in the hot pool. Being hot and wet will make a pleasant change from cold and wet.

22

Mountains of Colour
Kerlingarfjöll and Landmannalaugar

After a tense Houdini-like struggle and much swearing in the tiny toilet cubicle next to the cafe, I emerge, victorious, with my bikini on under my bike gear. I traipse over to the hot pool at the opposite end of the car park and strip off my layers again.

A stream flows down a gentle rocky slope, boiling and sulphurous, crystallised white at the edges where it has dried up. I'm fixated by the milky blue pool with clouds of steam swirling above it. I carefully step into the pool with the other red-faced tourists.

I exhale loudly as the hot water envelops me. *This is what a hot pool is meant to be like!* After five minutes, I have an overwhelming urge to jump into a pool of invigoratingly cold water. It's not a comfortable bath that you can lie in forever, getting sleepy.

There are two pipes sending water into the pool from opposite ends. Most people are congregated nearer the one. I edge closer to the other. There's a definite temperature gradient. I stupidly stick out my hand towards the pipe and immediately retract it. The water is scorching.

It's too hot to stay submerged for long. As more people leave, I move nearer to the other pipe and revel in the cold water gushing from it. First, I splash it over my arms. Then I forget all pretences of sharing this refreshing area with anyone and sit right next to it. The cold water runs over my shoulders and down my back. I edge away for a few minutes, get all hot and breathless and dive back to the cold pipe. With legs stretched out into the centre of the pool, my feet are roasting and my head is cool. It's blissful.

Hini is sitting on the side of the pool dangling his legs in the water. The situation could only be improved with an ice-cold beer in my hand. Hini agrees. Being immersed in water has also whetted our appetites. I'm ravenous.

Parboiled and hungry, we get out. I step carefully over the rocks, dripping to the bench where I left my gear. I squeeze my wet feet into my sodden boots until they're suctioned on fast. It'll be a fight to get them off again. I grab my towel and wrap it round me like a sarong. Then I stomp across the car park to the toilet and shower block to change. I am not surprised by the odd looks other people give me. I look ridiculous. The bikini, towel and bike boots combination is never going to catch on as a fashion statement. Why they didn't think to put the ablutions block next to the pool, I don't know.

'This place was not designed by Germans,' Hini jokes, arms overflowing with bike clothing.

Before entering the cafe, we remove our boots. In the entrance hall, the walls are hidden behind a multicoloured drapery of waterproofs. The floor is scattered with boots and shoes of all shapes and sizes, like the entrance to a mosque at prayer time. There's barely space for the two of us to stand. When someone else tries to enter, the door squashes Hini into the wall like a swatted fly. I hop backwards into the main hall, still wrestling to remove my suctioned boot. *This place was definitely not designed by Germans.*

We order a liquid lunch, each item with its merits but entirely non-complementary. We drink beer because we have been talking about how it would have tasted so refreshingly good while sweating in the hot pool. We eat a hearty soup because it's the most affordable yet filling food. We end the meal with coffee because we're in Iceland, everyone drinks coffee, and there are free refills.

The wall behind the counter with the coffee and hot water dispensers is covered with a collage of maps from around the world. While Hini pours another mugful, I peruse Ireland, Australia, Sweden, West Africa, India, South America, Britain. Places I've been, places I want to visit. Then we take seats at the other end of the cafe in front of the full frame windows giving a good view of a wet, cold and grey

Kerlingarfjöll and Landmannalaugar

Iceland that I've no interest in exploring right now. The Highlands is a bleak place in foul weather.

Hini is not deterred by the blanket fog or rain. He only has two weeks and must make every day count. We ride on towards Kerlingarfjöll, clueless as to what we'll find because Hini had not planned on coming this way and I've not planned much at all. It's a case of the blind leading the blind. In the thick cloud and with raindrops smeared across my visor, it's difficult to see much besides the potholed trail ahead. We come to a large building, several smaller huts and a campsite. Hini is convinced there'll be a cafe here. First, we ride the few remaining kilometres up into the mountains to the end of the trail.

The clouds lift to reveal striking orange, snow-capped mountains with steaming vents. There's a footpath down the mountainside. I walk it, careful not to slip on the slick clay. Hini's boots have no grip though, and he's forced to turn back. It's warmer in the valley bottom, sheltered from the wind and heated by the steam coming from the rust-coloured ground. Iceland's landscape is often described as lunar; this seems more like Mars.

Close to the bubbling mud pools, a noxious stench of sulphur fills the air. I quickly pull up my neck-scarf over my nose and mouth and step away. I'd rather be breathing in the intoxicating aroma of coffee. Striding back up the hill in all my bike gear, I'm soon sweltering, generating heat comparable to this geologically active area. Mid-way up, I stop to unzip my jacket and catch my breath.

I apologise to Hini for taking so long. He must have gotten cold waiting for me in the wind and rain, but he dismisses it with his big smile. I don't think anything could faze him. We return to the campsite, where the combined effect of coffee and apple pie whilst warm and dry is too comforting even for Hini to consider riding further in the rain today.

ICELAND Serow Saga

I'm thoroughly enjoying travelling with Hini. He rides at a similar pace, enjoys stopping for photos and videos as I do, and is very easy to get along with. It doesn't matter that his English is not perfect and I do not speak German; language is not always a barrier to communication.

We ride together, not needing to worry about the state of the trail ahead or what rivers there may be. When the trail becomes too steep and sandy, we unload bags, haul them up ourselves, then ride on. Hini has to give me a running push; the Serow's tyres are too worn and have insufficient grip. It's hard, sweaty work, but we love it. Through it all, we're both smiling.

I am not riding with Hini because I need someone to get me through the ride or the day. But together we can tackle harder terrain, ride without the fears that going solo inevitably evokes. We have each other for backup and company. We are both capable of succeeding individually. Knowing this, yet working as a team, we are even stronger. For the first time in months, possibly years, the confident, independent, self-assured me who cycled through Africa and Siberia alone, had always managed and was happy to look after herself has reappeared.

We ride southeast from Kerlingarfjöll towards Setur, then turn southwest deeper into the tephra desert. The yellow-green mosses growing along the river courses are shockingly bright in contrast to the undulating black sands, which are beautiful even under the dreary grey sky. My black waterproof jacket with fluorescent stripes down the arms is a perfect camouflage. Hini's fresh-eyed fascination with every plant, rock and view in this otherworldly landscape renews my enthusiasm. After two months riding through Iceland, I'd begun to forget how unique the environment is.

We see only two other vehicles coming from the opposite direction. They are big trucks kitted out for overland expeditions. We stop alongside and, straining our necks, peer up to the driver leaning out of the window. They have teamed up for safety to drive these

Kerlingarfjöll and Landmannalaugar

remote trails. It's not until the end of the day when we hit tarmac that we begin to see people again. We briefly visit Gullfoss, the popular waterfalls on the Golden Circle tourist route in the south, then find a campsite to stay at.

There is a web of dotted 4x4 track lines on my map to explore nearby. So the next day, we leave all but our tools and some food in our tents and set off for a day-ride unburdened by luggage. The bike is now easier to handle and manoeuvre. I ride faster than usual, the suspension able to cope with the ruts and bumps better with the reduced weight. After months of riding the Serow on these types of trails, I'm finely attuned to its ability for handling the terrain. I know precisely when to change gear to maintain maximum momentum, know when to give full power to get it up a steep hill and when to feather the throttle to ease the bike along without the wheels slipping on loose rocks or in deep sand. The bike may not be fast up hills, but I know that it will keep plodding along.

Today it's my turn to help Hini push his bike. On a steep hill with loose rocks, his back wheel slips and the bike topples over. His bike is much taller; he can only toe the ground, which offers less stability than being flat-footed as I am on the Serow. He can't then pull away, the higher torque engine causing the rear wheel to spin in the dirt. With a helping hand, he's soon on the move again.

We finish the ride with a dip at Hrunalaug, the hot pool Einar took me to. Now I'm the tour guide. I warned Hini where we were going and brought my bikini and towel this time. The following day, Hini rides to Reykjavík for a whistle-stop tour of the city. Not only does he meet Einar, but Birgir too. He sends me a photo of them all having lunch. It's a small community.

Hini is eager to ride to Landmannalaugar. We take one of the few trails in the area I've not ridden and loop via Krakatindur, a lone volcano. The black rock driven out of the moss-tinged tephra with an imposing, jagged peak makes me think of Mordor's Mount

ICELAND Serow Saga

Doom. A sense of some imminent threat overshadows me; although, Hini seems unaffected, keen to take a break here.

From riding over the undulating black sands, we enter an arena of colour, the dark hills splashed with red and orange, the water-nourished mosses bursting brightly in the valley. We cross a couple of shallow streams and stop to take photos. When ready to ride on, I remount and lift the bike off its side-stand, having to jerk the handlebars to free up the front wheel, which is embedded in the gravelly plain beside the water. I notice an unusually large amount of free play in the steering, the wheel movement lagging and less pronounced than the motion of the handlebars. Having checked the top bolt on the steering stem is tight, I set off cautiously, unable to do anything else to improve it.

We ride past Landmannalaugar and continue south on the Fjallabaksleið Nyrðri (F208) late into the evening. Unbelievably, the landscape in the gentle light is more beautiful than the last time I rode this way. Like Einar, I doubt I'd ever tire of returning and feasting on these views. The only distraction is the continuous vibration of the handlebars, the rhythmic wobbling more perceptible on the smoother trail.

Camping at Hólaskjól, the manager tells us that we might see a northern lights display tonight. The aurora borealis is more commonly associated with winter but occurs occasionally in August. In the dusk, I stare hard at the sky. If I squint and concentrate, I think I can see the faintest green tinge, but it could just be some wispy clouds. In a month, the darkness will be complete and more spectacular displays will become visible. I have seen so many beautiful aspects of Iceland, I don't mind that this striking face of the night remains masked.

I'm concerned about the wobbling handlebars, due to the worn headset bearings, and front forks that are now drained entirely of oil. Hini also notices that some spokes are very loose again, which surely doesn't help. I tighten the ones that aren't too rusted. When I find some discarded concrete blocks, I stack them beneath the bike's engine. This lifts the front end, so I can true the wheel. As the engine is still haemorrhaging, I do the daily oil top-up to finish.

I don't want to risk ruining Hini's last days of riding in the Highlands. It would be foolish to head off onto remote trails with an ailing bike. I still need to ride home, another couple of thousand kilometres away. My trail riding adventures in Iceland are, I fear, at their end.

Once packed, we hug each other, and I wave goodbye as he rides out of the campsite and disappears into the distance. Remembering my exploration of this area several weeks ago, I'm excited for him. If he enjoys it half as much as I did, he'll have a great time. I'm not sad that he's leaving; a week ago we didn't know each other, but now we're friends and that doesn't change because we're going in different directions. It's easy to stay in touch. I'll miss his company, but I'm equally looking forward to travelling solo again. It'll take some time, but gradually the images, impressions and ideas that occupy my mind daily will encroach to fill the emptiness he leaves behind.

Back to the Ring Road, I ride west past Vík to the Dyrhólaey peninsula, the southernmost point of the mainland. Looking across Reynisfjara, the black sand beach, I can see the distinctive basalt column stacks rising out of the ocean just off the coast. Being here reminds me of Leo, who was walking from the north to the south of the country. It only took him three weeks from Ásbyrgi, where I last saw him, to reach this point. It's taken me two months, albeit by a more convoluted route. I had said to Leo that I was taking the easy way; looking back, it hasn't been effortless. He was right in saying that neither journey was more or less worthy. Whether travelling on foot or by motorbike, bicycle, 4x4, horse or boat, each has its pros and cons, risks, rewards and challenges. Though, whereas Leo only had a short bus ride to Reykjavík to catch a flight home, my journey is still far from its end.

ICELAND Serow Saga

I camp in Vík and go for a walk in the hills behind the town. Caffeine-fuelled enthusiasm offsets my lack of fitness. Unfortunately, painkillers do little to combat my troublesome knee, an old injury I aggravated while riding with Birgir and his son.

Iceland is breaking us. I can't walk far because of my knee, can't write the manuscript because my laptop is broken, can't trail ride because my bike needs repairing. Exhausted in the afternoon, I wander aimlessly around the service station shop and buy an expensive woollen hat to replace the one I lost recently. If only I could replace the broken parts on my bike as readily. It's my only souvenir, but a good one.

Hand-knitted woollen clothing is popular in Iceland. Many locals and tourists alike wear the thick woollen jumpers with a geometric pattern of zigzag and diamond shapes that circles the neck and shoulders, which makes them easily identifiable as Icelandic. Known as *lopapeysa* (lopi sweaters), they are named after the yarn used. Produced from the fleece of the killer sheep, it's made up of two layers of wool. The wet-resistant, long and coarse outer layer is processed together with the soft, short insulating fibres of the inner layer to create lopi.

Knitting probably came to Iceland in the sixteenth century, but the lopapeysa is a twentieth-century tradition. It originated at the time when imports and mechanization began to replace hand-knitting, and people were looking for ways to use the wool and their skills. The long, dark winter nights were conducive to this indoor activity, where an ability to count stitches is more crucial than being able to see the curved needles and wool.

The lopapeysa has recently become fashionably popular as a symbol of Icelandic identity in an increasingly homogenous global world. With it, knitting has undergone a revival. What was a solitary hobby has become a group activity. Clubs now meet socially to knit and share ideas. In many villages, the clothing produced is sold in

Kerlingarfjöll and Landmannalaugar

local shops or community centres, the proceeds going back into the community.

Unnur often knitted in the evenings when I stayed with her and Högni. Unable to do many activities due to a pending operation, she had taken it up to keep occupied. Perhaps I should take up knitting.

There is only one region of Iceland that I've left to explore: the southeast. Fortuitously, there is only the tarmac Ring Road through it, so I can't be tempted by too many rough trails, the only ones being short off-shoots.

The road goes across Skeiðarársandur, a sixty-kilometre stretch of barren, gravel plains, heading directly towards the foot of Vatnajökull. This was the last section of the Ring Road to be completed in 1975 when several bridges were constructed over the shifting glacial waters. Intrigued by a giant metal structure covered in graffiti, I stop for a break. A family is scrambling over the huge girders that project out of the ground like the wings of a downed plane.

It's a section of the bridge that was destroyed in 1996 when an eruption beneath Vatnajökull caused a massive glacial flood. Icebergs up to around 1,000–2000 tonnes were carried downstream and washed away the road. The bridges had been built six metres above the ground to allow the passage of ice in the event of a flood, but the size and force of the flow were greater than estimates. This twisted, contorted girder stands as a monument to man's ongoing struggle for progress in the face of the indomitable forces of nature.

Like every other tourist travelling this region, I stop to see Jökulsárlón, probably Iceland's most famous glacial lagoon. The parking area is crowded with cars, 4x4s, buses and people. Thoughts about the safety of my bike and equipment enter my head for the first time in weeks.

There is little crime in Iceland. I quickly became as complacent as Einar, leaving my tank bag on the bike and only taking my credit card to pay for goods. I continue to lock my helmet to the handlebars, but

ICELAND Serow Saga

only to prevent it being accidentally knocked off and to stop curious Japanese tourists trying it on and taking selfies next to the Serow whilst ignoring the beautiful waterfall behind. After forgetting to take the key on a couple of occasions, I now leave it in the ignition. Then I know where it is and don't have to rummage through my jacket pockets to find it.

Here, I take the bike key with me and walk to the ridge overlooking the lagoon. Icebergs ranging in size from a bus to a small bird float in the still, blue water reflecting the sky. Fragments of ice drift with the outlet current towards the sea, where they will break up in the waves and finally melt in the warmer saltwater.

I ride an F-road nearby that goes up towards the southern edge of Vatnajökull hoping to find solitude. Instead, at the head of the trail, I find a base where a tour company runs 4x4 and skidoo trips onto the ice, super-sized 4x4s lined up outside an imposing concrete building. A few people are milling around the entrance, dressed in more insulated clothing than I had for the Siberian winter. The wind has a vicious bite. It is cold now the sun has dropped behind the mountains, but it's not *that* cold. This is August in Iceland, not the North Pole.

I descend back through the barren craggy terrain to where water flows and cottongrass grows. I see a small tarn with a track running to it. Late in the evening and with a mist creeping over the hills from the west, closing in around me, it's time to camp. There's no one around; it's lovely to be alone once more.

23

A Reindeer and More Rain
The Southeast

I wake early, put on my down jacket, pull on my boots and crawl out of the tent. The cold air nips. The fog has gone. The sky is clear, reflected perfectly in the still water, not a ripple or wave disturbs it. In the first light, the muted colours remind me of autumn in Scotland.

There's a reindeer, a beautiful stag grazing on the light vegetation among the quarried rocks. He hasn't seen me. I stand motionless, not wanting to disturb him, only to observe. I wish I could move through the wilderness undetected. When other animals do not flinch or twitch or flee in your presence, it's as though you are a part of nature itself. Oh, to be a leaf on a tree or berry on a bush, the featherweight dandelion seed floating in the wind, even the wind itself!

His coat is short with a glossy sheen of good health, a greyish-beige broad neck and shoulders, deepening to a rich chocolate tone along his back and flanks. The stark white rear looks like he's leant back against a recently whitewashed wall.

I move away silently, stepping slowly and quietly. The stag lifts his head, antlers sweeping through the air until they stand upright to alert attention. We both freeze, eyes locked on each other, zooming in until nothing else exists in our fields of view. It's not fear I see in his eyes but the realisation that he is not alone. This place is only big enough for one of us. It's as though there is a moment of resignation when the stag's head lowers just an inch before he steps down from the quarried rocks and casually trots off across the trail with his four dainty white socks and dark hoofs at the end of shapely legs.

He stops once to stare back and see that I haven't moved, then continues past a tumbling mountain stream and up the hillside. I lose sight of him amongst the rises and dips in the rough terrain of dry, tussocky grass and rocks.

A mix of emotions washes over me; wonder and amazement that I've had the privilege to see a reindeer, uneasiness of being an intruder in his home, and sadness that I disturbed him and forced him to take flight, even though it didn't seem like fleeing, rather a casual goodbye. Considering that reindeer are still hunted, I am surprised by the animal's lack of fear or urgent flight.

Reindeer were introduced to Iceland in the 1800s and widely distributed across the country, but their numbers have dwindled. Today, they are only found in the east. People living in the East Fjords seem particularly proud about this fact. Primarily, the reindeer inhabit the hills around Snæfell. This is the southernmost extent of their range, which spreads as far as Vopnafjörður on the north coast.

The dawn chill goads me back to the warmth of my sleeping bag and a good book. After two brews of coffee, the sun makes its appearance above the hills. As soon as the light hits the tent, the greenhouse effect immediately makes it too warm and claustrophobic, a rarity I revel in.

It's several days since my last shower. I contemplate a dip. Knowing the sun will be a short-lived delight, with the forecast of rain and chill of a day's riding ahead, I content myself with the luxury of a wash with water heated on the stove. There have been too few occasions when it's been warm enough to roll up my sleeves to the elbow, let alone strip off completely. The sun's gentle touch is warming as I dry in the light breeze before dressing.

I wander past three sheep: a ewe and her two plump, almost fully grown lambs. They are as scared and skittish as ever and freeze in terror on my approach. The ewe scrambles up the hillside while her panic-stricken lambs race past me, fleeing as though their lives depended upon it, never stopping to look back. They are more fearful of humans than the undomesticated reindeer.

The Southeast

The hillside drops away steeply into the flat-bottomed valley. A veined river takes a meandering route through the gravelly flood plain before emptying into the sea. On the opposite hillside, a group of white farmhouses are nestled under the cliffs surrounded by a geometric pattern of arable fields.

I can hear water flowing between rocks, though the only visible indication of a stream is the bright yellow moss lining the channel; elsewhere it's a pistachio silver-green fur. I take long strides, stepping over the rivulets of water trickling towards the tarn, my feet crunching over the sand and pebbles.

I hold many beautiful images of Iceland and experiences from this summer in my mind. The most vivid, those that stir the strongest feelings, are the thrill of riding remote tracks and crossing glacial rivers in the Highlands, and the deep tranquillity of wild camping in solitude, concerning myself only with what I sense in nature. The two experiences are at opposite ends of the emotional spectrum: one self-centred, adrenalin-fuelled excitement; the other, looking out into the world feeling peace and calm. This morning with the stag is how I shall remember the Iceland I feel a part of, not the one I've been riding across like a modern-day Viking conqueror.

Despite the beauty of this place, melancholic waves wash over me, dampening my contentment. It's only another fifty kilometres to Höfn. Then the only route to Seyðisfjörður to catch the ferry is along part of the Ring Road that I've ridden both ways already. The sun retreats behind a thickening wall of cloud, which soon releases the rain. Wondering how to spend my last days in Iceland, I remember Ásgeir telling me about Lónsöræfi to the northeast of here. It's accessed via an F-road that Norbert had recommended riding. If I can – if the bike can – I'll ride to the trailhead, then hike to the first mountain hut in the wilderness area.

I ride a hundred kilometres around the Ring Road, past Höfn and into familiar surroundings. Thankfully it's not windy or as wet as when I was here just over two weeks ago. I turn onto a gravel road and ride inland, passing from sheep-filled farmland into wilderness. The trail narrows and winds along one side of the wide valley. The sun illuminates the orange-red rhyolite mountains opposite, across the broad gravel plain with the glacial Jökulsá í Lóni River braided through it. It's beautiful, more so with each view that opens up as I weave along the track.

The trail descends onto the flood plain and becomes hard to follow, the way indicated occasionally by a painted rock until even those disappear near the confluence. I need to cross the river; I'm on the south side, and my map shows the route goes into the northern valley, which is where the hiking trail starts. Both Norbert and Ásgeir had warned me the river may be too deep to cross, but I have to see for myself.

Several tracks are faintly visible over the dry rocky bed. I try one, then another and another, but wherever they meet water, it's too deep and too fast. A couple of times, I find a place to cross the first strand of water only to be thwarted further on by a raging torrent. Each time I have to man-handle the bike over the rocks to turn it around. It's physically exhausting and causes intense pain in my left elbow and forearm, a repetitive strain injury caused by all the trail-riding. I sit down to eat lunch and rest my tired body before trying again.

In the end, I have to accept defeat. Disappointed, I turn back and pitch my tent with beautiful views of the valley and colourful mountains, which compensate for failing to reach the hiking trail. I read; I doze; I make tea. Then I sleep fitfully despite overwhelming exhaustion.

My inflatable mattress is pancake flat within ten minutes of inflating it these days. There must be a material defect because air is escaping from innumerable holes in the seams. Sleeping on the hard, cold ground for weeks has taken its toll on my body. I need a full night's sleep without waking every couple of hours to roll onto my other side because I'm cold, stiff and aching.

The Southeast

The last faint vestiges of warmth have vanished, summer snapped shut for another year. I feel the cold more and more each day. It's not a freezing cold of winter, a worthy opponent that confronts you head-on, its icy fingers like drawn swords that must be defended against. This is a damp chill that gradually wears down your defences like the volcanic tephra grinding on the bike's brake pads. It sneaks up on you unawares, grabbing you from behind and smothering you until its chill seeps deep into your bones.

I make one last cup of coffee, pack up the tent and ride. According to my map, there's a jeep track that shortcuts over the mountains. The bike and I are in no fit state for more trails, but I can't help myself.

Off the highway again, I dismount to pull back a wire gate, ride through and replace the wooden stake that holds it taut. I cross an old bridge over a gully with water gushing down the smooth rock bed. The concrete is crumbling away at the edges; the iron railings are rusted, mangled and ripped away at one end. Beyond, the trail uphill is loose and rocky. The back wheel slips and spins. The engine whines in first gear. Slowly, so slowly, we inch forward. I ride the inside track, hugging the hillside for fear the trail could give way and the bike slide off. When the incline eases, I speed up, change into second, then third, but soon have to slow again. It's rough and bumpy where water has created gullies and rockslides.

The trail narrows round a bend. The back wheel spins and spins on a glistening wet rock, slides left in the gravel, gains traction briefly only to be halted when the front end hits a step up. It's too steep. I need to be in first gear, not second, but it won't go and the bike is faltering. I tap and tap on the gear shift. Finally, it slips into … neutral. *No!*

I jam on the brakes, but the tyres have no grip and the bike slides backwards, closer towards the steep drop off the trail into the valley. *Shit.*

It grinds to a halt a little too close to the edge for comfort. I look down to where I could have ended up; with no head for heights, I feel distinctly uneasy. This time, the bike obliges and we pull away in first. I can smell the clutch burning.

I stop on a flatter section to decide what to do. I am beginning to lose faith in my bike. As with horses, you must have trust to enjoy the ride. The thrill of riding this short trail is not worth the risk of getting stuck or the bike breaking beyond repair. Cautiously I turn around, inching the bike forward then back until I'm facing downhill. I retrace my tracks slowly, using a low gear because the rear brake is ineffectual. The volcanic sand has worked its way into the drum and mixed with water from the river crossings into an abrasive paste.

The front wheel catches a rock and wrenches the handlebars. Pain sears through my forearm from the elbow. It doesn't matter how much I want to keep the bike upright, my hands loosen their grip, the wheel jerks to the right, and the bike topples over. The Serow is a sorry sight, sprawled on the ground like an injured animal waiting to be put out of its misery; even the best mechanic in the world can't help it here. I heave it upright and ride on.

There's one area of the East Fjords I've bypassed each time I've visited because it was always raining. I've ridden all the other trails on my map in the eastern half of Iceland. I want to discover what this last area unknown to me has to offer. With the perpetual raincloud that hangs over the East Fjords, I am soon wet through.

I stay at the community campsite in Neskaupstaður. My tent is soon sopping, looking as forlorn and dejected as a stray cat on a doorstep. I take refuge in the dry room, put the kettle on and pull a chair up next to the radiator to warm up. A twenty-something young woman enters. She looks far too clean and well-dressed to be camping, as though she's walked straight out of a North Face catalogue. The space is too small to not make conversation.

'Miserable day, huh?' I comment.

'Yes,' she sighs. 'It's too cold and wet for camping. I'm looking forward to going home now.' Her face brightens up at the prospect.

The Southeast

'I'm beginning to feel the same,' I agree, although she doesn't look bedraggled or tired enough.

'How long have you been here?' I ask.

'I hired a camper van with my boyfriend for a week. We've driven from Reykjavík,' she tells me. Then she adds with noticeable relief, 'Only three days left.'

How I wish I had my van with a bed to crawl into! I keep quiet and pull the chair closer to the radiator.

It never occurred to me before the trip that I could have driven my van here and transported the Serow in the back. For driving the main roads and well-maintained gravel roads, a camper van is a sensible choice. It offers a warm and dry escape from the inclement weather, the one thing lacking about motorcycle touring and camping. Then I could have explored the Highlands on the Serow on short trips, travelling light when the weather was favourable, always knowing there was a cosy van to return to where I could brew a cup of tea and change into warm, dry clothes every few days. I'm getting soft with age.

'You know, it's Iceland's worst summer in one hundred years,' she informs me with an air of authority, as though she's lived every one of those wet summer days. *She has no idea.*

'I had heard,' I comment off-handedly.

Outdoors for most of the eleven weeks I've been here, I've seen how the landscape and life have changed throughout a season, acutely aware of the subtle changes from one week to the next. At some point, the plover stopped calling and the puffins left their burrows. The spring lambs have grown into killer sheep. The horses have fattened on the lush grass they've been grazing free all summer, but now they're being rounded up and taken back to the farms. The fields have been cut, the hay baled. The withering grass that only a month ago was vibrant green and full of nutrients has turned a yellowish sheen. Berries have grown and ripened on the bushes. I see people out collecting them wrapped up in jackets, wearing hats and scarves.

ICELAND Serow Saga

Summer has come and gone in the blink of an eye. The snow finally melted from the mountaintops, but this last week they received their first fresh dusting, a sure sign that winter is approaching fast. And the dark nights have returned.

After a rest in the warm and dry, I feel revived, my enthusiasm renewed. I want to feel the thrill of riding one more trail and marvel at one more beautiful sight. I have to ride; I have to see.

I take the old road over the mountain. The air temperature drops with every metre climbed. My fingers are numb before the top. It reminds me of the cold during my early days in Iceland. Back down at sea level, I follow the coastline until the road diverges inland. Then I cross over the finger of hills and into Viðfjörður, then Vöðlavík, and back up the valley. Water streams down the hillside, dark rocks glistening. Rays of sunlight break through the bruised-black sky. The misty rain shimmers like fine netting wavering in the breeze.

Thawing out in the bakery cafe at Reyðarfjörður, I peruse my map, deciding which way to go next. I'd like to ride to the lighthouse at Dalatangi, Unnur's favourite road, the one that I turned back on during my first rainy days in the country. I'm also only one fjord away from where Unnur and Högni live. I want to visit them before I get the ferry. I'd better message them.

I briefly look up from my phone. To my surprise, Unnur is standing in front of me. If only I could have imagined the sun into being and banished the rain as easily.

'I came into town for a meeting and saw your bike outside,' Unnur explains.

'I was just going to message you!' I exclaim.

'Where are you staying tonight?' she asks.

'I'm not sure. Tomorrow's my last full day.'

'It's up to you, but you can stay with us and have a relaxing day tomorrow. You know you're always welcome.'

The Southeast

'I was thinking I'd ride to Dalatangi. If I go now, I could be at yours later this evening,' I reply.

Over the pass, I ride down the switchbacks and past the waterfalls to the coastline where I turned back the last time. It's clear now; sun breaks through the clouds intermittently, illuminating the hillsides and the rusting trawler that's beached in the shallows of narrow Mjóifjörður. I ride alongside the shore to the eastern end of the fjord and park at the end of the trail beside the squat, rectangular, bright orange lighthouse still in use today. It replaced the original one built in 1895, Iceland's oldest standing lighthouse, a smaller hut perched on a rocky mound just beyond.

Balanced on the exposed rocks, the wind freezing my cheeks, I look out across the choppy sea. There is no more land in sight; this is the end of my exploring in Iceland. Somewhere over the horizon, the ferry will take me home to a future filled with more adventures. First, I turn around and ride to Unnur and Högni's, which feels like my home in Iceland.

I'm content to do little on my last day except drink coffee, chat with Unnur and stare out across the fjord from the warm side of the window. Miraculously, it has stopped raining here. The sun even breaks through the clouds. It tempts me from the comfort of the sofa to walk around the village. It's not as warm out as it looked. It's what the Icelanders call 'window weather'. I get as far as the cafe, then return to the warmth of home. I won't be fooled again.

I unfold my map of Iceland. With a highlighter, I mark all the roads and trails I've ridden this summer and stare at the blank spaces. I can't say whether it's the empty areas of unfinished business or the threaded lines of memory along verdant fjords and over mountains, across lava fields and glacial rivers, past volcanoes and through canyons that will draw me back.

The next morning, I wave goodbye, ride to Seyðisfjörður and board the ferry. It's relaxing to be on the move without requiring any effort from myself and with no concerns about the Serow. I catch up on my journal and reminisce about the journey. After a good night's sleep, I wake up in the dark couchette. I've never been so thankful for or slept so well on a sweaty, plastic-covered mattress. I go upstairs to the top deck for fresh air, push open the heavy metal door and am confronted by the most beautiful vision - blue sky! *So that's what it looks like.*

The deep blue sea stretches to the horizon, razor-sharp and still. The ferry glides effortlessly over the gently undulating ocean, up and down, up and down; breathing, alive. Fulmars soar by with ease, their wings tipped against the wind, free. And a feeling swells inside me: I have been released. It's not that Iceland had been holding me a prisoner. I felt freer there than I have in a long time. It was as though Iceland, in its enormity, intensity and harshness, had enveloped me until I had become a part of it.

Tribute

Yamaha Serow XT225
~95,000 kilometres (1992 - 2019)

- The trusty little bike made for big adventures -

Manufactured in Japan in 1992, my Serow was imported to the UK with 8,000 kilometres on the clock in 2014. I purchased it immediately as a first motorbike and had it fitted with a long-range fuel tank and hand guards in preparation for long-distance overland travel.

Usually fully loaded and often off-road, it got me up and down the UK several times, across Europe twice and through Africa.

Apart from the engine seizing once (sheared starter clutch bolts), the bike always started and never failed to get me to my next destination, despite acquiring various ailments. During its life, broken or worn parts were replaced, including the rear shock absorber, starter motor, starter clutch, clutch plates, about sixteen broken spokes, wheel bearings, several chains and sprockets, numerous blown headlights and four sets of tyres.

Sadly, the ride around Iceland contributed to it's demise. It made the journey back to the UK, albeit leaving a trail of oil in its wake, but needed too much work for another big journey. The corroded wheels and broken spokes, the leaking front forks with seized seals, the worn piston rings, the broken starter motor and the dodgy wiring would all need to be replaced and the carburettor refurbished.

I took the Serow for its final ride last winter, exploring some of the Pyrenees for a week. After 95,000 kilometres, through thirty-six countries on two continents, it had earned its retirement.

Rather than gathering dust in a dingy garage and not wanting to give up completely, the Serow has instead donated some of its intact organs to the next incarnation. Its spirit lives on in an identical bike I've found recently, which I plan to ride in search of new adventures.

Glossary

The following is a list of some Icelandic words and their definitions.

Austur - east
Bær - farm
Brú - bridge
Dalur - valley
Djúp - deep inlet, long fjord
Drangur - rock column
Ey / Eyjar - Island / islands
Eyri - Sand spit
Fell / Fjall - mountain
Fjörður - fjord
Fljót - large river
Flói - bay
Foss - waterfall
Heiði - heath
Hellir - cave
Höfði - headland
Hraun - lava
Hver - hot spring
Ísland - Iceland
Jökull - glacier
Kirkja - church
Laug - warm pool
Leið - route
Lón - lagoon
Nes - headland
Mörk - woods/fores

Norður / Nyrðri - north / northern
Reykur - smoke
Staður - place
Suður / Syðri - south / southern
Tjörn - lake, pond
Vatn - lake
Vegur - road
Vestur - west
Vík - bay
Völlur / vellir - plain, flat land

Acknowledgements

Many people helped me during my travels and with producing this book. No words can express my gratitude, no matter how big or small the input. I am privileged and lucky to be surrounded by great friends and family; you know who you are. It is impossible to mention everyone here; though, I'd like to name a few individuals.

For the kindness, generosity, help and support I received during my travels, special thanks to Polly and Ivo at Motocamp, Unnur and Högni, Einar, Birgir and Fjóla, and Hini.

For invaluable input, advice and guidance on the manuscript, I thank my editor Jen Barclay, Iain Harper, Sam Manicom, Unnur Sveinsdóttir, Einar Valur Einarsson and, of course, my mum.

LEAVE A REVIEW

I would appreciate it if you would rate and review this book on Amazon. It is with your feedback that I can become a better writer. If you enjoyed it, please tell your friends and family about it, even spread the word on social media.

I am always interested to hear from you. Tell me what you thought of my books or just write and say 'Hello'. If you are inspired to go on your own adventure, feel free to ask me questions about it. I could not have begun any of my journeys without the help and knowledge of those more experienced than me. I hope that now, in turn, I may be able to help others.

If you'd like to read more about my other adventures, past and present, or get in touch, see my website:

www.HelensTakeOn.com

You can also find me on Facebook and Twitter:

www.facebook.com/helenstakeon

www.twitter.com/helenlloyd

MORE BOOKS BY THE AUTHOR

Desert Snow - One Girl's Take On Africa By Bike

Desert Snow is the story of one girl, one bike and 1,000 beers in Africa. By daring to follow a dream and not letting fear prevail, Helen cycled across the Sahara, Sahel and tropics of West Africa, paddled down the Niger River in a pirogue, hitch-hiked to Timbuktu and spent three months traversing the Congo, which she thought she may never leave...

A lot can change in 2 years, cycling 25,000km from England to Cape Town. So can nothing. Helen takes you with her on the journey through every high and low of her memories and misadventures. She describes a continent brimming with diversity that is both a world away from what she knows and yet not so different at all.

A Siberian Winter's Tale - Cycling to the Edge of Insanity and the End of the World

A gripping adventure travel book about Helen's most challenging journey by bicycle.

In the depth of winter, she spent three months cycling solo across one of the most remote, coldest inhabited regions of the planet - Siberia.

In temperatures down to -50°C, she battled against the cold, and overcame her fear of wolves and of falling through the ice of a frozen lake. Yet, alone in a hibernating land with little to stimulate the senses, the biggest challenges were with her mind.

Helen portrays her struggles with solitude in this sparsely populated region whilst weaving a story brimming with characters she met on her journey along the Road of Bones.

www.ingramcontent.com/pod-product-compliance
Lightning Source LLC
Chambersburg PA
CBHW022100090426
42743CB00008B/672